ROBERT W. BLAKE, JR.
AND BRETT ELIZABETH BLAKE

BECOMING A TEACHER

USING NARRATIVE AS REFLECTIVE PRACTICE

A CROSS-DISCIPLINARY APPROACH

PETER LANG
New York • Washington, D.C./Baltimore • Bern
Frankfurt • Berlin • Brussels • Vienna • Oxford

Library of Congress Cataloging-in-Publication Data

Blake, Robert W. (Robert William).
Becoming a teacher: using narrative as reflective practice.
a cross-disciplinary approach / Robert W. Blake, Jr., Brett Elizabeth Blake.
p. cm.
Includes bibliographical references and index.
1. Teachers—Training of. 2. Teaching. 3. Narrative inquiry (Research method)
I. Blake, Brett Elizabeth. II. Title.
LB1707.B53   370.71'1—dc23   2012000536
ISBN 978-1-4331-1331-4 (hardcover)
ISBN 978-1-4331-1330-7 (paperback)
ISBN: 978-1-4539-0588-3 (e-book)
ISSN 1058-1634

Bibliographic information published by **Die Deutsche Nationalbibliothek**.
Die Deutsche Nationalbibliothek lists this publication in the "Deutsche
Nationalbibliografie"; detailed bibliographic data is available
on the Internet at http://dnb.d-nb.de/.

© 2012 Peter Lang Publishing, Inc., New York
29 Broadway, 18th floor, New York, NY 10006
www.peterlang.com

Printed in the United States of America

To my family, Jennifer, Mackenzie, and Matthew. You provide me stories to last a lifetime. I love you all.

—rwb

In the glorious quiet of early morning, the Sisters of Charity of St. Vincent de Paul begin to hum and to chant—the soft sounds of song sweeping over me in the darkness—as I continue to write—finding peace and solace in their music and the fact that I remember that I am once again in Paris.

I dedicate this book to the Writing across the Curriculum group at St. John's University (especially our facilitators, Anne Ellen Geller, Harry Denny, and Derek Owens, who referred to us as the "work-hard/play-hard" group) who gave me the opportunity to come back to Paris, where I found a renewed inspiration in my writing, through the beauty all around us, and in new friends.

Merci du bas de mon coeur!

—beb

CONTENTS

Foreword

More Teacher Lore

In 2012, the twentieth anniversary of the publication of *Teacher Lore: Learning from Our Own Experience* (Schubert & Ayers, 1992), it is gratifying to see that the idea persists and has longevity of interest. I commend Bob Blake and Brett Blake for their efforts in this volume. I fondly recall the days when they were doctoral students in the Ph.D. Program in Curriculum Design, which since became the Ph.D. Program in Curriculum Studies at the University of Illinois at Chicago (UIC).

In this foreword I want to situate the book historically, so that others might build upon the spirit of its contribution. After developing a framework for narrative inquiry into teacher lore, Blake, Blake, and their contributors provide original inquiry and insight for teacher education by focusing on a set of topics previously not treated extensively in teacher lore literature (special education, art, science, technology, reading, ELL, and migrant education), with special emphasis on the symbiosis of theory and practice and cultural context in relation to teacher identity. The chapters join a burgeoning body of literature that pushes the lore of teaching in new directions—expanding the frontiers of narrative inquiry (e.g., He, 2003; He & Phillion, 2008; Carger, 2008; Clandinin, et al., 2009; Schubert, 2009; Goodson, Biesta, Tedder, Adair, 2010; Reynolds, in press; Barone & Eisner, 2012).

I want to begin by sharing a precursor of teacher lore from thirty years ago. In the early 1980s I taught a special topics doctoral seminar on *Progressive Education*. We studied the history of progressive education stemming from the works of John Dewey and those who built upon and influenced the integration of theory and practice he developed at the University of Chicago Laboratory School, which Dewey founded in 1896. His wife, Alice Chipman Dewey, was the director or principal of the Lab School until 1905, and the lore she created doubtless influenced Dewey's early writings: *My Pedagogic Creed* (1897), *The School and the Society* (1899), *The Child and the Curriculum* (1902a), and *The Educational Situation* (1902b).

Dewey's conceptualization of the Lab School was doubtless influenced by one of his foremost doctoral students, Ella Flagg Young, who completed her Ph.D. with Dewey in 1900 and was fourteen years his senior. A long-time teacher and principal in the Chicago Public Schools, having started teaching in 1862, when Dewey was three years old, she became the first woman superintendent of the Chicago public schools as well as the first woman president of the National Education Association. The lore Dewey received from interactions with Young must have been enormous, especially the urban dimension, given that Dewey grew up near Burlington, Vermont and taught in Oil City, Pennsylvania. Dewey's urban lore was doubtless influenced by another progressive educator, Jane Addams who worked in curriculum outside of schools, as founder of the first and most well-known settlement house, Hull House in Chicago. It is fair to call Addams the mother of social work in America and to call her a teacher in a profound sense. As a member of the Board of Directors of Hull House, Dewey learned the lore of teaching those in poverty from diverse immigrant backgrounds. Experiences with Alice Chipman Dewey at the Lab School, along with interactions Addams and Young were surely influences on Dewey's (1916) *magnum opus* on education, *Democracy and Education*. Dewey always wanted the Lab School to remain an experimental place for discovering and imagining educational ideas and did not want it to be a demonstration normal school for teacher education as was Francis Parker's normal school. Nevertheless, it would be fair to say that Dewey had sufficient interactions with Parker to merit him as part of Dewey's teacher lore. Dewey, however, was most concerned with teaching-learning situations as microcosmic societal experiences or democratic communities in which interest and will or effort (as published by Dewey in 1913) were integrated in the mutual pursuit of growth as *teachers* and *learners* negotiated *subject matter* and *milieu*—to draw from Joseph Schwab's (1970) four commonplaces of practical enquiry. In fact, during his first decade at Columbia University, Dewey and his daughter Evelyn (Dewey & Dewey, 1915) traversed the country to find schools that exemplified such educational experience, calling them *schools of tomorrow*. A central feature in the teacher lore of such schools was a broad and deep interpretation of science that Dewey (1929) expressed thusly:

> The sources of educational science are any portions of ascertained knowledge that enter into the heart, head, and hand of educators and which, by entering in, render the performance of the educational function more enlightened, more humane, and more truly educational than it was before. But there is no way to discover what is "more truly educational" except by the continuation of the educational act itself. The discovery is never made; it is always making (76–77).

This image of educational science or inquiry can be consider relative to another kind of teacher lore that influenced Dewey's (1933) image of teaching—a fictive one, regarding Utopians he claimed to have visited—a Deweyan episode so intriguing to me that I spent the better part of two years writing a book about it called *Love, Justice, and Education: John Dewey and the Utopians* (Schubert, 2009).

In my course on progressive education we studied others in the movement, especially William Heard Kilpatrick, Jesse Newlon, L. Thomas Hopkins, Harold Rugg, George S. Counts, Boyd H. Bode, as well as the less acknowledged progressive women educators such as Margaret Wells, Mary H. Lewis, Ann Shumaker, Sara E. Chase, Helen Parkhurst, Patty Smith Hill, and Caroline Pratt. These and other women educators offered more in the way of teacher lore than did the men who concentrated more on theoretical aspects.

In 1927, Volume 1 of the 26th Yearbook of the National Society for the Study of Education (Rugg, 1927) published what could be called a compendium of progressive practices. Moreover, at about the same time The Progressive Education Association, founded in 1919 to develop and extend Dewey's work, began planning a monumental study, called The Eight Year Study (Aikin, 1942) to compare high school and college experiences of progressively educated students with those who were educated traditionally. The final volume in the five-volume Eight Year Study set consists of stories, one could say lore, of the thirty schools that participated—a huge book of nearly 800 pages (Thirty Schools, 1942). The study pointed not only to the relative benefits of progressive education, compared with traditional education, but to the value of teacher experimentation in the search for ways to respond to interests and needs of students through democratic teacher-pupil planning (see Kridel & Bullough, 2007). If I were teaching this seminar again I would add considerable study of

African American educators who spanned the progressive era (e.g., W.E.B. Du Bois, Anna Julia Cooper, Carter G. Woodson, Horace Mann Bond, Ella Baker, Septema Clark, Fannie Lou Hamer) and challenge the class (including myself) to look for complementarities and critiques of tenets of progressivism.

When the students in my seminar on progressive education completed the class their evaluations of the experience were positive; however, they were dis-heartened with the lack of progressive orientations in the schools, education-al policy, and teacher education. They pointed out that progressive theory and practice was treated as an anathema in the time of ascendency of *A Nation at Risk* (National Commission on Excellence in Education, 1983), wherein teach-ers were accused of being as likely as a foreign invaders to destroy the United States. Students also pointed to their desire to experience progressive educa-tion, not just learn *about* it. They expressed skepticism as to whether it was pos-sible to experience it in large organizations, such as schools and universities amidst the trappings of syllabi, preordained objectives, tests, schedules, and grading. So, while the students were glad to have had flexible assignments in the seminar on progressivism, they wondered if I would practice what I preached and if I would convene a democratically oriented progressive study group. I could not decline. To do so would negate my advocacy of progressive education. Despite the added load, I wanted to do this study group.

After only a few meetings of the study group, during which students lament-ed the policy mandates that prohibited progressive practice, we all noted that we should do something more than lament. We talked about teachers who had made profound positive differences in our lives, as well as some who had dele-terious effects. We reflected on our own elementary, secondary, or collegiate teaching careers and shared the influence we recalled having on students—and they on us for that matter. So, we decided to make our Study Group a center to advocate, hopefully inspire the study of teachers. We conceived of such study as different from "research on" teachers. Rather, we wanted it to be research with teachers about teaching and teachers' lives. We were distressed that career teachers have often spent between twenty to forty years in classrooms, inter-acting with students. Yet, ironically we seldom heard of educational researchers simply asking experienced teachers what they have learned from that experi-ence. Against this backdrop, we also talked of the powerful writing of first-per-son accounts of teachers: Caroline Pratt (1948), Sylvia Ashton-Warner (1963), John Holt (1964), Jonathan Kozol (1967), Herb Kohl (1968). We did not naively think that what teachers would have to say is neglected *truth* about teaching; however, we did decide that it would be worth listening to them.

We called our project The Teacher Lore Project. Lore, of course, refers to knowledge or belief. We wanted to put the knowledge or beliefs of teachers on the table for consideration by any who want to know about teachers and teaching. We saw this as consonant with progressive values of starting with experiences, interests, and concerns of those most involved and democratically engaging them in the process of understanding themselves. We saw it as a contribution to curriculum studies, too, because we deemed the teacher an integral part of curriculum. In fact, we sometimes referred to the teacher as the curriculum, though we knew that was overstating the case. We trusted that the lore of teachers would contribute to teacher education in a manner not served by more traditional research. We thought about multiple ways to invite teachers to participate and conjured up different approaches to inquire into what their experience taught them. The emphasis on invitation is a key here, and one of our participants said it well, emphasizing that teacher lore is *an invitation, not an inventory* (Melnick, 1992, p. 81).

As we invited teachers to participate in the Teacher Lore Project, for which we gained approval from our Institutional Review Board and funding from in-house research grants generously provided by the Chicago Area School Effectiveness Council of the Center for Urban Education Research and Development at UIC, we decided to speak and write about the project. We presented about the work of our study group and the burgeoning dissertations that evolved from it at several conferences: The Bergamo Curriculum Conference, American Educational Studies Association, Association for Supervision and Curriculum Development, and the American Educational Research Association. William Ayers (1989), a new faculty member at UIC, who had just published a book about six exemplary pre-school teachers, became a valuable part of our study group. I was invited to write about the Teacher Lore Project in a book on stories that lives reveal through narrative and dialogue by Carol Witherell and Nel Noddings (Schubert, 1991), and in that chapter tried to show how tenets of theory for teacher lore were influenced by the philosophy of John Dewey and related theoretical perspectives. We also published about teacher lore in numerous venues that would hopefully reach a broader audience of educators: telling how the idea emerged from a study group on progressive education in *Teaching Education* (Schubert, Thomas, Wojcik, Zissis, Hulsebosch, Koerner, & Millies, 1987); arguing that perspectives of teachers are neglected in understanding curriculum and supervision in ASCD's *Journal of Curriculum and Supervision* (Schubert, 1989), Guided by such theoretical constructs, participants in the study developed dissertations on teacher lore that were characterized in a special issue of the *Kappa Delta Pi Record* (Schubert, Hulsebosch, Jagla, Koerner, Millies, 1990), focusing on the need to attend to the experiential knowledge of teachers. The culminating event was the book that Bob and Brett Blake are continuing: *Teacher Lore: Learning from Our Own Experiences* (Schubert and Ayers, 1992), joined by Janet Miller whose *Creating Spaces and Finding Voices* (Miller, 1990) was an inspiration. In addition to chapters in *Teacher Lore* by Bill Ayers and myself, key participants from the Teacher Lore Project shared central ideas from their dissertations, each in a separate chapter: Mari Koerner, Virginia Jagla, Suzanne Millies, Carol Melnick, and Patricia Hulsebosch. Numerous other students at UIC built dissertations around teacher lore, including Brett Blake and Bob Blake in literacy and science, respectively. Others extended the work into the lore of leadership and supervision or into focus on the lore of students and their lives (for additional citations see Schubert, 1992, Schubert, 1993, Schubert and Lopez (1993), and Ayers and Schubert (1994).

I was pleased to say that the teacher lore work has continued under many guises. I was pleased to see Gretchen Schwarz (Schwarz & Albert, 1998; Schwarz, 2001) reach out to educators through a publication with the highly populated Phi Delta Kappa with direct reference to our teacher lore project. Indicating continued use of the topic, *Teacher Lore* was selected for re-publication in the Classics in Education Series of Educators International Press (Schubert & Ayers, 1999). Additionally other similar work evolved during roughly the same period to call attention to teachers as sources of insight about teaching: continued work on teachers and teaching by Ayers (1993, 1995, 2010; Ayers & Ford, 1996; Ayers, Ladson-Billings, Michie, & Noguera, 2008) *personal practical knowledge* of teachers, Freema Elbaz, Michael Connelly, and Jean Clandinin (Elbaz, 1983; Connelly & Clandinin, 1988; Connelly & Clandinin, 1990); narratives of in-between and exile by work by Ming Fang He and others (He, 2003, 2010; He & Phillion, 2008; Ivor Goodson's use of the term *teachers' lives and careers* (Goodson & Ball, 1985; Goodson, 1992, 2008); educational criticism by Tom Barone (2001, Barone & Eisner, 2012); stories of early career teachers by Robert Bullough, Jr. (1989, 2001, 2008, Bullough and Baughman, 1997), All of this work on and of teachers was legitimized when Cathy Carter (1993) summarized much of the early work on teacher stories in *Educational Researcher* as basis for research on teachers and teaching. Today there is an entry in the Sage *Encyclopedia of Curriculum Studies* entitled "Teacher Lore Research" (Brown, 2010).

This volume, like our *Teacher Lore* (Schubert & Ayers, 1992) twenty years earlier, is another call to share the breadth, depth, nuance, and complexity of stories, to heed the *call of stories* (Coles, 1989), and to engage in *making stories* (Bruner, 2003). Such work can go far to provide counter-narratives to the puerile and too often inimical mandates offered under the label of school reform. Here, teacher lore is offered for the improvement of teacher education and need to see *teacher education* in two lights; one is of course the education of teachers, and the other (less emphasized) is for the education of the public and policy makers about and through teachers.

So, many thanks to you, Bob and Brett, for moving teacher lore onward with skill, intelligence, and creativity.

References

Aikin W. M. (1942). *The story of the Eight Year Study*. New York: Harper & Brothers.

Ashton-Warner, S. (1963). *Teacher*. New York: Simon & Schuster.

Ayers, W. (1989). *The good preschool teacher*. New York: Teachers College Press.

Ayers, W. (1993, 2001, 2010). *To teach: The journey of a teacher*. New York: Teachers College Press.

Ayers, W. (Ed.). (1995). *To become a teacher*. New York: Teachers College Press.

Ayers, W. & Alexander-Tanner, R. (2010). *To teach: The journey, in comics*. New York: Teachers College Press.

Ayers, W. & Ford, P. (Eds.). (1996). *City kids: City teachers*. New York: The New Press.

Ayers, W., Ladson-Billings, G., Michie, G., & Noguera, P. A. (Eds.). (2008). *City kids, city schools*. New York: The New Press.

Ayers, W.C., and Schubert, W.H. (1994).Teacher lore: Learning about teaching from teachers. In T. S. Shanahan (Ed.), *Teachers thinking, teachers knowing: Reflections on literacy and language education* (pp. 105–121). Urbana, Il: National Conference on Research in English and the National Council of Teachers of English.

Barone, T. E. (2001). *Touching eternity: The enduring outcomes of teaching*. New York: Teachers College Press.

Barone, T. E. & Eisner, E. W. (2012). *Arts-based research*. Los Angeles: Sage.

Brown, P. U. (2010) Teacher lore research. In C. Kridel (Ed.), *Encyclopedia of curriculum studies* (pp. 863–864). Los Angeles, CA: Sage.

Bruner, J. (2003). *Making stories. Law, literature, and life*. Cambridge, MA: Harvard University Press.

Bullough, R. V. (1989). *First year teacher*. New York: Teachers College Press.

Bullough, R. V. (2001). *Uncertain lives: Children of promise, children of hope*. New York: Teachers College Press.

Bullough, R. V. (2008). *Counternarratives: Studies of teacher education and becoming and being a teacher*. New York: Teachers College Press.

Bullough, R. V. & Baughman, K. (1997). *"First year teacher" eight years later: An inquiry into teacher development*. New York: Teachers College Press.

Carger, C. (Ed.). (2008). *Before there were numbers: The power of narrative inquiry*. A special edition of the journal, *Thresholds in Education* 34(1&2, Spring–Summer).

Carter, K. (1993). The place of story in the study of teaching and teacher education. *Educational Researcher, 22* (1), 5–12, 18.

Clandinin, D. J., Huber, J., Orr, A. M., Huber, M., Murphy, M. S. (2009). *Composing diverse identities: Narrative inquiries into the interwoven lives of children and teachers*. New York: Routledge.

Coles, R. (1989). *The call of stories: Teaching and the moral imagination*. Boston: Houghton Mifflin.

Connelly, F.M. & Clandinin, D. J. (1988). *Teachers as curriculum planners*. NY: Teachers College Press.

Connelly, F. M. & Clandinin, (1990). Stories of experience and narrative inquiry. *Education Researcher, 19* (5), 2–14.

Dewey, J. (1897). *My pedagogic creed*. New York: E. L. Kellogg.

Dewey, J. (1899, revised 1915). *The school and the society*. Chicago: University of Chicago Press.

Dewey, J. (1902a). *The child and the curriculum*. Chicago: University of Chicago Press.

Dewey, J. (1902b). *The educational situation*. Chicago: University of Chicago Press.

Dewey, J. (1913). *Interest and effort in education*. Boston: Houghton Mifflin.

Dewey, J. (1916). *Democracy and education*. New York: Macmillan.

Dewey, J. (1929). *The sources of a science of education*. New York: Liveright.

Dewey, J. (1933). Dewey outlines utopian schools. *New York Times*, April 23, p 7. Also in Boydston, J. A. (Ed.), *The later works (1925–1953) of John Dewey*, Volume 9 (pp. 136–140) Carbondale, IL: Southern Illinois University Press, 1989.

Dewey, J. & Dewey, E. (1915). *Schools of tomorrow*. New York: E. P. Dutton.

Elbaz, F. (1983). *Teacher thinking: A study of practical knowledge*. London: Croom Helm.

Goodson, I. (Ed.). (1992) *Studying teachers' lives*. London and New York: Routledge.

Goodson, I. (2008). *Investigating the teacher's life and work*. Rotterdam: Sense Publishers.

Goodson, I. & Ball, S. (Eds.). (1985/1989). *Teachers lives and careers*. London and New York: Falmer/Open University.

Goodson, I., Biesta, G., Tedder, M., Adair, N. (2010). *Narrative learning*. London: Routledge.

He, M. F. (2003). *A river forever flowing: Cross-cultural lives and identities in the multicultural landscape*. Greenwich, CT: Information Age Publishers.

He, M. F. (2010). Exile pedagogy: Teaching in-between. In J. A. Sandlin, B. D. Schultz, & J. Burdick (Eds.), *Handbook of public pedagogy: Education and learning beyond schooling*. (pp. 469–482) New York: Routledge.

He, M. F., & Phillion, J. (Eds.). (2008). *Personal~passionate~participatory inquiry into social justice in education*. Charlotte, NC: Information Age Publishing.

Holt, J. (1964). *How children fail*. New York: Delta.

Johnson, M. (1987). *The body in the mind*. Chicago: University of Chicago Press.

Kohl, H. (1968). *36 children*. New York: Signet.

Kozol, J. (1967). *Death at an early age*. Boston: Houghton Mifflin.

Kridel, C., & Bullough, R. V. Jr., (2007). *Stories of the Eight Year Study: Reexamining secondary schooling in America*. Albany, NY: State University of New York Press.

Melnick, C. R. (1992). The out-of-school curriculum: An invitation, not an inventory. In W.

H. Schubert & W. Ayers (Eds.), *Teacher lore: Learning from our own experience* (pp. 81–105), New York: Longman.

Miller, J. L. (1990). *Creating spaces and finding voices.* Albany, NY: State University of New York Press.

National Commission on Excellence in Education (1983). *A nation at risk.* Washington, DC: Government Printing Office.

Parker, F. W. (1894). *Talks on pedagogics.* New York: E. L. Kellogg.

Pratt, C. (1948). *I learn from children.* New York: Harper & Row.

Reynolds, W. M. (Ed.). (In Press). *Curriculum of place.* New York: Peter Lang.

Rugg, H. O. (1927). *Curriculum making: Past and present.* Twenty-sixth Yearbook of the National Society for the Study of Education. Part I. Bloomington, IL: Public School Publishing Company.

Schubert, W. H. (1989). Teacher lore: A neglected basis for understanding curriculum and supervision. *Journal of Curriculum and Supervision, 4* (3), 282–285.

Schubert, W. H. (1991). Teacher lore: A basis for understanding praxis. In C. Witherell, C. & N. Noddings (Eds.), *The stories lives tell: Narrative and dialogue in education* (pp. 207–233). NY: Teachers College Press, Columbia University, 207–233.

Schubert, W. H. (1992). Personal theorizing about teachers' personal theorizing. In E. W. Ross, J. Cornett, & G. McCutcheon (Eds.), *Teacher personal theorizing* (pp. 249-264). Albany, NY: State University of New York Press.

Schubert, W. H. (1993). Teacher and student lore: Their ways of looking at it. *Contemporary Education, 65* (1), 42–46.

Schubert, W. H. (2009). *Love, justice, and education: John Dewey and the Utopians.* Charlotte, NC: Information Age Publishing.

Schubert, W. H. & Ayers, W. C. (1992). *Teacher lore: Learning from our own experience.* White Plains, NY: Longman.

Schubert, W. H., Hulsebosch, P. L., Jagla, V. M., Koerner, M., Millies, P. S. (1990). Theme Issue: School culture/teacher lore, *Kappa Delta Pi Record, 26* (4), 98–127.

Schubert, W.H. and Lopez, A.L. (1993). Teacher lore as a basis for in-service education of teachers. *Teaching and Teachers' Work, 1* (4), 1–8.

Schubert, W. H., Thomas, T. P., Wojcik, J.T., Zissis, G., Hulsebosch, P., Koerner, M., and Millies, P. S. (1987). Teaching about progressive education: From the course to study group? *Teaching Education, 1* (2), 77–81.

Schwab, J. J. (1970). *The practical: A language for curriculum.* Washington, D.C.: National Education Association.

Schwarz, G. (2001). *Teacher lore.* Bloomington, IN: Phi Delta Kappa.

Schwarz, G. & Albert, J. (Eds.). (1998). *Teacher lore and professional development for school reform.* Westport, CT: Bergin & Garvey.

Thirty Schools. (1942). *The thirty schools tell their stories.* New York: Harper & Brothers.

Witherell, C. & Noddings, N. (Eds.). (1991). *Stories lives tell: Narrative and dialogue in education.* New York: Teachers College Press.

Acknowledgments

Without the dedication and hard work of the following people at Peter Lang Publishing this book would not have been possible. Thank you to Patricia Mulrane Clayton, Bernadette Shade, Sophie Appel, Heather Boyle and Phyllis Korper. We thank Chris Myers for his patience, humor, and concise ("guy talk") responses to our many questions. A special debt of gratitude to Shirley Steinberg for taking the time to read our initial proposal and believing that what we had to say was pertinent and timely. Finally, our years at the University of Illinois at Chicago would not have been the same without the insight of Bill Schubert and Bill Ayers, who envisioned that teaching is a profession worthy of pursuit, and continue to champion the value of teacher voices as we consider what is worthwhile to know and experience.

Introduction: What Are Narratives and Why Use Them in Teacher Education?

ROBERT W. BLAKE JR. & BRETT ELIZABETH BLAKE

We all have stories to tell, and yet the meaning, or even the "value," of these stories or narratives is always open to interpretation. Today, the term *narrative* is not only used in educational circles but also in popular culture circles as well as in intellectual cultural circles (often termed the "cultural elite")—as can be seen on someone's Facebook page or in the pages of *The New Yorker* magazine. For example, a recent piece in the "The Talk of The Town" section called "Life Stories" by Ian Frazier (2011) describes a program called Theatricalizing the Personal Narrative begun in an upstate New York prison, in which inmates told stories that took "technical skill" and could "become draining" but eventually, as they "pushed through," turned into art (p. 21). In popular cultural circles, all one needs to do is to conduct a Google Internet search with the keyword "narrative" and one of the sites that pops up is called News for Narrative. For example, an August 1, 2011 search at this site revealed these five articles:

- "Five Ways to Understand the Harry Potter Narrative"
- "Thou Shalt Not Defy the Narrative on Israel"
- "The GOP's False Fiscal Narrative"
- "The Jeter Narrative"
- "Canadian Media's Narrative of the Afghan War Suspiciously Like a Fairy Tale"

You can even have the word narrative added to personalize your Google home page. Let's face it. In today's society, you're really not cool unless you have a narrative—your own personal narrative—as expressed through Twitter, Facebook, a blog, or in the pages of the news media we read.

So why this emphasis on narratives in teacher education? Twenty years ago, *Teacher Lore: Learning from Our Own Experience* was published and quickly became an alternative to the traditional notions and models of research, inquiry, and teacher knowledge. Genres such as action research, teacher as researcher, educational criticism (Eisner, 1991), reflective practice, and narrative research (Clandinin, 2004; Kohler-Riessman, 1993, 2008) all link to this groundbreaking work, and educational and social science researchers alike embraced the notion that "the greatest potential of 'teacher lore' resides in an oral tradition among teachers who exchange and reconstruct perspectives together" (Schubert and Ayers, 1992, vii). Using a format that highlights teachers' own words, "sometimes by telling stories of teaching experience," Schubert and Ayers (1992) remind us (and celebrate) the value of teachers' experiences, knowledge, and voices. Several years later, we, the editors, began the process of collecting narratives or stories from our students, student teachers, and teachers in an effort to understand better what Schubert and Ayers began focusing on—the purpose of narrative in education.

Today, twenty years later, teachers' voices have been supplanted by state and national mandates; by policies and policy makers who demand "scientifically based" data and outcomes; by a government that takes money from schools that already have few resources; by media that are complicit in chastising teachers for their failure to properly educate children. Like Schubert and Ayers (who were our former professors at The University of Illinois at Chicago), we see the potential of narrative as a means to counter the mandates of the government and other policy makers and once again engage teachers in reflective practices. We see the potential for teachers to construct and reconstruct the stories and experiences that take place in their classrooms into a narrative that is instructive, useful, and promising to students and to other teachers who read these narratives and use them to understand and enhance their own teaching. It seems to be a propitious time to return to the discussion we highlighted earlier: Narrative is simply back in style.

We see this book as an attempt to build upon what our former professors and mentors, Schubert and Ayers, started and envisioned, which is that both preservice and in-service teachers will find themselves going through these pages as they struggle to create their own classrooms and their own understandings of what it means to become a teacher across all grade levels and subject areas, such as science, special education, or urban English language learners (ELLs). We also hope that this book can serve as a "reminder" to those of us in teacher education that the very mandates that control so much of our curricula, funding, and publishing decisions can be reconstructed to reflect what we know is good teaching—what we have learned to be good practice—and what we know works in spite of standardized testing and accountability measures that declare the opposite.

Narrative as Reflective Practice

Written reflections are but one way to analyze and assess the practice of teaching. In preservice teacher education, for example, we often find professors asking students to "journal" or reflect on their teaching experiences as a means to better not only their own learning but also to assess their students' learning. Teacher preparation programs are often accused, however, of focusing primarily on the theory of teaching, or the ideal of teaching, in which students are expected to simply transfer what they have learned at the university into their classroom experience. On the other hand, schools tend to focus on the "now," pragmatic experiences, or the reality of teaching, with little perceived connection to theory. The difficulty, as Bryan and Abell (1999) pose it is, "How do teacher educators go about helping their students to articulate, analyze, and refine their beliefs about teaching and learning?" (1999, p. 122).

We can also ask how do we move beyond an application-of-theory-model (Korthagen & Kessels, 1999, p. 4) to help teachers (pre- and in-service) to bridge theory and practice? In science, Trumbull (1999) uses narratives to discuss the adjustment novice biology teachers face in becoming teachers and their attempt to bridge theory and practice. She suggests:

> Once they [pre-service teachers] complete teacher education programs, new teachers enter schools where practices engender particular conceptualizations of teaching. The conceptualizations of teaching that are promulgated in these different settings are not all consistent. A lack of consistency across contexts can impose stresses on new teachers and render their professional development complex. . . . (p. xv).

From Trumbull's viewpoint, the strength of these stories is their ability to provide us a better understanding of how these new teachers " . . . manage the contradictions across different conceptualizations? How do they succeed in their contexts of practice?" (p. xv).

This book highlights not only how the use of narratives links theory to practice but also showcases the richness and reality of these experiences, which may not be apparent in a more formal presentation of the classroom experience. We agree with Bruner (1985) in his suggestion that the narrative and paradigmatic ways of knowing are two "modes of cognitive functioning" (p. 97). Whereas the paradigmatic focuses on science to seek objective truth, the narrative, being context sensitive, seeks "truth-likeness" (p. 97). He (1985) suggests that "good narrative is full of human factivity—wanting, opining, decrying" (p. 106) and that "great narrative is an invitation to problem finding, not a lesson on problem solving" (2002, p. 20).

The goal of narratives, therefore, is not to produce "truth" in an objective, empirical, scientific sense but to create "believability" through the construction of good stories. Kohler-Riessman (1993) asserts that "individuals recapitulated and reinterpreted their lives through story telling" (p. vi) and that "narrativization assumes point of view. . . . [where]. . . . facts are an interpretive process" (p. 64), with differing accounts about the same event evident from different authors. Politics of religion aside, one account or story by different authors is clearly represented in the gospels of the bible ("Matthew," "Mark," "Luke," and "John"). In *The Case for Christ*, Strobel (1998) points out that narrative as an oral tradition predates written books and the printing press, and that narratives, or stories, were passed along for the purpose of imparting lessons. Although obvious differences exist among the four gospels the four versions preserve the main components and importance of the story, and the differences are related to the individual narrator's view of the events through the contexts of his own experiences. The lens through which a story is told is embedded in the lived experiences of the storyteller, and the creation of meaning, or "believability," rests with the individual reader as she relates the story to her personal contexts and experiences in life. By encouraging an analytical, reflective process, we seek to gain insight into how teachers "manage the [theory-practice] contradictions across different conceptualizations" (Trumbull, 1999, p. xv) of teaching.

The Professional Stance

In becoming a teacher, we also encourage students to construct (and "seasoned" teachers, perhaps, to "reconstruct") a narrative around what that act of becoming means. Referred to throughout this book, we define a *professional stance* as a set of beliefs that a teacher (whether novice or veteran) constructs as she juxtaposes her original personal theory of teaching with the realities of her everyday practice. We portray narratives as a means for reflecting on practice, for assessing what one believes and does in teaching, and to use narratives as a means to help individuals reconstruct their *personal theory* into a professional stance (see Blake & Haines, 2009).

We each begin with our *theory* of teaching, a set of personal beliefs constructed from the association of prior experiences, which includes those gained in classroom situations and university coursework, and influenced by and possibly changed by new experiences in the classroom. We label this new set of beliefs—the ones that allow teachers to function in the pragmatic day-to-day tasks of the profession—the professional stance. As part of the ever-changing process of teaching, the professional stance is a reconstruction or reorganization of personal theory, which happens as beliefs are manifested in the practice of full-time teaching. This stance is influenced by many factors (see Figure 1.1), is used as a means to bridge theory and practice, and allows us to examine practical issues of teaching while incorporating theory within that process (Blake & Haines, 2009).

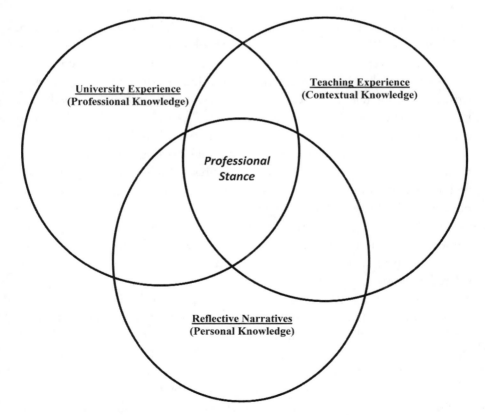

Figure 1.1 Constructing a Professional Stance Through Narratives

One purpose of using narratives as a means to articulate beliefs is to aid teachers as they link beliefs and theories with actual classroom practice. As a teacher gains experience, she reconstructs her personal theory relative to the culture of schooling. The professional stance is ultimately the central guiding system of beliefs that influences what the teacher does in the classroom.

Organization of the Book

There are a number of books that focus on teachers' narratives of their practice and what we can glean from these stories (Ayers & Ayers, 2011; Blake, 2004; Jalongo & Eisenberg, 1995; Miller, 2005; Mack-Kirschner, 2004; Trumbull, 1999; Schubert & Ayers, 1992). There are also books on how to undertake narrative inquiry (Clandinin & Connelly, 2000; Ritchie & Wilson, 2000; Lieblich, Tuval-Mashiach, & Zilber, 1998; Kohler-Riessman, 1993, 2008) and ones that provide historical and contemporary information of the role that narratives play, and have played, in everyday life (Bruner, 1986, 2003; Polkinghorne, 1988). There is even a textbook that uses narratives to exemplify the methods of teaching elementary/middle school science (Koch, 2009).

Because we believe in including many voices, in the pages that follow in this book, we include "new" teacher researchers as well as more "seasoned" ones (from 2 years experience in the classroom to 60 years); arts and counseling in education teachers as well as foundations and social studies educators; all of whom in some way have used narrative in their classrooms. We have also tried to draw authors from across the country, representing what we hope is a unified national view of the urgency of once again listening to teachers' voices and narratives. We believe that our book is unique in that it focuses on narrative as being instructive in various disciplines across various grade levels—complementing books on narrative already written. (See Table 1.1 for a list of selected works beginning with the year 2000, which is, however, in no way to be considered exhaustive or comprehensive.)

We have attempted to organize the 10 chapters of this book into themes. Although we would never insist that one needs to read each chapter in order, we do believe that there is a thematic structure to what we have presented, however fluid it may seem. With that in mind, Chapter 2 begins our journey by sketching out the historical roots of narrative, stretching back to antiquity. Chapters 3 and 4 focus on two disciplines that we have deemed to be more traditional and the resultant narratives, and Chapters 5 through 10 introduce the new potential of narrative in such areas as digital narratives, narratives among counselors in education, and narratives from our English language learners.

Table 1.1 Selected Works Beginning with the Year 2000

As research and research methodology

Gubrium, J. F., & Holstein, J. A. (2009). *Analyzing narrative reality*. Thousand Oaks, CA: Sage.

Ritchie, J. S., & Wilson, D. E. (2000). *Teacher narrative as critical inquiry: Rewriting the script*. New York, NY: Teachers College Press.

Reissman, C. K. (2008). *Narrative methods for the human sciences*. Thousand Oaks, CA: Sage.

Clandinin, D. J., & Connelly, F. M. (2000). *Narrative inquiry: Experience and story in qualitative research*. San Francisco, CA: Jossey-Bass.

As preservice foundations

Alsop, S., Bencze, L., & Pedretti, E. (Eds.). (2005). *Analysing exemplary science teaching*. New York, NY: Open University Press.

Lyons, N., & LaBoskey, V. K. (Eds.). (2002). *Narrative inquiry in practice: Advancing the knowledge of teaching*. New York, NY: Teachers College Press.

Miller, P. C. (Ed). (2005). *Narratives from the classroom: An introduction to teaching*. Thousand Oaks, CA: Sage.

As middle-level inquiry

Malu, K. F. (Ed.). (2010). *Voices from the middle: Narrative inquiry by, for, and about the middle level community*. Charlotte, NC: Information Age.

As an international perspective

Mattos, A. M. A. (Ed). (2009). *Narratives on teaching and teacher education: An international perspective*. New York, NY: Palgrave Macmillan.

And as biography, life history, case study, and teacher autobiography

Ayers , R. & Ayers, W. (2011). *Teaching the taboo. Courage and imagination in the classroom*. New York, NY: Teachers College Press.

Ayers, W. (2001). *To teach: The journey of a teacher*. New York, NY: Teachers College Press.

Blake, B. E. (2003). *A culture of refusal: The lives and literacies of out-of-school adolescents*. New York, NY: Peter Lang.

Kozol, J. (2000). *Ordinary resurrections: Children in the years of hope*. New York, NY: Crown.

Kozol, J. (2009). *Letters to a young teacher*. New York, NY: Three Rivers Press.

To be specific, Robert W. Blake Sr. begins Chapter 2 by highlighting our past—the writings of Homer, Herodotus, and Thucydides, whom the author, suggests literally "invented the genre we call narrative." Then, he moves into the classroom, which he shares with us techniques to write the memoir, a special kind of narrative that can "call forth bright images, conjure up sharp senses, and awaken profound feelings." Chapter 3 looks at preservice special education teachers as they reflect on their student teaching or internship experiences. In this chapter, Darlene Fewster using such wonderful thematic descriptors as "Crayons in the box" and "Who moved the cheese?" reminds us how these students' narratives serve as "powerful mechanisms for learning about the rewards and challenges of teaching students with diverse learning needs." Chapter 4 takes us into the science preservice classroom, where students reflect on their field experiences. Beginning with a wonderful story about his young daughter, Mackenzie Grace, Robert W. Blake Jr., presents us with not only a model for teaching science but also an avenue through which we can openly reflect and analyze "good" science teaching through the lens of "becoming a science teacher." Blake reminds us how crucial these things are in being able to say, "Elementary science is an endangered species."

Chapter 5 introduces us to using the arts in school counseling education. Helen Garinger and five of her graduate counseling students wrestle with the notions of using "artistic endeavors to engage students, convey ideas, and provide an alternative to talk therapy." In conclusion, Garinger reminds us that one of the greatest challenges in this field is indeed to "get teachers and counselors to use the arts in a narrative capacity." Chapter 6, written by Sandra Schamroth Abrams, takes us into her preservice secondary-level, state-required language acquisition course with majors in history, math, science, and English. In this chapter, Schamroth Abrams explains how "21st century technologies have provided dynamic opportunities to construct personal and collective narratives," leading into what she terms a "third space" in which students' digital, reflective narratives "advanced their thinking about education and practice through online interactions." Mary Beth Schaefer begins Chapter 7 vividly by taking us into one of her seventh-grade English language arts (ELA) classrooms. Using "narrative inquiry as a window to Reader Response" in an actual middle school classroom, Schaefer reports that the seventh-grade students and she as a teacher, through narrative, "changed everything about power and learning in the classroom."

We believe our journey into new realms for narrative reflection in the form of "digital stories" begins in Chapter 6, perhaps moving us beyond the so-called traditional disciplines (but in which we tell stories) and continues in the narratives in Chapters 8 to 10, in which we find ourselves, students, and teachers appearing in more "contested" spaces like migrant workers' camps, graduate social foundations classrooms, and urban in-school and out-of-school contexts. We see these chapters as fluid, reflecting our attempt to highlight the ways we can now apply *critical* interpretations in forming this overall perspective of ourselves. which we call a professional stance.

Specifically, in Chapter 8, Julie Carter explores one example of the use of story, or "critical incidents," as a pedagogical tool for teacher development in her graduate social foundations course. She argues convincingly that using these critical incidents can help both pre-and in-service teachers to "locate themselves with education and to imagine socially-just places" as they become teachers and reflect on their own lives as ways to reflect on those of their students. In Chapter 9, Elizabeth Quintero offers us a new model by which to support the early-childhood learning of migrant farmworkers' children. Referred to as "listening, dialogue, and action," we see how this model can allow pre-service teachers to move from narrative study to action in their attempt to strongly support these children (and other ELLs) in their content-learning experiences. Quintero eloquently reminds us of all parents' "profound hopes [for the] voices of possibility" of their young children.

To conclude, in Chapter 10, Brett Elizabeth Blake, situates narrative in a globalized context, drawing on research on "voice" and "cultural texts" from a critical perspective. Blake shows us how both teachers of urban students and of urban/ELL students can move closer to a more authentic "cultural identity" through the use of story and reflection and naming and challenging institutionalized ideas around bullying, discrimination, and racism.

The boundaries of disciplines have gotten blurred in elementary, middle, and both pre- and postsecondary classrooms today, and expectations are that the material on high-stakes state and national assessments is increasingly cross-disciplinary at every level. As such, we urge you, the reader, to invoke a critical stance to *all* that you read here, so that, like Schubert and Ayers (1992), we, too, can discover and/or rediscover the power of a narrative and that, as they put it, through story or through a student's or teacher's own words:

> . . . the secret of teaching [can be] found in the local detail and the everyday life of teachers; teachers can be the richest and most useful source of knowledge about teaching; those who hope to understand teaching must turn at some point to teachers themselves. (Prologue, v)

References

Alsop, S., Bencze, L., & Pedretti, E. (Eds). (2005). *Analysing exemplary science teaching.* New York, NY: Open University Press.

Ayers , R. & Ayers, W (2011). *Teaching the taboo. Courage and imagination in the classroom.* New York, NY: Teachers College Press.

Ayers, W. (2001). *To teach: The journey of a teacher.* New York, NY: Teachers College Press.

Blake, B. E. (2003). *A culture of refusal: The lives and literacies of out-of-school adolescents.* New York, NY: Peter Lang

Blake, R. W. Jr. (2004). *An enactment of science: A dynamic balance among curriculum, context, and teacher beliefs.* New York, NY: Peter Lang.

Blake, R. W. Jr., & Haines, S. (2009). Becoming a teacher: Using narratives to develop a professional stance of teaching science. In A. M. A. Mattos (Ed.), *Narratives on teaching and teacher education: An international perspective.* New York, NY: Palgrave Macmillan.

Bruner, J. (1985). Narrative and paradigmatic modes of thought. In Elliot Eisner (Ed.), *Learning and teaching the ways of knowing. Eighty-fourth yearbook of the national society for the study of education: Part II* (pp. 97–115). Chicago, IL: University of Chicago Press.

Bruner, J. (1986). *Actual minds, possible worlds.* Cambridge, MA: Harvard University Press.

Bruner, J. (2003). *Making stories: Law, literature, life.* Cambridge, MA: Harvard University Press.

Bryan, L. A., & Abell, S. K. (1999). Development of professional knowledge in learning to teach elementary science. *Journal of Research in Science Teaching, 36*(2), 121–139.

Clandinin, J. (2004). *Narrative inquiry: Experience and story in qualitative research.* Hoboken, NJ: Wiley.

Clandinin, D. J., & Connelly, F. M. (2000). *Narrative inquiry: Experience and story in qualitative research.* San Francisco, CA: Jossey-Bass.

Eisner, E.W. (1991). *The enlightened eye: Qualitative inquiry and the enhancement of educational practice.* New York, NY: Macmillan.

Frazier, I. (2011, August). Life Stories. *The New Yorker,* 21.

Gubrium, J. F., & Holstein, J. A. (2009). *Analyzing narrative reality.* Thousand Oaks, CA: Sage.

Jalongo, M. R., & Eisenberg, J. (1995). *Teachers' stories: From personal narrative to professional insight.* Hoboken, NJ: Wiley.

Kagan, D. M. (1992). Implications of research on teacher belief. *Educational Psychologist, 27*(1), 65–90.

Koch, J. (2009). *Science stories: Science methods for elementary and middle school teachers.* Florence, KY: Wadsworth.

Kohler-Riessman, C. (1993). *Narrative analysis: Qualitative research methods: Series 30.* Thousand Oaks, CA: Sage.

Kohler-Riessman, C. (2008). *Narrative methods for the human sciences.* Thousand Oaks, CA: Sage.

Kooy, M. (2006). The telling stories of novice teachers: Constructing teacher knowledge in book clubs. *Teaching and Teacher Education, 22*(6), 661–674.

Korthagen, F. J., & Kessels, J. P. (1999). Linking theory and practice: Changing the pedagogy of teacher education. *Educational Researcher, 28*(4), 4–17.

Kozol, J. (2000). *Ordinary resurrections: Children in the years of hope.* New York, NY: Crown.

Kozol, J. (2009). *Letters to a young teacher.* New York, NY: Three Rivers Press.

Lieblich, A., Tuval-Mashiach, R., & Zilber, T. (1998). *Narrative research: Reading, analysis and interpretation*. Newbury Park, CA: Sage.

Lyons, N., & Labosky, V. K. (2002). *Narrative inquiry in practice: Advancing the knowledge of teaching: Practitioner inquiry series*. New York, NY: Teachers College Press.

Mack-Kirschner, A. (2004). *Powerful classroom stories from accomplished teachers: Stories from the classrooms of accomplished teachers*. Thousand Oaks, CA: Sage.

Malu, K. F. (Ed). (2010). *Voices from the middle: Narrative inquiry by, for, and about the middle level community*. Charlotte, NC: Information Age.

Mattos, A. M. A. (Ed). (2009). *Narratives on teaching and teacher education: An international perspective*. New York, NY: Palgrave Macmillan.

Miller, P. C. (Ed). (2005). *Narratives from the classroom: An introduction to teaching*. Thousand Oaks, CA: Sage.

Munby, H. (1984). A qualitative approach to the study of teacher's beliefs. *Journal of Research in Science Teaching, 21*(1), 27–38.

Polkinghorne, D.E. (1988). *Narrative knowing and the human sciences*. Albany, NY: SUNY Press.

Ritchie, J. S., & Wilson, D. E. (2000). *Teacher narrative as critical inquiry: Rewriting the script*. New York, NY: Teachers College Press.

Schubert, W. H., & Ayers, W. C. (Eds.). (1992). *Teacher lore: Learning from our own experience*. New York, NY: Longman.

Strobel, L. (1998). *The case for Christ: A journalist's personal investigation of the evidence for Jesus*. Grand Rapids, MI: Zondervan.

Tabachnick, B. R., Popkewitz, T. S., & Zeichner, K. M. (1979). Teacher education and the professional perspectives of student teachers. *Interchange, 10*(4), 12–29.

Trimmer, J. (Ed.). 1997. *Narration as knowledge: Tales of the teaching life* (pp. ix–xv). Portsmouth, NH: Boynton Cook.

Trumbull, D. J. 1999. *The new science teacher*. New York, NY: Teachers College Press.

· 2 ·

Tell Me a Story

The Forms and Uses of Narrative

Robert W. Blake Sr.

Storytelling—or *narrative*, which seems to be used interchangeably with the word *story*—is as old as language itself. But even though the word story has assumed so many shapes and purposes over the centuries, it is still the default term for explaining meaningful experiences and difficult ideas.

Conscientious parents tell us stories in order to teach us how to behave; in effect to introduce us to our culture and a worldview. Recent research tells us that storytelling for children is essential if they are to become literate, fully functioning citizens in this globalized world. And as children hear these stories verbatim time and time again, they learn to expect a particular structure, with the bad guys always being beaten up by the good guys. Later, as they grow up, they experience stories in the movies, read books in print and electronic form, and may read human nature stories in newspapers. (We are told that someone in *The New York Times* invented the "anecdotal lead" for all news stories as well as with editorials and op-ed pieces.)

In this chapter, I first discuss how the earliest writers of narrative—three iconic authors of antiquity, Homer, Herodotus, and Thucydides—literally invented the genre of storytelling. Their stories are so powerful that we still enjoy reading, studying, and seeing versions of them in theaters, such as in the very successful movie *Troy*, a version of Homer's *The Iliad*, which opened in 2004 and in the *Three Hundred Spartans*, which came out in 1962 and later became a graphic novel, simply called *300*. Both movies are based on Herodotus's account of the 300 Spartans battling against thousands of Persians at the pass of Thermopylae. The three ancient innovators of narrative I shall be taking into account are:

- *The Iliad* by Homer, which is generally known as the greatest epic poem in literature but also the most tragic;
- *The Histories* by Herodotus, the author known as the "father of history"; and
- *The History of the Peloponnesian War* by Thucydides, the author who considered that his history was "done to last forever."

Next, I introduce kindergarteners through adults to a successful, classroom—tested way to compose a type of narrative we know as the "memoir."

Three Iconic Narratives by the Ancients

How have the shapes and purposes of narratives morphed over the centuries? Why is it important for us to learn how they evolved? One answer is that if students become knowledgeable about several outstanding kinds of narratives, they may broaden their understanding of a wide range of possible kinds of narratives as well as make sense of contemporary narratives and even write their own narratives. In order for students to understand the salient characteristics of the following narratives, I recommend that they read the subsequent summaries carefully, write out short responses to what they have read, and discuss their findings with other students. The general topics they might attend to are listed in Table 2.1.

Homer's *The Iliad*: How the Greeks Were Educated

Robert Fagles (Homer, 1991), a recent translator of *The Iliad* from the ancient Greek to contemporary English, sums up his idea of the fundamental meaning of the poetic epic as follows: "The rage of Achilles—its cause, its course, and disastrous consequences—is the theme of the poem, the mainspring

Table 2.1 Suggested Writing Prompts for Readings

Introduction

Name the author of the narrative, including relevant information about him or her and the age in which he or she lived.

Meaning

First, write out a simple, one- or two-sentence statement of the general meaning of the narrative. Then, after you have read about the narrative and thought about its influence throughout the ages, write out a longer reaction of several pages. What for you is the deeper meaning of this complex narrative? What ideas and conclusions have you come away with from your reading, either explicit or implied?

Characteristic Form

What is the distinctive structure of the narrative? Describe how it is put together, and tell how its form is related to the meaning of the narrative.

Reputation

What is the present-day reputation of the narrative and its author? Why has the work lasted? How was the narrative originally received?

of the plot" (p. 3). However, the theme of war and its unremitting scenes of death and destruction is only one aspect of the epic. Throughout the poem, we find example after example of the warrior's wish for a peaceful life.

It is believed that *The Iliad* was created by a single poet called Homer rather than being developed over the ages by a series of minstrels. Although we have no records of the life of Homer, the people of seven Greek cities were convinced he was born in their city. It is generally accepted, however, that he was born in Ionia, on the eastern Aegean Sea. Scholars do agree that the epic—originally handed down orally for centuries—was first written in an alphabet invented by the Greeks in the late-eighth or early-seventh century B.C.E. (The abbreviation B.C.E., which stands for "before the common era," contains the traditional abbreviation B.C., which stands for "before Christ"; Blake & Blake, 2005, p. 51)

What was the author's—or authors'—purpose in telling this tale? What do we take away from the epic poem, either in terms of what the author explicitly tells us or what we find implicitly revealed in the epic? According to Knox (Homer, trans. 1991), director emeritus of Harvard's Center for Hellenic Studies in Washington, DC, the title *Iliad* simply means "a poem about 'Iliam' (i.e., Troy)," (p. 3), and it has been known as *The Iliad* ever since the Greek historian Herodotus called it that in the fifth century B.C.E.

Here are the opening lines of Book One of *The Iliad*, "The Rage of Achilles." The lines lay out quite forcefully one major meaning of the epic:

BOOK ONE: "THE RAGE OF ACHILLES"

Rage—Goddess, sing the rage of Peleus son Achilles,
murderous, doomed, that cost the Achaeans countless losses,
hurling down to the House of Death so many sturdy souls,
great fighters' souls, but made their bodies carrion,
feasts for the dogs and birds,
and the will of Zeus was moving toward its end.
Begin, Muse, when the two first broke and clashed,
Agamemnon lord of men and brilliant Achilles.

Was there ever an opening to a story as gripping as this one! As Knox, a classical scholar (Homer, 1991), points out, "These two poles of the human condition, war and peace, with their corresponding aspects of human nature, the destructive and creative, are implied in every situation and statement of the poem..."(62).

But back to the deeper dual meanings of *The Iliad*. With constant horrendous battles and individual contests, we have the ever-present "warriors'" dream of peace, a normal life beyond war. According to Knox (Homer, trans. 1991):

These vivid pictures of normal life, drawn with consummate skill and inserted in a relentless series of gruesome killings, have a special poignancy; they are one of the features of Homer's evocation of battle which makes it unique: exquisite balance between the celebration of war's tragic, heroic values and those creative values of civilized life that war destroys. (p. 62)

We acknowledge these two contradictory phases of life in the heroic epic in the most piercing way when we encounter the "great and massive shield" created by the crippled Smith, god of fire, the great artificer Hephaestus. First, Homer (trans. 1991) has him create a "great and massive shield" using "all his craft and cunning, a work of gorgeous immortal work" (p. 483). What does Homer have

Hephaestus include on the magnificent shield for Achilles? Of course, war has its place on the shield, but if we can lay aside looking at the images of battles and deaths for a few moments, we find on the shield Homer's idea of a peaceful community.

What is Hephaestus's design for the shield? He places on it the earth, the sky, the sea, the "inexhaustible blazing sun," and the "moon rounding full." (Homer, 1991, p. 483) He forges two cities, one with "weddings and wedding feasts"; the other with men struggling over the "bloodprice for a kinsman murdered" (p. 483).

> And he forged a king's estate where harvesters labored (p. 485)
>
> And he forged a thriving vineyard loaded with clusters, bunches of lustrous grapes in gold (p. 485)
>
> And he forged on the shield a herd of longhorn cattle (p. 486)
>
> And the famous cripple Smith forged a meadow deep in a shaded glen for shimmering flocks to graze (p. 486)
>
> And the crippled Smith brought all his art to bear on a dancing circle, broad as the circle Daedalus once laid out on Cnossos' spacious fields for Ariadne the girl with lustrous hair (p. 486)
>
> Here young boys and girls, beauties courted
> With costly gifts of oxen, danced and danced . . .
> A breathless crowd stood round them struck with joy (p. 487).

According to Knox (Homer, 1991), in the end, Homer closes with the dance, "that formal symbol of the precise and ordered relations of people in peaceful society" (p. 62).

Here then, Homer depicts aspects of the Greek culture other than that of the wrath of Achilles and of unremitting violence, human waste, and destruction. If there is the honor and acclimation for the great warrior, there is always the deeply felt warrior's dream of peace.

Although *The Iliad* is a terrific read, a tale of the rage of Achilles and how it affects all the characters around him, one of the purposes of the poem is a didactic one, in that it taught the ancient Greeks how to behave as citizens. For according to Blake and Blake (2005), it was created "to pass on to citizens a certain worldview, a common history they needed to share in order to survive as a cohesive people" (p. 58).

There is another element of *The Iliad* that deserves consideration: A great deal has been made of the fact that the characters in the poem are "high-born," "nobles," or exceptional people. But the characters in *The Iliad* were selected not for snobbish reasons. Indeed they exist to teach lessons on *how not* to behave as well as *how* to behave. The poem includes characters of great importance because, by their actions, they exemplify two related Greek laws, the public laws, or *noma,* as well as family or private laws, known as *ethos,* the Greek word from which we derive the modern English word "ethics." "In effect, Homer's epics united all the citizens of the *poleis* (city-states)—in spite of their constant arguments and skirmishes—into a single, proud people" (Blake and Blake, 2005, p. 54).

Characteristic form

The Iliad was originally recited, or sung orally to preliterate audiences as poetry with regular hexameter lines of verse consisting of six metrical feet. Why such an unusual form? Because we all know we can memorize regular verse more easily than we can remember irregular prose, especially, prose such as we encounter, for instance, in works of abstract philosophy, like Plato's *The Republic*. Not only is it epic in poetry, but it also has other fairly regular features that allowed minstrels to learn its some 15,693 lines of verse by heart.

Another way to ease memorization of *The Iliad* was its "recurring epithets," the repeated labels that identified each hero, king, queen, nobleman, beautiful woman, god, or goddess. For instance, whenever Agamemnon appears, the descriptive term "lord of men" or "wide-ruling" appears, and the great warrior Achilles is regularly identified as "brilliant," "godlike," or "swift-footed."

We are told that these recurring epithets are used not to underline the fact that Achilles is "godlike." Rather, it may be that the familiar epithets were chosen because a particular item fits a line of meter. When the minstrel is reciting the poem and doesn't know how to finish a line of poetry, he simply plugs in an epithet that belongs in that spot and is related to the appropriate character.

Reputation

What is the reputation of *The Iliad*? For Knox (Homer, trans. 1991), "*The Iliad* remains not only the greatest epic poem in literature but also the most tragic." He continues:

Homer's Achilles is clearly the model for the tragic hero of the Sophoclean stage; his stubborn, passionate devotion to an ideal image of self is the same force that draws Antigone, Oedipus, Ajax and Philoctetes to the fulfillment of their destinies. Homer's Achilles is also, for archaic Greek society, the essence of the aristocratic ideal, the paragon of male beauty, courage and patrician manner—the "the splendor running in the blood," says Pindar [Greek lyric poet]. (p. 63)

The Histories by Herodotus: The Father of History

Although we know little of the life of Herodotus, he was recognized by the ancients as well as by many moderns, with his title—first given by Cicero (Roman statesman and philosopher, 106–43 B.C.E.)—the "father of history."

Herodotus was born about 490 B.C.E. in Halicarnassus, a city located on the southwest coast of Asia Minor. He traveled throughout the ancient Mediterranean world, visiting Egypt, Africa, the Black Sea, and several Greek city-states. He sojourned in Athens for a while, we are told, and gave readings to sizable audiences, recounting his extensive adventures, and he became friends with the playwright Sophocles, the author of the universally acclaimed play *Oedipus Rex* among many others. Herodotus died "some time" between 425 and 420 B.C.E.

Meaning

What was the subject matter of *The Histories?* Why was Herodotus's work called *The Histories?* First of all, the original meaning of the word *history* is a "narrative of events; a story" (*The American Heritage Dictionary of the English Language*, 4th ed., s. v. "history"). The word history, then, is just another word, meaning story. Our word history originates in the Greek word *historia,* for the original word *historein,* which means "to inquire."

We need to remember that Herodotus was in unknown territory when he wrote *The Histories.* He single-handedly invented a genre of history as he went along. Translated by Aubrey De Sélincourt (Herodotus, 2003), Herodotus

lived in a time when categories of knowledge had not been rigidly separated, and his work ranges over many fields and includes geography, anthropology, ethnology, zoology, even fable and folklore. His work defies easy categorization: like Homer, Herodotus is a world unto himself. (p. xiv)

Herodotus states about himself that "[he] aimed to write about human achieve-ments, and [he] also wants to write about the great and monstrous deeds" accomplished by the Greeks and barbarians (the word "barbarian" was not pejo-rative but simply a word for peoples who could not speak Greek and made noises liked this: "ba, ba, ba").

When Herodotus studied people, he was concerned about all aspects of their culture: their monuments, religious beliefs, customs, how they made a liv-ing, and the natural wonders of the country. We also find in *The Histories* sto-ries he picked up along the way, accounts we would now describe as folktales, much like the fairytales later written by the Brothers Grimm. For De Sélincourt (Herodotus, trans. 2003), "Many of Herodotus' readers can sense that whatever his shortcomings as a historian—in the modern sense of the word—he is a story-teller of the first rank" (p. xvi).

Because of his love for the marvelous, the unusual, and the fantastic, he was criticized by his contemporaries "as a tall-story teller"; he was considered both the "father of history" and the "father of lies." No wonder so many of his fol-lowers loved to learn about his exaggerations and make-believe tales! Herodotus, however, is best known as a historian for his treatment of the wars between the Persians and the Greeks. According to Marincola (2003), in his preface to *The Histories*, Herodotus reports being interested especially in "why the two peoples the Persians and the Greeks, fought each other" (p. xvi). His accounts of the sea battle at Salimas and the battles of Marathon and Thermopylae have become legendary.

From the battle at Marathon between the Spartan Greeks and the Persians, we get the apocryphal story of the messenger Pheidippides, a professional long-distance runner, who ran to the city of Sparta to proclaim a Greek victory over the Persians and then dropped dead.

Our modern tradition of a long-distance marathon of 26 miles and 385 yards (41.3 kilometers), named for the battle at Marathon, comes to us from Herodotus's treatment of the battle in *The Histories*.

When the Greek forces met the overwhelming Persian forces, on the plain of Marathon, we sense why the account of the battle has lived on for centuries. Here is Herodotus's (trans. 2003) description of the battle:

> The Athenians came on, closed with the enemy all along the line, and fought in a way
> not to be forgotten; they were the first Greeks, so far as we know, to charge at a run, and
> first who dare to look without flinching at Persian dress and the men who wore it; for
> until that day came, no Greek could hear even the word Persian without terror. (p. 401)

At the battle of Thermopylae, the Greeks had repulsed the Persian hordes until a Greek traitor told the Persian King Xerxes about a pass behind the Spartan lines. When Leonidas, the commander of the 300 Spartan warriors who remained to fight the Persians, learned of this treachery, he released all the Greeks except the 300 warriors, who would not retreat because they were honor bound to fight to the death.

From the battle of the Spartans, several sayings have survived. At one point the Spartans were told that "When the Persians shot their arrows, there are so many of them that they hid the sun." Unmoved, a Spartan merely remarked, "This is pleasant news that the stranger from Trachis brings us: if the Persians hide the sun, we shall have our battle in the shade" (Herodotus, 2003, pp. 494–495).

The Spartans fought the Persians to the last man, and when their swords were destroyed, they fought with hands and teeth. The Spartan dead were buried where they had fought. For the fallen Spartans, a special epitaph with the following inscription was erected: "Go tell the Spartans, you who read: We took this order, and here lie dead." (Herodotus, trans. 2003, p. 495).

Herodotus treats in some detail the naval battle between the Persians and the Greeks at Salamis, an island on the Hellespont, also referred to as the Dardanelles, the name of the strait connecting the Aegean Sea with the Sea of Marmara. The Battle of Salamis was another victory for the Greeks. Here, Herodotus (trans. 2003) describes how the Greeks out-fought the Persians:

> The greater part of the Persian fleet suffered severely in the battle, the Athenians and Aeginetans accounting for a great many of their ships. Since the Greek fleet worked together as a whole, while the Persians had lost formation and were no longer fighting on any plan, that was bound to happen. (p. 529)

Herodotus (2003) goes on to report , "A few days after the battle of Salamis, Xerxes' army began its withdrawal, marching into Boetian by the same route as it had taken during its advance." (p. 540)

Although a Greek writer named Hecataeus of Miletus—who flourished around 500 C.E.—is the first Greek to use prose to chronicle Greek tradition and customs, Herodotus apparently learned this method and may have made use of some of the sources his predecessors had gathered. Herodotus also used all kinds of skills to write his *Histories*, such as firsthand observations. He also interviewed what he considered to be reliable sources. In cases for which he had no data or credible witnesses, he wrote what he thought might have happened.

According to Marincola (2003), because he used

> all of these [methods] as needed, Herodotus stands out as a pioneer in the field of his-
> torical research and methods. . . . Because written records were almost non-existent,
> Herodotus, with few exceptions, was unable to use written sources, a necessity for all
> modern historians. In spite of this lack, we should credit him with a great accomplish-
> ment. . . . his achievement is impressive indeed, for it was put together from vast
> resources done over a better part of a lifetime of travels throughout the Mediterranean.
> (p. xx1)

Characteristic form

How did Herodotus arrive at the creation of a structure out of the great mass
of material and references he had collected? As we noted in the description of
the three great Greek victories over the Persians, it is apparent that one of the
themes of *The Histories* was the Greek wars against the invading Persians.

We find in *The Histories* recurring references to the theme of retribution and
vengeance. Herodotus also displayed a common Greek belief in hubris (*hybris*),
which is any act of insolence or overweening pride that inevitably leads to
destruction (the Greek word is *nemesis*). Closely related to hubris is the idea of
the instability of human fortune.

Another repeated theme is related to reliance on a wise advisor or an ora-
cle. Both the oracles and dreams appear as metaphors, but a problem with oracles and dreams is that many times the advice comes too late. It should be noted
that Herodotus essentially holds that human actions are often not the result of
oracles or dreams but are decided by human actions alone.

What point of view did Herodotus have in *The Histories*? Marincola (2003)
points out that it might be surprising to us that unlike other historians of his
age, he wrote in the first person and was not shy about giving strong opinions.
By contrast, later historians (and their modern descendants), with few excep-
tions, have written primarily third-person narratives (p. xxviii)

Reputation: What was Herodotus's place as a history writer?

During the period in which he wrote, Herodotus was immensely successful, and
his works were continually copied over the ages. At one time, the entire body
of *The Histories* was divided into the nine books that appear in present-day edi-
tions. He was indeed known as the "father of history" by a great many people.
At the same time, no one was more criticized than was Herodotus.

He was accused of reporting events that had never occurred and of telling tall tales. In the first century C.E., the biographer Plutarch, in an essay entitled "On the Malice of Herodotus," found fault with the entire *Histories* for the author's prejudice against certain peoples—other than the Greeks—and mainly for his lack of actual facts. However, "this work," writes Marincola (2003), "and the copious criticism served up throughout antiquity, merely remind us of Herodotus' popularity and the fact that for all the criticism his work was read and debated, and no one ever replaced him" (p. xxx).

In modern times, Herodotus was attacked because he didn't write history in the manner that contemporary historians were used to. Some critics even went so far, for instance, as to accuse him of never even visiting Egypt, about which he had written reams of papyrus. Others were convinced he had made up all his alleged travels. The most deadly criticism was that Herodotus wasn't even a historian at all, at least as compared to what modern histories should be. In summary, in the view of one critic, Detlev Fehling, "Herodotus is more writer of fiction than of history" (Marincola, 2003, xxxi).

Once we take Herodotus's work for what it is, a sweeping account of how the people of his time lived and produced the richness of the era, we understand why he was—and still is—so popular. From here, we might better appraise Herodotus's great accomplishments that encompass the whole world in which he lived. As Marincola (2003) sees it:

> Herodotus called the deeds narrated in his history 'great and worthy of wonder': it is a description that just as easily applies to the historian himself. For he did nothing less than attempt to fashion for his contemporaries (and in a different way, for those who still read him) a portrait of themselves and of others, and of the vast world, both physical and metaphysical, within which their actions take place. (xxxiii)

The History of the Peloponnesian War by Thucydides

We are told that Thucydides was "probably" born in about 460 B.C.E. and died in "about" 400 B.C.E. . The most important influence on Thucydides's life, without a doubt, was the Peloponnesian War fought between Athens and Sparta from 431 to 404 B.C.E., with a barely observed seven-year truce. For most of his life, all Thucydides knew was war, suffering, and destruction. He took an active part in the war and was appointed a general (the Greek word for general officer is *strategos*, from our word *strategy*, meaning a military maneuver), but he failed to follow an order and, as a result, was ostracized for 20 years—a common punishment for the Greeks, who believed nothing was as bad as not being allowed to live as a citizen of Athens—and died a few years after he was allowed to return to Athens.

From the little Thucydides tells about himself and from an "unreliable" biography credited by a person named Marcellinus (Finley, 1972), Thucydides was

> humorless, pessimistic, skeptical, highly intelligent, cold and reserved, at least on the surface, but with strong inner tensions which occasionally broke through the impersonal tone of his writing in savage whiplash comments . . . Not that he was indifferent to language and its nuances; on the contrary, correct use of language was for him a moral question, its debasement a symptom of moral breakdown. (p. 9)

Meaning

In his introduction to Book One of *The History of the Peloponnesian War*, Thucydides (1997) gives his reason for writing the work:

> Thucydides the Athenian wrote the history of the war fought between Athens and Sparta, beginning the account at the very outbreak of the war, in the belief that it was going to be a great war and more worth writing about than any of those which had taken place in the past. (p. 35)

Thucydides (1997) also makes clear his famed intention for writing about the war in Book I: "My work is not a piece of writing designed to meet the needs of an immediate public, but was done to last forever" (pp. 48, 49).

Now that we have some idea of how he wrote his masterpiece, what was it all about? Again, we turn to his own words and sense on his overwhelming wish to write *History* in order to understand the reason for the interminable conflict between Sparta and his home city-state, Athens, for literally his entire life.

Thucydides (trans. 1997) starts *History* by remarking that the greatest war for the Greeks up to this point was against the Persians, but that this extended conflict was over after two naval and two land battles:

> The Peloponnesian War, on the other hand, not only lasted for a long time, but throughout its course brought with it unprecedented suffering for Hellas. Never before have so many cities been captured and then devastated, whether by foreign armies or by the Hellenic powers themselves (some of these cities, after capture, were resettled with new inhabitants); never had there been so many exiles; never such loss of life—both in the actual warfare and in internal revolutions. (p. 48)

Characteristic form

Thucydides, according to some critics, wrote in a complicated style; according to some, the elaborate sentences may reflect his deep respect for the Greek language. For Thucydides, the correct use of language was a moral imperative. To gather material, he depended on firsthand responses from informants and was constantly seeking out eyewitnesses to the war. Although he read all the available books dealing with the conflict, there were few in this era.

Because he was writing a version of history involving a completely new content and style, there is no reference by Thucydides in *History* that would answer these questions:

- What should a history be about? What information should be included?
- How could any history be worth a lifetime of very hard work?

The answer to these questions may very well have been that Thucydides, while writing his work was searching for these answers. What we might consider as obvious solutions appear far from apparent for the author because the writing of history was still in its infancy.

Modern writers have criticized Thucydides for not making more of written documents, which are supposed to be the foundation of all contemporary historical research. It appears the Thucydides didn't use documents—scarce as they were—because he was more concerned with people.

Unlike Herodotus, Thucydides relied not on what gods, oracles, or omens told him. History, for him "was in the most fundamental sense a strictly human affair, capable of analysis and understanding entirely in terms of known patterns of human behavior, without the intervention of the supernatural" (Finley, 1972, p. 20).

In order to make clear the complexity of what was not revealed, especially the narrative aspects of the *History*, one of Thucydides's major techniques was the use of speeches. As Finley (1972) points out:

> ...to lay bare what stood behind the narrative, the moral and political issues, the debates and disagreements over policy, the possibilities, the mistakes, the fears and the motives, [Thucydides's] main device was the speech. It was a device he employed with variety and artistry. (p. 25)

During the winter of the first year of the war, the Athenians, as was their custom, conducted a public funeral for those warriors who had been the first to die in the war. The only exception to this practice was for those who died at Marathon, who were buried on the battlefield itself because they were considered absolutely out-standing based on their achievement (Thucydides, trans. 1997, p. 143).

I include an excerpt of one of the most famous of the speeches from the *History*, the "Funeral Oration," by the legendary Athenian leader Pericles, who died in 429 B.C.E. What follows is just one aspect of Athenian culture excerpted from the full speech by Pericles and recorded by Thucydides:

SELECTION FROM PERICLES' FUNERAL ORATION

Our love of what is beautiful does not lead to extravagance; our love of the things of the mind does not make us soft. We regard wealth as something to be properly used, rather than as something to boast about. As for poverty, no one need be ashamed to admit it: the real shame is in not taking practical measures to escape from it. Here each individual is interested not only in his own affairs but in the affairs of the state as well: even those who are mostly occupied with their own business are extremely well informed on general politics—this is a peculiarity of ours: we do not say that a man who takes no interest in politics is a man who minds his own business; we say that he has no business here at all. . . . Others are brave out of ignorance; and, when they stop to think, they begin to fear. But the man who can most truly be accounted brave is he who best knows the meaning of what is sweet in life and of what is terrible, and then goes out undeterred to meet what is to come. (Thucydides, trans. 1997, p. 147)

Reputation: How was Thucydides's *History* thought of in his day? What is its reputation today?

In his day, Thucydides was taken to task by many critics. For instance, he was faulted because the subject of the Peloponnesian War was not considered appropriate for a book on history. The first, and one may say the most necessary, task for writers of any kind of history, is to choose a noble subject and one pleasing to their readers. In this, Herodotus seems to me to have succeeded better than Thucydides who, according to Finley (1972) "writes of a single war, and that neither glorious nor fortunate, one which, best of all, should not have happened, or (failing that) should have been ignored by posterity and consigned to silence and oblivion" (p. 30).

Critics and writers of the modern world have a much different view of Thucydides's *History*. A Latin version of *History* was published between 1450 and 1452. The first translation in French was published in 1556. As a result, Thucydides became required reading for students pursuing a classical education. The English philosopher and political theorist, Thomas Hobbes, published an English edition of the *History* in 1628. Eventually the *History* became required reading for those dedicated to a political education in Victorian England.

Because of the disastrous war that loomed over Thucydides from childhood virtually until the end of his life, he perceived the war from an overwhelmingly personal perceptive. His ideas about the war turn out to be few and simple but of all-consuming significance. According to Finley (1972):

> [Thucydides] had a pessimistic view of human nature and therefore of politics. Some individuals and some communities, by their moral qualities, are entitled to positions of leadership and power. But power is dangerous and corrupting, and in the wrong hands it quickly leads to immoral behaviour, and then to civil strife, unjust war and destruction. These were familiar themes among poets and philosophers. The genius and originality of Thucydides lay in his effort to present them in a new way, by writing contemporary history, and in the artistry of the presentation. (p. 31)

"My Early Memory": Students Writing a Memoir

My use of an "early memory" as a prompt for writers of all ages came about like this: I first noticed a short piece by the writer Jerome Agel (1975) in *The New York Times Magazine* called simply "First Memory." The writer had discovered several pieces written by noted people relating their earliest memories.

Arthur Miller, probably best known for his Pulitzer Prize–winning play, *Death of a Salesman*, contributed this memory

> I was probably 2 or 3; I don't know. I was on the floor; my mother, in a long woolen dress that reached to her ankles, was speaking into a wall telephone. I tugged at her hem: a shaft of sunlight crossed her shoe (p. 274).

Mikhail Baryshnikov, the Soviet-born ballet dancer, who danced for and later directed the American Ballet Theater, related this memory: (Agel, 1975)

> I was very young and it was a sunny day in Riga, Latvia, and my mother and I were outside. I couldn't walk very well yet and I was holding onto my mother's skirt for support and looking up at her. I remember that she was wearing a dress of chiffon with yellow and purple flowers. I remember her ash blonde hair and bright blue eyes and thinking how incredibly beautiful she looked in the sunlight (p. 274).

I thought such a prompt would be a natural to start off students of all ages writing. All of us, of course, have memories, so no one would be anxious about having nothing to write about. Later, I read an interview with the writer Bernard Malamud about something to the effect that all writers have two funds of experiences to draw from: early childhood and the rest of their lives.

Early memories, it would seem to follow, call forth bright images, conjure up sharp senses, and awaken profound feelings. Such an exercise, I thought, might very well produce great raw stuff for storytelling. With this assignment, I asked students to write about the first time they could remember, but I found their memories, although frequently vivid and intense, to be invariably brief and underdeveloped.

So I now asked them to think about *any* early memory, not necessarily the earliest, and directed them to recall a special day when they were either terribly frightened or enormously happy. I recalled Thornton Wilder's play *Our Town*, in which Emily has recently died and returned in spirit to a single day in her life. She is told to pick a "happy day," but then Mrs. Gibbs, a character in the play, tells her, "No, at least choose an unimportant day in your life. Choose the least important day in your life. It will be important enough" (Act III). Can it be that any single day would be miraculous enough for anyone to enjoy a heightened consciousness of having lived a full life?

Why, then, such a prompt? Because virtually all beginning writers share the common fear of finding a topic and writing about it. Chances are, these students have known only academic assignments found in textbooks and valued by certain teachers. It is doubtful such neophyte writers had ever learned that writing anything at all is only the first step, what is commonly described as *first drafting*—the first stage in which we just start off writing without worrying about mechanical problems, such as spelling, punctuation, usage, or even the validity of ideas. What happens is that as our uninhibited consciousness kicks in, and as the early memory takes shape, words and phrases appear magically on the paper or on the computer. I start off such a process with this short the following simple introduction

Writing about an early memory

Our childhood memories remain with us for all our lives. In many cases, when we think about and feel our early childhood memories, we are amazed at how intensely some of them stand out. In this memory, a mature woman writes about an early fearful experience she had carried all her life and one that might very well have affected her feelings about her relations with her father.

This is what June wrote

My Earliest Memory
I had been asleep. Someone—my father, I suppose—snapped on the wall switch. I sat up in bed, surprised and confused by the blinding light. I sensed that the loud noise in my dream had been the door knob that had been crashed against the bedroom wall.

People were shouting outside in the hallway. A woman was crying. I think I was not aware, then, that there were anger and hate in those sounds. There was only my fear in that room. It was a smothering fear that I didn't want to take in. I remember that I held my breath and shut my eyes as tightly as I could. I crawled deep down inside myself into a little black hole where no one could reach me. But my father shook me and made me look at a suitcase. He asked me if I wanted him to go away. And I answered from that walled-in place that I wanted him to stay. He left the room, then. I took my fear down under the blankets and curled up with it. Nothing more got in. When I was a grown woman with children of my own, I finally asked my mother about that night. She didn't remember it. But I have never forgotten it—or the realization that I had lied to my father.

Because I wished for nothing to break the spell in the classroom after the student had read her early memory to her classmates out loud, I immediately set them to a task. I instructed:

Now write about an early experience you can remember, a time when you were either terribly frightened or enormously happy. Step back as an adult and let the child who was once but is no longer you, now another, separate person, tell the story through your eyes.

When the students turned out the first draft, I asked them to read over what they'd written and think about how they might improve—in other words, revise—their first draft. I suggested the following questions to use as guides for revision:

- *Total Effect:* What was the total effect I wanted to achieve? Happiness? Fright? How well did I pull it off?
- *Strong Emotion:* Does the memory reflect strong emotions? How did I feel? Did I reveal my feelings? Did I say or imply that I was sad or frightened or happy?
- *Point of View:* Have I maintained my point of view consistently? If I write as a child, have I used words and sentences consistently that a child would use?
- *Mechanics:* Now at the last stage of writing about your piece, after you have revised your memory in ways you felt good about, read over the revised draft and proofread your story. Look for misspelled words, grammatical errors, and any other surface mistakes that would prevent a reader from concentrating not on mechanical problems but rather than paying attention to the meaning of your piece.

There are several reasons why I asked students to write about an early memory. They may not realize it at this time, but this early memory is, in fact, a memoir—a kind of writing directly related to the basic genre of narrative, also called story, autobiography, diary, and journal, as well as the term currently in vogue, memoir. The reasons, then, for having students write about an early memory are as follows:

1. Primarily, I would like the writers to become aware of the use of narrative, not by memorizing its abstract features but through an experience with writing about personal memories and sharing reactions with other people. At the same time, I want students to internalize the writing process by learning how it works by choosing a topic of powerful personal interest. Later, they will be introduced to the following technical elements of the writing process: (a) *prewriting*, which includes all the preparations for writing, like thinking, reading, talking to people, and taking notes; (b) *first drafting*, which involves letting sentences spill out onto the paper or computer;(c) *revising*, which involves making significant alterations, such as switching between points of view, changing voice, and significantly revising openings and closings; and finally (d) *proofreading*, which involves checking for surface errors, such as spelling, punctuation, and awkward sentences.

2. I have learned that the early memory prompt for neophyte writers *is* a foolproof exercise because we all have early powerful memories and have little hesitation in retrieving experiences and writing about them with gusto.

3. On a deeper level, I want the students to recognize how the experience of this childhood memory has affected them as people. In other words, I want them to reflect on the ways in which recalling a traumatic early memory might contribute to their present-day way of looking at themselves and ultimately on how the memory might affect how they deal with other people, especially direct relatives.

4. And last, as students think carefully about significant early memories and move toward finding thoughts, words, and sentences to express their understanding of these memories, they may learn about making sense of important episodes in their lives by following such a process as described above. We don't learn to write about events and feelings—as many misguided teachers believe—

by first memorizing abstract elements related to writing, such as character, setting, point of view and theme. Making sense of these general elements of writing comes not *before* writing itself but only *after* much experience with lots and lots of actual writing. As a result, students may come to grasp the incredible richness of one of the primary kinds of storytelling, the memoir.

Reflective Questions

1. Writing about an early memory may be a sure way to come to understand ourselves and the people around us. Why is this kind of writing, known as a memoir, so powerful?

2. If you have written an early memory about a lasting happy memory, you might now write an early memory about a frightening time in your childhood.

3. Why do you suppose *The Iliad* was written? What was its purpose?

4. Why was *The Iliad* written in poetry? Why not in prose?

5. Write an alternative ending to *The Iliad* with the Greeks and Trojans agreeing to make peace. How do the leaders work this out? What becomes of Achilles, Agamemnon, Priam, Hector, Paris, Helen, and Andromache?

6. Herodotus writes about many different groups of people, their customs, and their cherished stories. Write out an account of one of the tales told by one of your relatives.

7. Herodotus wrote about three of the best-known battles ever fought by the Persians and the Greeks, the battle on the plain of Marathon, the naval battle at Salamis, and the battle at the pass of Thermapylae. Pick one battle and describe it. Why did the Greeks, even if all the 300 Spartans were killed at Thermapylae, honor the battle?

8. What are called "comic book" tales about superheroes, such as Batman, Iron Man, and Superman, are enormously popular today. Write your own story about one or another of these characters of your choice. Of course, with such narratives, anything goes, but the hero—male or female—must always take care of the villains. Who knows, your story might appear on TV or in the movies.

References

Agel, J. (1975). First Memory. *The New York Times Magazine*, Endpaper, October 26, 1975.

Blake, B. E., & Blake, R. W. (2000). *Literacy and learning: A reference handbook*. Santa Barbara, CA: ABC-CLIO.

Blake, B. E., & Blake, R. W. (2005). *Literacy primer*. New York, NY: Peter Lang.

Finley, M. I. (1972). *History of the Peloponnesian war*. New York, NY: Penguin.

Herodotus. (2003). *Herodotus: The histories* (A. de Sélincourt, Trans.). New York, NY: Penguin.

Homer. (1991). *The Iliad* (R. Fagles & B. Knox, Trans.). New York, NY: Penguin.

Marincola, J. (2003). *Herodotus: The histories* (Introduction). New York, NY: Penguin.

Thucydides. (1972). *History of the Peloponnesian war* (R. Warner & M. I. Finley, Trans.). New York, NY: Penguin.

· 3 ·

Developing a Sense of Becoming a Special Educator

DARLENE FEWSTER

Theoretical Introduction

What does being a special educator mean to you? For many of us, it means making a difference in the life of a student with a disability. It means providing services in the general education classroom as well as in many other settings, such as the special education classroom or a separate special education school. Special education means providing services and supports to meet the academic needs of students identified to have disabilities (McLeskey, Rosenberg & Westling, 2010). According to Kauffman and Hallahan (2005), there are several factors that make special education different from general education, including: (a) the intensity of the services provided, (b) the structure of the classrooms, (c) the curriculum taught during certain portions of the school day, (d) collaboration between the special educator and the other support school staff, and (e) monitoring of student progress. The education for many students with disabilities takes place in their neighborhood school in a general education classroom, the inclusion classroom. In general, the inclusion classroom consists of students with a range of disabilities (see Table 3.1), as well as students from cultural and linguistic diverse (CLD) backgrounds. These students include students who are at risk for school failure, students from diverse cultural and linguistic backgrounds, students with disabilities who are eligible for services under Section 504, a civil rights statute in the Rehabilitation Act of 1973 that prohibits discrimination against individuals with disabilities, and students who are gifted and talented. In essence, special education means specially designed instruction that meets the needs of students with diverse learning needs. It may include providing specific materials, teaching techniques, assistive technology, and specially designed classrooms. The array of special education services can range from a few provisions made by the student's general education classroom teacher to 24-hour residential care in a special facility. Placement options include: (a) a general education classroom in which the teacher makes necessary accommodations, (b) general education with consultation, (c) itinerant services from a specialist, (d) resource room services, (e) self-contained classes, (f) day school to meet the needs of various students, (g) residential school, and (h) hospital or homebound instruction. Federal law under the Individuals with Disabilities Education Act (IDEA) calls for placement in the least restrictive environment (LRE), which means that students with disabilities are required to be placed in an environment closest to the general education classroom.

In a typical school of 1,000 students, approximately 114 students will be identified with disabilities (U.S. Department of Education, 2007), as presented in Table 3.1. Approximately 106 of these students will have mild disabilities that include learning disabilities, speech and language impairments, and attention deficit hyperactivity disorder, and about eight will have significant disabilities, such as intellectual disabilities and multiple disabilities. If you are a general educator, you will probably have one or more students with mild disabilities in your classroom each year. As a general educator, you will collaborate with a special educator on matters of developing and implementing instruction based on the individualized education program (IEP) for students with disabilities (see Figure 3.1). To that end, you will become an integral member of the student's IEP team. Your team may also include a school psychologist, a speech and language pathologist, a physical therapist, an occupational therapist, and parents/guardians.

Table 3.1 Disability Categories

Disability Category	Description
Specific Learning Disability	• Diverse category of disabilities in which students have difficulty making adequate progress in school in areas that include literacy or mathematics.
Speech or Language Impairments	• Characterized by difficulty in the audible production of sound, letters, or words and with understanding the meaning of words.
Intellectual Disabilities	• Students with these types of disabilities function at various cognitive levels and experience difficulty with adaptive behavior skills.
Emotional Disturbance	• Students with this type of disturbance exhibit a range of behaviors that include internalizing behaviors and externalizing behaviors and to a marked degree.
Autism Spectrum Disorder	• This type of developmental disability significantly affects verbal communication and social interaction.
Hearing Impairments and Deafness	• Students with hearing impairments may have some residual hearing that may be used to understand oral speech • Students who are deaf lack residual hearing.
Orthopedic Impairments	• Students with these impairments have physical limitations that may be caused by a congenital anomaly, disease, and/or impairment from other causes.
Visual Impairments Including Blindness	• Students are blind or have significant visual impairments.
Deaf-Blindness	• This dual disability results in impaired hearing and vision.
Traumatic Brain Injury	• This type of injury to the brain is caused by an external force, and results in total or partial functional disability or psychosocial impairment, or both.
Multiple Disabilities	• Multiple disabilities refers to students who have disabilities in one or more areas. • This range of disabilities often results in severe impairments and significant educational needs.

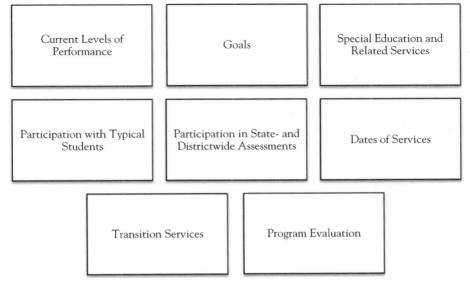

Figure 3.1 Elements of the Individualized Education Program

Teachers who pursue a degree in special education do so for the purpose of work-ing with students with various disabilities. For some special educators, the preference is to teach students with high-incidence disabilities (e.g., learning disabilities), whereas for others it is to teach students with low-incidence dis-abilities, such as autism spectrum disorders (ASDs). In either case, the desire to teach students with disabilities requires a set of skills, a body of knowledge, and dispositions (e.g., caring, committed, and collaborative) in order to make a difference in the academic achievement and social-emotional development of the students.

Special educators are expected to be the ultimate "team players" in the school by collaborating with families, general educators, and other service providers, while having the answer to every question posed regarding students with disabilities. Special educators are often viewed as "the person" who (a) has knowledge of special education legal matters and identification procedures; (b) can develop an effective instructional plan for students with disabilities; (c) ini-tiates and maintains collaborative relationships with families, general educa-tors, and service providers; (d) coplans and coteaches with general educators; and (e) serves as teacher-scholar in providing research-based, effective instruc-tion to students with disabilities. In order to fulfill the vast array of responsi-bilities expected of special educators, one needs to examine the preparedness

of the special educator. Knowledge, skills, and dispositions of the special educator are taught, cultivated, and reinforced and, to some extent, innate. The
ability to be a teacher, particularly a special educator, first requires the *desire* to
teach and then the *ability* to teach. The innate desire to make a difference in
the life of a student with a disability comes from within the individual, whereas
the ability to teach can be taught and eventually cultivated. Many would
argue that even the ability to teach is somewhat innate and improves with training and experience. The special educator is trained not only in pedagogy but
also in the process of teaching. Aside from the desire to teach and, of course,
the determination to make a difference in the life of a student with a disability, what makes an effective special educator? There are basically two responses
to this question: First, the desire to teach is paramount in being effective and
the second requirement is excellent teacher preparation.

Context of Study

College students who are enrolled in teacher preparation programs are generally
required to master a range of liberal arts courses combined with a theory and
methods course in the area of their particular focus. For example, at a large met-
ropolitan university in the state of Maryland, teacher education students are
required to take a variety of courses in different content areas, while concentrating on courses that focus on *how* to teach students with disabilities (see Table 3.2).

Table 3.2 Sample Undergraduate Program for Special Education Majors

Year 1	Year 2
English	Mathematics
Social Studies	Psychology
Science	Technology
	Cultural Awareness
Year 3	**Year 4**
Assessment	Special Education Internship (*Source*
Literacy	*of Intern Narratives*)
Assistive Technology	Special Education Internship
Curriculum and Methods	Seminar
Special Education Internship*	

For the first two years of the four-year teacher education program, students take courses in English, social studies science, mathematics, technology, and cultural awareness. During the third year, students enroll in courses that lead to the internship experience, including formal and informal assessment, methods courses, classroom management, and an internship experience in which the students are placed in schools two days per week. The fourth year of the program requires that the students complete an internship in multiple class settings. This capstone experience, the internship (traditionally called *student teaching*), is one in which the student works with a mentor teacher and gradually assumes the responsibilities of the "lead" teacher.

It is during this experience that the student develops a sense of being a special educator. The transition from "student to teacher" occurs at various points of the internship and is influenced by many factors. For many teacher education candidates, the transition occurs during the internship experience, which is the clinical capstone experience whereby the intern learns, collaborates, teaches, and conducts action research. The internship experience for special education interns generally involves placement in a professional development school (PDS),[1] which is a public school in a county or city school district. The PDS is one that is identified through a university-designated process and is a partner with the university regarding the preparation of preservice teachers and provides a range of professional development opportunities to practicing teachers. Special education interns may also be placed in special education classrooms or in separate schools that provide intensive services for students with the types of multiple and severe disabilities shown in Table 3.1.

Upon entering the internship experience, special education interns have completed courses on theory and methods, and during the internship demonstrate competency and ultimately mastery in a wide range of professional responsibilities. One of the main skills necessary to improve on the art of teaching is the ability to reflect on one's teaching. To that end, interns reflect on their experience while in their internship placement. Interns are required to reflect on any and all of the following:

- daily lessons,
- classroom management issues,
- collaboration with mentor teachers,
- contributions to IEP team meetings,
- use of technology,
- administration and interpretation of assessments data, and

- relationships with the school administration, other support staff, and, of course, the parents.

The reflections of special education interns become a way to ascertain how they view themselves as teachers and at the same time, the reflections serve as a powerful mechanism for learning about the rewards and challenges of teaching students with diverse learning needs. Interns' reflections serve as power tools for the preparedness of special educators, as well as for clarifying their beliefs about their role as teachers and the responsibilities required to be an effective special education teacher.

Method

A review of the reflections of more than 30 special education interns was conducted. The reflections are in-depth narratives written by the interns that address issues ranging from college coursework to actual teaching experiences at the PDS sites. The interns submitted reflections to their university supervisor each week during the final internship experience, the purpose of which was to provide the intern the opportunity to discuss issues regarding what they had learned about themselves as they fulfilled the responsibilities of a special education teacher. Although many different themes emerged from the narratives, some of them will be presented to offer a personal and candid view about what issues concern special education preservice teachers. What follows are the seven main themes that emerged from the students' reflective narratives:

1. *Theme 1: Different Crayons in the Box.* This involves what interns say about teaching students at various grade levels and forming attachments to their students.
2. *Theme 2: Being a Team Player.* This involves what interns say about their mentor teacher and professional collaboration.
3. *Theme 3: Landing on Your Feet.* This involves what interns say about classroom management.
4. *Theme 4: Who Moved the Cheese?* This involves what interns say about the importance of being flexible.
5. *Theme 5: Enhancing Technology Through Technology.* This involves what interns say about using technology in teaching.
6. *Theme 6: Understanding the Connection between Assessment and Instruction.* This involves what interns say about how assessment impacts teaching.

7. *Theme 7: Getting the Job. It's Show Time.* This involves what interns say about preparing for the interview, the position, and becoming a special education teacher.

Narratives from Special Education Interns

I will now provide the actual reflective narratives written by the interns, from which each of these themes derived:

Theme 1: Different Crayons in the Box: What Interns Say About Teaching Students at Different Grade Levels and Forming Attachments to Their Students

Abby

This placement is allowing me to experience a completely different learning environment. I am learning how I can differentiate my lessons to meet the needs of students ages 13 to 16 with varying abilities. With the differing abilities, it can sometimes be challenging to find activities that my students can be successful with while learning that is on a level they can understand. My mentor teacher is allowing me to try new things in my teaching and allowing me to learn from them. . . .

This is my first week back at Red Apple Middle School. It has been a big change again, this time going from very young students to students who are much taller than me. This sort of switch is teaching me to be flexible and open to new things, which is a large part of what special education is all about. I am still really enjoying the middle school aged students. My classroom management skills are broadening since I have had the opportunity to work with a wide age range of students. The younger and older students both have tested my limits to see what they can and can't get away with. The students in middle school understand that I am a relaxed person, but they also understand that we have work that must be done, too.

Amy

During the first week, it seemed like students weren't sure who I was or why I was there. By the end of this week, I felt like they had accepted my presence in the classroom. When I returned to the classroom after seminar on Thursday, the students screamed my name and ran over from their learning centers to give me a hug. I was gone for 3 hours, but they acted like I was gone a month. I remember that I wasn't sure about working in a pre-K because I knew there would be a lot of challenging behaviors. I have seen all of the challenging behaviors I feared and behaviors I didn't even imagine. I leave school each day physically exhausted from running after 3 & 4 year olds and crawling on the floor all day. But I didn't anticipate all the hugs I would get from students. Or the excitement I would feel when a student suddenly starts signing the words to "Simon Says" or clapping his hands at the end of the "Hokey Pokey." I hate to sound clichéd, but those moments really do make the challenging times worthwhile.

It's hard to believe that this rotation is already over. I am both joyful and a little sad that it is time to move on to my next rotation. On one hand, 3 and 4 year olds are not my favorite age group to teach. I am not a big fan of singing in the classroom and I did not enjoy picking up little kids all day. Some of those children are quite heavy and quite strong when they are resisting sitting on a chair. On the other hand, the TEACCH model is a wonderful method, and it was exciting to see the amount of progress students could make in relatively short periods of time. In these past eight weeks I've learned so much about making every single minute in the classroom count.

It was very hard to say goodbye to these students. We didn't make a huge deal out of my coming departure with the 3-year-old morning group because it's a little beyond their understanding. However, the 4 year olds in the afternoon gave me a good-bye card with all of their pictures on it. They even signed their names they best they could. When they gave me the card they were falling over themselves to make sure I knew which scribble was their signature. It was adorable. The hardest thing about student teaching is working so hard to build rapport with the students, and then having to leave in eight weeks. Not only is it particularly difficult to establish rapport with students on the autism spectrum, but also some of these students have parents who come and go in their lives. It made me feel a little sad to think that those students were just starting to trust me and then I had to leave.

Alexandra

My mentor teacher has told me that she thinks I over-prepare for lessons. She is concerned that I will not be able to prepare such extensive lessons when I have the additional responsibilities of running my own classroom. I appreciate where that concern is coming from but I have to disagree with her. Of course I just smiled and gave my usual, "You have a good point. I'll give that some thought," type of response. I just feel that it is better to be over-prepared than under-prepared. Because of my over-preparation last week, I was ready to move on to more advanced concepts if students mastered the week's objectives sooner than I expected. They did not, but I felt more comfortable knowing that I could deal with that situation if it arose. Also, because of the large amount of preparation I did for last week's lessons, I did not have to run around this weekend preparing for next week. All of my preparation is already finished and I spent this weekend organizing my paperwork for my various projects and getting ready for my next rotation. If I were actually running a class of my own, then I would have been able to use the time to get a head start on IEPs and progress reports. In addition, knowing that I had so much work done ahead of time allowed me to deal with the usual stresses of teaching with a clear head.

I know that feeling prepared makes me more confident. And I know that feeling prepared and confident makes me a better teacher. All of us must find a working style that allows us to feel comfortable in the classroom. If it were up to me, I would have had every single one of my lessons for this rotation prepared by the end of my second week. My mentor prefers to take things week by week. Although my mentor teacher felt I over-prepared this week, it actually contributed to my feeling more comfortable with my ability as a teacher.

Alexandra Preparing for the Field Trip

This has been a very busy week. The students went to Very Special Arts Festival on Thursday so we spend almost the entire week preparing them for their trip. We discussed and role-played appropriate behavior. We reviewed maps of the park at Oregon Ridge so that the students would know what to expect. We spent several days making sure the students knew the names of their peer buddies. We invited the peer buddies to our classroom for one of the class periods so that the students could get to know one another. We talked at length about what the students should do if they get lost. We worked all of these things into just about every teaching mod this week. We reviewed peer buddy names during the opening presentation each day. Some of my fellow student teachers sometimes make comments to me like, "Oh it must be nice to go on field trips all of the time," as though it is all about fun and games. It is fun, but there is a tremendous amount of work that goes into the preparation for each trip. It was exhausting and I was a little glad when the trip was over so we could stop talking about it.

Alexandra Preparing for the Unexpected

Our school is having major roofing work done, and as a result, hydrogen sulfide gas is leaking into the school. The administration's response has been to completely shut off the entire ventilation system. We have no windows whatsoever in the school, and the special ed classrooms are completely closed off. For the entire week, we've all had headaches, upset stomachs and burning eyes from the hydrogen sulfide gas. Plus, everyone has been lethargic from the general heat and stuffiness of the classroom. Several afternoons we've had to take all of the students outside just to get some fresh air. One day the three self-contained special education classes went outside together. We set up three areas out on the front lawn and divided all of the students into three groups. The students then moved through the three areas in circuits. In one area, the students sat and listened to one of the teachers read a book about Spring. Another group played lawn bowling and the third group practiced line dances. I accompanied one group of students through all three circuits. I was so impressed to see how the three teachers threw together these activities with absolutely no notice. I definitely had the impression that the sky could be falling around them yet these teachers would still continue to teach. It was a lesson for me in the need to be prepared for absolutely anything that might happen.

Kelly

Laura, my mentor teacher, observed me this week, and she was impressed by my math lesson. She was impressed by how I was able to think quickly on my toes as the students quickly comprehended the content, and how as the beginning of the lesson, I have been consistent in asking the students some of the terms and concepts from the days before.

Using knowledge from my coursework at the university, I was quite successful in designing lessons to meet the needs of students with learning disabilities, behavioral problems, and those students with intellectual disabilities. This week, I designed and implemented a series of science lessons based on the concept of *universal design for learning* (UDL). The lesson included activities for the different learning styles of my students. Even though it took a lot of time to design the lessons, it was worth the effort because the students really enjoyed the activities, and, based on the results of the post-test, they learned a lot! It was great to actually use knowledge that I learned in my coursework at the university.

Theme 2: Being a Team Player: What Interns Say About Their Mentor Teacher and Professional Collaboration

Abby

This has been yet another busy week at Smiley Face Elementary School. This week I have really learned the pros and cons by co-teaching with a general education teacher. It is very nice to have 2 adults in the room, especially for behavior issues. It is also nice to have 2 adults to provide support for student's individual needs and to be able to utilize small group instruction with differentiation. I have also realized a few cons with co-teaching. It is difficult to instruct when numerous adults are talking at the same time. The class that I am in has 4 adults now; the general educator, the special educator, and personal assistant, and myself. I find that I am competing with the voices of the other adults when giving instruction. The other adults in the room are there to support the students' needs when I am teaching. I am finding that when the other adults are providing support, they talking such a loud voice to individual students, that it is a distraction to others and me. The students have difficulty learning when there is numerous adults talking, and I find myself having to repeat instruction. Planning lessons also has some difficulties to it when co-teaching. I have realized the importance of being open to new suggestions. The general educator I am working with has been teaching for a long time and is very set in her ways. Sometimes it can be difficult for her to allow me to try something new to engage the students into learning. Discovering the pros and cons with co-teaching is very important because it is helping me become an effective teacher.

Kelly

My mentor teacher has high expectations of me and requires a lot of hard work. I am learning the importance of team work. In the beginning of my internship experience, it was very hard for me to delegate responsibility to the instructional assistant (IA) in the classroom. The IA is the person who works closely with my mentor teacher. I work with both my mentor teacher and the instructional assistant. I am designing lessons for all of us to teach, which requires an extraordinary amount of my time. I am learning to collaborate with many other people in the building too. I work with the speech-language pathologist closely for one of my students and the crisis-intervention specialist for another student. Each day, things are getting better for me.

Amy

All of the staff and faculty at William James Elementary School have been very helpful during my time there. They have never hesitated to answer any of my questions, let it be regarding teaching styles or how to fix the copy machine. Sometimes, I am hesitant to ask questions of the other members of the support staff but I am feeling more confident. I spent a lot of time working with the general education teacher and my mentor teacher. I have learned a lot from my mentor teacher about working with others and to help all of my students.

Sarah

In my Classroom Management class, I learned about many different models of collaboration and am trying to figure out which one works best for me. I can see the advantages of the teacher-parent-student model. Working closely with my mentor teacher, I have learned that everyone in the school needs to be a team-player, which means that everyone in the building is responsible for educating all of the students, regardless of their ability.

Theme 3: Landing on Your Feet: What Interns Say About Classroom Management

Abby

I am really growing in the area of classroom management. Many of my students have disruptive behaviors that I am learning to manage. My mentor teacher is fabulous when it comes timeto suggestions and support when dealing with such behaviors. Most of my students are much bigger than myself, which is one reason why improving classroom management strategies are important.

Some of the students in my adapted class displayed inappropriate behavior this week such as profanity and fighting. This experience tested my classroom management skills. It also gave me practice for dealing with such inappropriate behaviors.

Sarah

As I take on more responsibility in the classroom, I realize how much I do not know about managing the classroom. So much of what I learned about classroom management techniques during my coursework simply is not appropriate or effective in an autism classroom. While trying to lead Circle Time on Friday afternoon, one of the students was alternating between banging his head on various objects, attempting to escape, climbing on shelves, and hitting people.

While this is typical behavior for him, it was much more frequent and intense than usual. The IA and I tried our usual methods of stopping these behaviors with no success. At one point, the student was actually climbing up my chair and over my back while I was trying to lead Circle. I really had no clue what to do about him, so I just kept teaching. Andrea intervened and suggested that we give a goldfish cracker to each student who was sitting nicely. This was effective at getting our eloping friend back in his chair. He still engaged in some disruptive behaviors, but the occasional distribution of goldfish distracted everyone long enough for me to get the lesson going again. I guess it's a good idea to keep a stash of emergency incentives to use when students need extra help gaining control of themselves in the classroom. . . .

While teaching this week, I noticed that in the afternoons the students weren't very responsive. I also began noticing more disruptive behaviors. I began to wonder if it was me. Maybe I was boring or maybe I was asking questions that were too difficult. The disruptive behaviors made me wonder if there was something wrong with my classroom management style. I asked Kristen about it and she assured me that it wasn't me. She kept telling me that I was doing fine and that this is how the students always are in the afternoon.

Amy

The students this week have been great as far as testing my patience, compared to last week. Last week, it seemed that getting the students' attention was near impossible, to the point where I felt like I had to stop every two minutes to get their attention. This week, all I had to do was give a look and they stopped. I am looking forward to an even better week next week.

Kelly

My goal this rotation is to find a happy median between being nice and being stern. I think if I can manage that, then I can manage anything.

Stacy

Throughout the week I had the chance to do a lot of co-teaching with Ms. Schwartz as well as independent teaching on my own. We found that co-teaching works well with the 1st graders since we have them for so long (almost 2 and ½ hours) they benefit from looking at a different person teaching them and doing different activities.

Theme 4: Who Moved the Cheese? What Interns Say About the Importance of Being Flexible

Stacy

Through my planning this week, I did completely learn what it means to be flexible in my teaching. I did have lessons planned, but based on each day and the students, I had to pretty much take those lessons and save them for another day. I never realized what being off for a week would do for the students as far as not retaining what it is that was taught just before the break.

Amy

The biggest thing that I have learned if I haven't learned anything else is that flexibility is key! I have to be flexible with changes in the schedule, working with other people, and in quickly changing my lesson when I need to change it.

Theme 5: Enhancing Technology Through Technology: What Interns Say About Using Technology in Teaching

Laura

I love using technology and infusing it in my teaching. At the university, I took an Assistive Technology course, which I learned about low-tech and high-tech methods that are effective in the classroom. For example, I frequently use Kidspiration, Inspiration, and other computer programs. At first, I thought that I would use a lot of high-tech stuff in my classroom. But, I quickly learned that the low-tech stuff is very effective. For example, for one student in my class who has a muscular control problem, I gave her a triangular-shaped rubber holder for her pencil. I felt so good seeing that she was able to write easier with the pencil holder.

Megan

There is so much technology at my school. I am fortunate to be doing my internship at such a great school. To help one of my students with dysgraphia, a writing disability, he uses a computer program to help him compose a paragraph. The program spell checks, grammar checks, and helps him write more detailed sentences. He loves working on the computer and is making great improvements.

Anna

I have adapted some books for my students. To help them with vocabulary and comprehension, I have adapted some books that include pictures and have simple sentences.

Kelly

Sometimes, I am very overwhelmed with all of the technology that we are expected to use in the classroom. I choose technology to improve my teaching. But that means that I have to spend a lot of time in deciding which kind of technology will make my lessons fun, interesting, and will help my students learn. I am feeling more confident each day!

Stacy

My mentor teacher compliments me all of the time about my ability to use technology. She has learned from me. This week, I showed her how I use Board Maker in my lesson and she was very excited. She asked me to show her some "tricks" in using the program. I was thrilled that my teacher asked to teach her!

Theme 6: Understanding the Connection Between Assessment and Instruction: What Interns Say About How Assessment Impacts Teaching

Lauren

When I took the two assessment courses at the university, I did not realize the importance of understanding that assessment affects teaching. This week, I administered the Woodcock-Johnson Test of Achievement to a student in my class. I was so proud of myself because I was able to administer the test, score it, and contribute the report that was written. I understood the results and talked to my mentor teacher about the results. I felt good about how I was able to administer the test.

Megan

This week was a great week. I spent a lot of time administering a formal standardized reading test, the Woodcock Reading Mastery Test. I learned about the test during one of my assessment courses. This time, the test results counted! I was a little nervous at first but did a good job. My mentor teacher was impressed that I was able to use the computer scoring program too! I am glad that we had to take two assessment courses.

Kelly

I was so busy this week. I had to plan lessons and to administer a formal stan-dardized, multi-subject text. I administered the Woodcock-Johnson Test of Achievement. It was so much work. My mentor teacher was impressed that I could score the test and use the CompuScore program.

Abby

I have been using a lot of different kinds of informal tests. For example, I gave my students a quick math probe on Monday. On Tuesday, I assessed one my stu-dents' reading ability by giving an Informal Reading Inventory, and on Wednesday, I gave a curriculum-based assessment for a group of students for their math skills. I learned about these assessments in my two assessment courses at the university. Next week, my class will be taking the statewide test and hopefully, I can observe as they take the test.

Amy

One of the main things that I learned during my internship is that assessment is very important. There are so many different kinds of assessment. There are formal tests like the Woodcock and there are informal tests that we give in the classroom every day. I am learning that assessment directly affects our teach-ing. Teachers use assessment to figure out if students really learn. The results are important to administrators, parents and, of course, teachers. Sometimes, I am overwhelmed by all of the assessments given to students. In special edu-cation, we give a lot of assessments to figure out if special education programs are making a difference for students with an IEP.

Stacy

Yesterday, I attended an IEP meeting with my mentor teacher. It was a great opportunity for me. I learned a lot about how assessment results are used in iden-tifying students who have a disability. At the meeting, the school psychologist shared information about a student's IQ, then another special education teacher discussed results from other tests, and a general education teacher discussed results of a reading test. It was interesting to learn how the results of different tests are included in an IEP. This experience was a very good one and I learned a lot.

Theme 7: Getting the Job. It's Show Time: What Interns Say About Preparing for the Interview, the Position, and Becoming a Special Education Teacher

Abby

This has been a very exciting week for me. I interviewed with Hadada County Public Schools on Monday. It was a very stressful day because I had 9 interviews. I was a little nervous the night before the interview because Harford is the county that I *really* want. Upon arrival at the interview I felt and looked professional. Many schools were very impressed with my portfolio, which made me very proud. Some principals didn't look at my portfolio, while others looked at it in depth. The main artifact that was the most impressive to the interviewers was the positive behavior support plan. The interviews really liked my data and organization....

I was called by HCPS on Thursday morning and was offered 4 schools! The schools I chose are very close to my home. I will be teaching .5 at Jamesville Elementary and .5 at North Hatford Elementary in kindergarten and first grade classes as an inclusion teacher. I am very happy that the interviews were very successful. I am proud of my accomplishments and am very excited to graduate and start my career!

Kelly

Through this week of complete chaos, I still managed to get everything done that needed to be done for my portfolio review. Between all of the hard work that I have put into my portfolio and making lesson plans and also going to the job fair at the Fair Grounds, I still have a strong feeling of accomplishment. I had the opportunity at the job fair to talk with several principals or school administrators. Many were very helpful in how I should go about talking to present myself better. I did manage to meet with the principal from Orville Elementary, and she seemed just as excited as I am for me to come and see the school soon. It is defiantly sounding promising to me. I did receive other promising words from Vanilla Villa and Beechwood Elementary Schools.

Sarah

This week was also a great learning experience because I got to see a number of different responsibilities I will have in the future. I worked with Ms. Schwartz on report cards, progress reports, and saw all the collaboration she had to have with other teachers in the school while doing these. I also got to see her test students with the Woodcock Johnson Test of Achievement, DIBELS, and the Test of Written Language (TOWL) . . .

I believe that the process of becoming a special educator is a very important one. I believe that in order for me to help myself in this process I need to do everything I can to learn new things and expose myself to materials and situations I will be encountering when I finally do become a teacher.

Stacy

My mentor teacher commented to me that I was over-planning for my daily lessons. This particular comment reminded me of something I read when I was looking for advice just before I started student teaching. I read an essay in which the author said, "Seek help and advice from everyone you can . . . and then only listen to what really helps." Many people will be quick to offer their profound words of wisdom on the teaching profession. Some of this advice will be useful while some of it will test your powers of tact in holding back from saying, "You're crazy." That one piece of advice was probably the most useful thing I did to prepare for student teaching.

Sarah

I know that when she is in the room, she is letting me do things on my own, but she has been able to comment as needed during a lesson, which is most welcome. With her not there and with the IA having to help in other classes, I was able to work on my classroom management skills. Students' behavior is completely different when she is in the room compared to when she is not, especially the fifth grade. The fourth grade behaved pretty much as I had expected, and they have learned early on in my student teaching this semester that I do not tolerate certain behavior in the classroom, so they are pretty much through with testing me.

Amy

I was sad to see my final day at Mary Ellen School come so soon. I really have gotten to know so many students and faculty that I am going to miss. When I first began my student teaching at this school, I wasn't quite sure how I would enjoy teaching younger students because I really enjoyed teaching the older ones so much. By the end of the 8 weeks, I really like teaching first graders! On my last day at the end of the day, my first grade inclusion class had a small celebration to say goodbye and good luck to me. I almost cried when 21 students gave me a huge group hug and were sad to see me leave....

I have learned a lot about myself as a teacher throughout my students teaching experience at Mary Ellen School. This experience has allowed me to truly understand that I am meant to be a special educator. I have positively impacted many students' lives over the past 8 weeks. I find myself applying and utilizing terminology and techniques that I have learned throughout my college experience. Attending co-planning sessions, Student Support Team meetings, Progress Monitoring meetings, and Staff meetings have all allowed me to apply the knowledge that I have gained through my college experience. I feel comfortable and confident when I think of myself as a professional.

Abby

Where has the time gone? It is so hard to believe that we have been working on the whole internship/student teaching experience since last summer. I remember when I started, it seemed like it would last forever. Now that it's over, it seems like it was an incredibly short time. Either way it was an incredibly valuable learning experience that helped me develop my teaching skills and more importantly, my confidence as a teacher.

It's hard to write journal entries about events that happened that contributed to becoming a teacher. When I first started student teaching, I was intimated because I wasn't sure I knew the "secrets" of being a teacher. It seemed like some kind of complicated thing that I wasn't quite sure about. These last eight weeks in the classroom made me realize that teaching is what I've been doing my whole life. Once I got into the classroom, I just focused on the individual students and did what I could to meet their needs. Eventually I realized THAT was the secret. Knowing your subject matter, understanding the students, and being focused on meeting their needs. Whew, that's not intimidating! I've been doing that forever.

Kelly

For the first time since I began student teaching, I finally feel like a special educator. This week was filled with all different tasks and aspects.

I knew I was officially a special educator when my mentor teacher had to be absent my second day back. She left me the day's work and I was 100% comfortable teaching the class the lesson. I knew what I expected from the students and I would not accept anything less. . . .

This week was definitely an intense week. I never realized how draining a day could be. As much as I may not think so, my students look up to me—despite their actions I know that they appreciate me being there. For the first time in a long time, I feel as though I truly am a special education teacher. I have become so much more aware of the needs of my students as well as determining beforehand whether or not a lesson will be effective. I can sense when a student is becoming frustrated as well as learn new techniques to help calm them down. The most important thing I have learned in this rotation is that you have to take things as they come. It is so crucial to be a flexible teacher and go with the flow.

The most important thing is to let the students know you understand and care. I feel as though I have developed a connection with my students. This week, we took a field trip to Towson University. I was so surprised to see the kids' reactions. They loved it. They had a great time and became so excited to see what a college is like. I think this was an awesome trip and hopefully it will impact their lives. . .

This was the last week of my first rotation. I cannot believe how quickly time went by. This has been an unbelievable experience and every day in the classroom was another wonderful teaching experience. I feel as though I have grown and matured in so many ways. I have learned so much and hope to take my new found lessons with me to my next rotation. All the children meant so much to me and I will really miss them. This rotation showed me that I can really handle any situation that is thrown at me. I learned that I can make the best out of any situation. I learned how important it is to learn to swallow my pride and take everything in stride.

Amy

I am learning more and I am feeling more involved with the students as well as the entire school. I really think that being there every day makes a huge difference. Last semester I would see the students, at most, twice a week and sometimes not even that. Now when they walk in the room they expect to see me there, which I like.

Kelly

The one thing right now that is keeping me from becoming the teacher that I would like to be is adjusting to having so many adults in the classroom. There are twelve students in the classroom, in which three have PAs (personal assistants) and there is also the IA (instructional assistant), Amy and myself. Amy has told me to instruct the IA and PA just as if I were the classroom teacher, but for the IA especially, I am not comfortable with this at this time. I have told Amy this, but it still remains an issue. The other issue in the classroom and having so many adults is that there is a constant lack of communication. Amy and I are always talking and generally always on the same page, and we will give the students one instruction and then the IA will give them another going against ours.

Sarah

The only thing at this point that might be keeping me from becoming the Special Education Teacher that I would like to be is the fact that I have not taken the Elementary Praxis II and did not realize until recently that I needed to take them in order to teach in a self contained classroom such as an ALS room like the one I am in now at Paul Harris Elementary. That is just a matter of taking the Praxis which I have registered for June 6th. In completing my projects and my portfolio, I feel like I have been trying to complete them all at one time, jumping back and forth, trying to work on them simultaneously, which does not work out. Over spring break, I am looking forward to being able to take a day or two to work on one and then the other and finally get everything done so after the break I will be able to focus on all of my lessons and the rest of the time that I have with my students.

I am working hard to be a good teacher. When I finish my internship and graduate, I know that I will have to take professional development courses so I can keep up with changes in the special education laws and procedures for doing things. My university supervisor and mentor teacher have informed me that good teaching results from a passion for teaching and self-reflection and improvement. So, I guess, I will a lifelong learner. I love teaching and want to keep up with the field.

Abby

Looking back, I can't describe any one experience as the definitive moment I felt that I had become a special education teacher. It was a gradual process and a collection of small experiences that told me I was on the right path. During my rotation in the pre-school autism class, my teaching skills really developed. I gained a lot more confidence in my ability to plan and execute a lesson for students in any age group. When that rotation ended, I probably would have said that I felt confident in my abilities, but now that I look back on that time I realize there was still something missing. I had the "technical skills" and certainly the professionalism to get the job done, but I didn't have that 100% confidence in my heart that I later developed.

During my rotation in the middle school I really started to feel like I was a special education teacher and not just a student. Maybe it was because I really enjoy students at that age group, or maybe it was because my mentor gave me the freedom to try lots of new things, or maybe both of those things. I found myself being able to adapt to last minute changes, take advantage of sudden learning opportunities, manage classroom behaviors, all while teaching a lesson and keeping to the bell schedule—without having to think about it anymore. I remember when any one of those tasks seemed intimidating, and now it just seems like a part of my day.

Toward the end of this experience, I realized that I actually looked forward to seeing the students each day. I remember how when I started I was so scared when I had to teach a lesson by myself. There was so much to juggle, so much to remember, and I was so concerned that I wouldn't be able to do it. By the end of this rotation, planning lessons was fun because I enjoyed what I was teaching and I couldn't wait to watch the students discover new ideas. When I realized that I was approaching my job with a sense of fun and excitement, that's when I realized that I had become a special education teacher. I hope I don't ever lose the passion for teaching that I feel right now.

Lauren

Finally, I feel like a teacher. Really! I love being with me students. Most people would prefer [not] to work with students who have an emotional disturbance, but I love the challenge of teaching these students. Most teachers . . . love to have only six students, but my six students require a lot of work! I have to be very patient with them and use different learning strategies for them to be successful. I have to try many different things with them. Sometimes, things are great and sometimes, I feel like I am not making much progress with my students. In the beginning, I was very frustrated because I felt like I was a good teacher. I have made a lot of progress and am very proud of myself. My confidence level increased as my mentor teacher gave me more responsibilities in the classroom. She was very reassuring and gave me a lot of positive feedback on my teaching.

Marissa

Ever since I was little, I wanted to be a teacher. My mother and grandmother were teachers. When I told everyone that I wanted to be a special education teacher, people told me that I would regret that decision. They told me that special education is a tough job and that I would have a lot of challenges. When I was in the third grade, there was a girl who had learning problems. I remember how the other kids teased her and I always remember that. As I grew up, I developed an interest in teaching children who do not learn like everyone else.

When I informed my parents that I was going to major in special education, they were very supportive. I have had great instructors at the university who encouraged me to do my best and to pursue special education. I worked hard in courses and in my internship and learned so much. I felt like I became a teacher when I was given all the responsibilities of a teacher. At the middle phase of my internship, I felt confident to work with other teachers and even parents!

Erin

I have always been a teacher according to my mother. When I was young, I made my little brother play school with me. He was not always interested because he wanted to play soccer when I wanted him to play school. When my friends visited me, we played school and I always played the role of the teacher. When I graduated from high school, I was the coordinator of a program for regular students and students with disabilities and I love it! So, it made sense for me to major in special education. I loved the courses even though some of them were very challenging. I learned a lot and used so much in my internship. My internship has been awesome. I had the opportunity to work with children at the fourth grade level and older kids in middle school. I really want to make a difference for my students. I love being with them and helping them. My mentor teacher has been so supportive. I am a teacher now and work hard to be a good one.

Discussion: Lessons Learned from Special Education Interns

Reflecting on one's teaching requires an honest analysis of accomplishments and challenges during the internship experience. It requires a deep look into the successes as well as the obstacles of the teaching situation. The interns begin their internship viewing themselves as "student," and at some point during the internship, the intern transitions from the traditional role of college student to that of practicing "teacher." This transformation of mindset occurs as the intern assumes the role of teacher. For some interns, the "aha" moment occurs midway through the internship experience, whereas for others it occurs toward the end of the capstone experience. Throughout the internship experience, interns identify what they have learned (i.e., lesson preparation, collaboration, classroom management, assessment, technology) and how they have grown professionally. They acknowledge clearly that their choice of pursuing special education is the appropriate one and that becoming a special educator means making a difference in the life of students with diverse learning needs. In their reflections, the interns identify the expectations required of them. They specify that instructing students with learning difficulties is a primary responsibility of their position. In addition, "managing serious behavior problems," using technology to enhance instruction, and knowing special education policies and procedures are essential to being an effective special education teacher.

Issues for All Teachers

An analysis of the interns' reflections reveals that although there are clearly certain issues that concern special educators, most of the responses did not differ significantly from the concerns of interns in general education settings. This particular group of interns seemed most concerned about the following issues: (a) classroom management, (b) meeting the needs of all students, (c) utilizing assessment data for lesson development, (d) collaborating with other members of the support team, and (e) securing a teaching position. It was obvious from reading the interns' reflections that they made the connection between the knowledge and skills they learned in the undergraduate teacher preparation program and the expectations for the special educator. Interns were successful in articulating that the knowledge and skills learned had a direct impact on their internship experience. For example, many interns attributed their success in using technology, collaborating with teachers, and using assessment data to their undergraduate coursework. For some interns, the transition from student to teacher occurred early in the internship experience, whereas for other interns, the transition occurred later as their teaching responsibilities increased. An analysis of the reflections reveals that interns had major concerns about their teaching and their ability to cope with challenging behaviors. As the interns were provided the opportunity to demonstrate their ability to teach and to collaborate, they became more confident and viewed themselves as "the teacher."

Reflective Questions

1. Why do you want to be a special education teacher? Who inspired you to pursue special education?
2. During the course of your teacher preparation program, what have you learned about yourself?

3. What makes an effective special education teacher? What qualities or dispositions do you possess for being an effective special education teacher?
4. What knowledge and skills do you hope to gain as a result of your teacher preparation program?
5. What are your main concerns about fulfilling the roles and responsibilities of being a special education teacher?

References

Kauffman, J. M., & Hallahan, D. P. (2005). *Special education: What it is and why we need it*. Boston, MA: Pearson Education.

Maryland State Department of Education. (2007). *Professional development school: Assessment framework for Maryland*. Retrieved from http://www.msde.maryland.gov/NR/rdonlyres/75608A85–6909–4BE3-A4D8-D08C759D0A5A/14214/PDSAssessmentFramework RevisedAugust2007.pdf

McLeskey, J., Rosenberg, M.S., & Westling, D. L. (2010). *Inclusion: Effective practices for all students*. Boston, MA: Pearson.

U.S. Department of Education. (2007). *Final regulations on modified academic* achievement standards summary (Federal register document 07–1700). Retrieved from http://www.ed.gov/policy/ speced/guid/modachieve-summary.html

Note

1. According to the Maryland State Department of Education (2007), "A PDS is a collaboratively planned and implemented partnership for the academic and clinical preparation of interns and the continuous professional development of both school system and institution of higher education (IHE) faculty. The focus of the PDS partnership is improved student performance through research-based teaching and learning."

· 4 ·

The Shallow End Is Boring

Getting Science Back into the Elementary Classroom

ROBERT W. BLAKE JR.

I have had a blast this semester. I loved going to internship every Wednesday, and I loved seeing the interest in science that sparked in 23 young students. This experience made me feel like being in a classroom is right where I need to be, and it confirmed that I am heading down the right path in fulfilling my dreams to become a teacher. I have learned so much from the students, and I was able to see for myself how much an 8 year old can really do. I couldn't have been more please [sic] with the way things went at Jacksonville Elementary and I am so thankful to have had such a wonderful team of science professors to help make me into the best science teacher that I can be. (Kelly, final reflection, Spring 2011)

Before the summer of 2011, my daughter, Mackenzie, was a timid novice swimmer. Although she took lessons and spent time in pools, she was adamant about *not* taking any more lessons and *not* going into the deep end. As a family, we joined the neighborhood pool for 2011. At first, my daughter and I would spend all of our time in the shallow end. I would either hold her or she would bounce around in 3 feet of water (she is 4 feet tall). We would play, dunk our heads, splash around, and "practice" various swimming skills. Occasionally, I would "back away" and let her maneuver on her own, yet, I *was always there*, and she *knew* this. She began to venture from the wall and swim any way she could. Using a hand-over-hand method, she would even move down the wall into the deeper parts of the pool and periodically don a life jacket to float in the deep end. One day, Mackenzie, my sister, and I were at the pool, and Mackenzie decided to go over to the deep end, which had a diving board. In a quick moment, without coaxing or cajoling she decided that she was going to jump off the board. She walked over, climbed the single step up to the board, and with no hesitation ran off into the deep end. She then did her best to swim to the side. While we did not teach her how to jump off the diving board per se or even to swim in the deep end, she knew from experience that she was safe and supported in her experiment. She had spent time in the pool and had "mileage" (a phrase we used in skiing teaching) under her belt. She practiced in the shallow end, saw others jump off the diving board, and decided that she too could do this. And she did. Over, and over, and over. Now, when asked if she wants to go to the shallow end, she comments, "The shallow end is boring."

Why Narratives

Using narratives as a means of storytelling, of recounting actual events, and of creating personal meaning and understanding relative to real-life contexts has a long history in human society (Bruner 1985, 1986; Matthiessen, 1978, 1988; Polkinghorne, 1988; Strobel, 1998). What is it about stories that attract us? What is their usefulness in "getting at" certain understandings of a person's life? In short, why do we care? In teaching, Schubert and Ayers (1992) argue, and I agree, there is value in the "desire of teachers to see their own experiential learnings and those of other teachers become acknowledged as worthwhile knowledge in the field of education. . . . *Conscientious teachers reflect seriously on their work. They think carefully about what they do and why they do it*" (emphasis added, pp. viii–ix). I assert, therefore, that there is no one better to understand the complexities of a process of teaching than those who do it. Narrative, however, as a mode thinking and even inquiry, as Bruner (1985) states, has "not seemed very attractive or challenging to most of us" (p. 105) and is not considered to be a viable form of inquiry of those who espouse to the traditional conventions of science.

But stories *can* be seen in what is considered "science." For example, *The Last Panda* is a narrative account of George Schaller's experience in studying the remaining great pandas of China. In this story, Schaller communicates the details of the panda's life and its tenuous future in nature. As a scientist, he values the conventions of scientific thinking but steers us toward his technical report for a detailed analysis of his "scientific" findings (for example, the number of dung samples he collected). In the actual story of *The Last Panda*, Schaller conveys in a personal narrative a gentleness and empathy toward the panda, traits rarely seen in scientific writings but that allow the reader to find meaning and to create a bond with the subject that is lacking in the traditions of science. Through his story, Schaller conveys the human character of science. He emphasizes that as humans, we do impose our own selves upon the study, and in doing so we bring a certain richness and reality that are not apparent in a more formal presentation of scientific data (Blake, 2004). Schaller (1993) argues that the traditions of science writing are

> lacking in . . . the human factor, the joy of discovery, the pleasure of new insight, the admission that research is sporadic and haphazard—and the fact that the information is not as objective as one would like to think. Statistics may help to describe the universe but not other beings: numbers cannot convey the quality of a creature; they cannot express love, anger, joy, and courage. (p. 105)

Why Reflections in the Teaching of Science

This chapter looks at the narratives of preservice elementary interns as they reflect on their experiences of teaching science in a third-grade classroom. There are two main reasons for doing this: First, as discussed briefly in Chapter 1, it provides preservice interns opportunities to make explicit the struggles they may have between the theories/beliefs of teaching science and their actual classroom practice. I want interns to move away from a strict "application-of-theory model" of teaching (Korthagen & Kessels, 1999, p. 4) and place a greater emphasis on reflection and analysis of their teaching. In addition to teaching and encouraging students to embrace a constructivist learning model (Karplus & Thier,1967; Bybee et al., 2006) and promoting inquiry in their science lessons, I want to encourage the notion of becoming a teacher, one who seriously reflects on her practice and who is conscientious as she betters herself as a teacher. These students are first and foremost elementary interns, generalists by profession, with little or no specialization in the teaching of science, yet they expect to and are expected to be good.

The second reason for looking at these narratives is directly related to this last statement. I agree with Conderman and Woods (2008), who argue that elementary science instruction is an "endangered species." Since the inception of the No Child Left Behind Act of 2001, science instruction at the elementary level has been cut by 75 minutes per week, only 25% of elementary teachers felt qualified to teach science, and 58% of 3,400 surveyed elementary teachers said that they did not have enough science professional development to carry out meaningful science instruction (Center for Education Policy, 2008; National Research Council, 2007). The testing data mirror these reports. In "Nation's Report Card" from 2009, National Assessment of Educational Progress (2011) finds that only 34% of fourth-grade students (sample size 156,500 students from 9,330 schools) had scores that reflected proficiency in science and of those only 1% scored at the advanced level. A comparison of the 1995 to 2007 science scores for the Trends in International Mathematics and Science Study (TIMSS) by the National Center for Educational Statistics (2011) finds that

> there was a lower percentage of U.S. fourth-graders performing at or above the advanced international benchmark in science in 2007 than in 1995 (15 v. 19 percent) . . . and that neither U.S. fourth- and eighth-graders showed any detectable change in science achievement in 2007 compared to 1995.

In the 2009 Program for International Student Assessment (2009) science exam, 15 year olds from the United States scored below average for the 34 members of the Organization for Economic Cooperation and Development (OECD), with 12 countries scoring higher at this age level and 9 scoring lower (National Center for Education Statistics, 2011).

As recently as May 2011, members of the Change the Equation group (2011; a network of more than 110 CEOs) sent a letter to the nation's governors asking for a "sustained commitment to improving STEM education from business leaders, government officials, STEM educators and other stakeholders through innovation, communication, collaboration and data-based decision making." In "Slow off the Mark," a report establishing the lack of preparation and a knowledge base of preservice elementary interns' teaching of math and science, Epstein and Miller (2011) make a clear statement regarding the need to emphasize science teaching in the elementary classrooms: "It is elementary school mathematics and science that lay the foundation for future STEM learning, but it is elementary school teachers who are often unprepared to set students on the path to higher-level success in STEM fields" (p. 2). They go on to say, "An interest in science can develop at a young age, and learning the fundamental principles of scientific inquiry is critical to success in secondary science courses" (p. 11).

The argument that little teaching of science is occurring at the elementary level is solidified by the congressional testimony of Harold Pratt (2009), former president of the National Science Teachers Association (NSTA), who states that we "must improve the quality and quantity of science provided at the elementary level. Increasing the number of science and math graduates relies more on our success at the elementary level than many people realize." In 2007, Pratt had also commented that it is a "flawed assumption" that ill-prepared elementary school children can simply 'catch up' in science once they are in middle and high school." Both the National Science Teachers Association position statement on elementary school science (2002) and the "National Science Education Standards" (National Research Council, 1996) call for elementary science instruction to:

- be offered daily;
- support inquiry and problem solving;
- enhance higher order thinking skills (analysis, synthesis, and evaluation) process skills (such as observing, classifying, measuring, interpreting, and predicting), and the ability to problem solve; and
- support the teachers and time necessary to provide hands-on experiences for children.

Relative to all of these reports and opinions by expert organizations, this chapter looks at what preservice elementary interns say about the teaching of science, a discipline that gets little emphasis in school curricula and an area that is often not in their "comfort zone" of content understanding, let alone teaching.

Contextualizing the Experience

The General Program Format

The narratives presented here come from *preservice interns* (the term used instead of *student* or *student teacher*) enrolled in an elementary teacher preparation program at a university in Maryland. As a four-year (eight-semester) professional program, candidates spend the first two years (generally as freshmen and sophomores) taking prerequisite courses and are considered "pre-elementary education majors." In this screened major, students apply and if admitted have two more years (four semesters) of prescribed course work (Table 4.1). State certification guidelines require 12 credits of content science, which is accomplished by having two four-credit science laboratory courses (biology and physical science) completed as prerequisites and then two more three-credit science courses taken in internship two (see Table 4.1). These final two science courses are considered part content (two credits per course) and part pedagogy (one credit per course). By adding the four credits from internship two to the eight credits taken as prerequisites, students satisfy the twelve credits of science content. The accompanying field course, *Teaching Science in the Elementary School*, during internship two is where students actually teach science in the elementary classroom (highlighted in Table 4.1). Here, interns are expected to combine all their content knowledge from previous experiences with the school's curriculum as they plan and implement science to elementary students. It is this field course that is the source of the narratives by preservice interns.

Fall Courses	Spring Courses
Typical Junior Year	
INTERNSHIP ONE	**INTERNSHIP TWO**
•Children's Literature	•Life Sciences for Elementary Teachers
•Foundations of Writing & Language Arts	•Earth/Space Science Elementary Teachers
•Language and Literacy Internship	(Each 2 Credits of Content)
•Principles/Practices of Instruction in Reading/Language Arts	•Teaching Science in Elementary School •Utilization of Instructional Media •Teaching Mathematics in Elementary School •Supervised Teaching Elementary School Math
Typical Senior Year	
INTERNSHIP THREE	**INTERNSHIP FOUR**
•Child & Elementary School Curriculum/Assessment	•Professional Development School Internship II (Student Teaching)
•Professional Development School Internship I	•Professional Development School Internship II Seminar
•Teaching Social Studies in Elementary School	
•Principles/Practices and Assessment in Reading/Language Arts	
•Curriculum/Methods of Inclusion	

Table 4.1 Sequence of Prescribed Courses in Elementary Education Professional Program

Model for Teaching Science

The model used in the Teaching Science in the Elementary Classroom is shown in Figure 4.1. The number of interns per classroom is determined by the combination of the number of interns enrolled and the number of classroom teachers willing to have interns. Each week for about 10 weeks, the intern plans and teaches a science lesson to a small group of students. Occasionally, there are only two or three interns per classroom, and thus team teaching and team planning frequently happens. At the very least, each intern is responsible for producing his own lesson plans and mini-unit.

The reflective narratives stem from these teaching episodes. The post-teaching reflections are required, and interns receive full credit for merely writing and submitting them. I encourage criticism from the interns, positive and negative, about the program and their experiences, and I ask them to write through the lens of *becoming a teacher of science*.[1] When the semester is complete, they submit a "final exam"; a summative reflection that is, again, required but not graded (see Figure 4.2). I provide prompts, quotes regarding science education, and "things to think about" but allow the interns the freedom to write about what they choose. I encourage an open and candid reflective analysis of their science teaching experience in the elementary classroom.

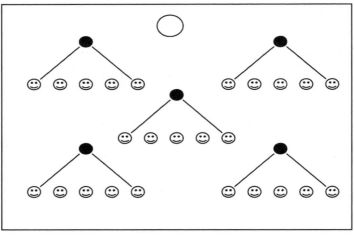

o = **Classroom Teacher**

● = **Intern**

☺ = **Elementary Students**

Figure 4.1 Model Used in the Teaching of Science in the Elementary Classroom

Figure 4.2 Final Exam for Teaching Science in the Elementary Classroom

Where do you stand on the issue?

PLEASE READ ALL FIRST

It is elementary school mathematics and science that lay the foundation for future STEM learning, but it is elementary school teachers who are often unprepared to set students on the path to higher-level success in STEM fields.

These STEM initiatives are worthy and useful, but the inadequate preparation of elementary school teachers is a "blind spot" in our portfolio of STEM programming.

Poor student achievement in science translates into dismally low adult scientific understanding.

NSTA EXPRESS, 5/11/2011
Slow Off the Mark: Elementary School Teachers and the Crisis in STEM Education

A new report from the Center for American Progress focuses on the current status of elementary science and math instruction and provides recommendations that stakeholders can consider to reform teacher training policies.

From the report:
The way we select and train our elementary school teachers is completely incompatible with our stated goals related to STEM [Science, Technology, Engineering, and Math] careers, economic growth, and innovation. Not only are many elementary school teachers ill-prepared to teach mathematics and science effectively, but current policies favoring elementary grade teaching candidates with little appetite for mathematics and science is tantamount to an anti-STEM initiative. Everyone seems to agree that we have a problem—that our country's economic future depends, at least in part, on raising our kindergarten-through-12th grade students' math and science achievement so that they can eventually progress into STEM careers. Where we are deficient, however, **is in the will to reorient our education system toward a greater focus on high-quality math and science instruction in the early years.**

Figure 4.2 Final Exam for Teaching Science in the Elementary Classroom (*continued*)

The report recommends that Congress, state legislatures, and state boards of education **reform their teacher training policies to:**

- Increase the selectivity of programs that prepare teachers for elementary grades
- Implement teacher compensation policies, including performance-based pay, that make elementary teaching more attractive to college graduates and career changes with strong STEM backgrounds
- **Include more mathematics and science content and pedagogy in schools of education**
- Require candidates to pass the mathematics and science subsections of licensure exams
- Explore innovative staffing models that extend the reach of elementary level teachers with an affinity for mathematics and science and demonstrated effectiveness in teaching them

The Center for American Progress is a nonpartisan research and educational institute dedicated to promoting a strong, just, and free America that ensures opportunity for all.

Read the full report (21 pages): http://www.americanprogress.org/issues/2011/04/pdf/stem_paper.pdf

Prospective teachers can typically obtain a license to teach elementary school without taking a rigorous college-level STEM class such as calculus, statistics, or chemistry, and without demonstrating a solid grasp of mathematics knowledge, scientific knowledge, or the nature of scientific inquiry. This is not a recipe for ensuring that students have successful early experiences with math and science, or for generating the curiosity and confidence in these topics that students need to pursue careers in STEM fields. (p. 1)

It is elementary school mathematics and science that lay the foundation for future STEM learning, but it is elementary school teachers who are often unprepared to set students on the path to higher-level success in STEM fields. (p. 1). . . *[Yet] strengthening our elementary school teachers in math and science is the first critical step in the right direction.* (p. 2)

These STEM initiatives are worthy and useful, but the inadequate

Figure 4.2 Final Exam for Teaching Science in the Elementary Classroom (*continued*)

preparation of elementary school teachers is a "blind spot" in our portfolio of STEM programming. Very few STEM initiatives focus explicitly on the need for better elementary level teaching in math and science, yet it is these early grades that lay the critical foundation for future student learning. Students' interest in math and science is often stimulated at a young age, and building solid skills early on is essential for successfully progressing to higher-level subjects. (p. 7)

An interest in science can develop at a young age, and learning the fundamental principles of scientific inquiry is critical to success in secondary science courses. (p. 11) [And]…

Adequate preparation in science is critical in order to teach subject-specific content knowledge, promote conceptual understanding, and build students' fluency with the fundamental processes that constitute the scientific method of generating new knowledge. Confidence is also very important. (pp. 11–12)

YOUR FINAL EXAM

After reading this text <u>AND</u> after reflecting on your experiences in Level II science please write a narrative essay (first person) that explains your thoughts on teaching science at the elementary grade level.

THINK ABOUT (but you do not have to respond to each)

- How has this semester helped you to be able to teach science in the elementary classroom?
    - o Compare/contrast your beliefs before level II and now.
    - o Use examples from your coursework and field experiences to bolster your statements.
    - o Tell a story about an experience that went well and why it did.
- What has been the best aspect(s) of Level II that has enabled you to teach science in the elementary classroom?
- What have been problems in your ability to teach science in the elementary classroom?
- What are your thoughts on the above text that indicates a "blindspot" or inadequacies in teaching science in elementary schools and in particular YOUR preparation to teach science?
- What can we (university and schools) do better to help you in this area of teaching?

Figure 4.2 Final Exam for Teaching Science in the Elementary Classroom (*continued*)

> ## TO DO
> - 3–5 page reflective narrative that talks about any of the above or anything else related to Level II science.
> - Submit via Blackboard and label file with your last name and final. Ex. Blakefinal.doc
> - Write in first person, tell stories about your teaching, and be honest.

My Class

During the spring 2011 semester, I had 12 elementary education preservice interns enrolled in my science field internship class. One student withdrew after two weeks for personal reasons, leaving a total of 11 interns for the remaining semester. All of the interns were female and were divided into groups among five classrooms. There was one classroom with three interns each and four classrooms with only two. Due to the small number of interns and a relatively large number of mentor teachers (five), each intern was responsible for seven to ten students based on the model presented in Figure 4–1. Often, however, groups did team planning and team teaching, providing each intern the experience of whole class instruction (teaching the entire class of third-grade students).

The elementary science curriculum in this Maryland county works according to a "kit" program. Self-contained kits, which include written curricular teacher guides, student workbooks, and all necessary materials, are sent to the school as requested by each grade level. During the spring 2011 semester, the science units were:

1. Matter: Just the Facts
   - focusing on states of matter and phase change
2. Moving Mountains
   - focusing on landforms, erosion, weathering, and the natural features of Maryland

Because there is no mandated state, county, or even school exam with which to evaluate whether the third-grade students learn the material, there is considerable flexibility in how the interns teach each unit. In fact, I encourage the interns to experiment with their own lessons as they practice to determine what is foundational to teach relative to the unit objectives. In addition, they are concurrently taking the two content/pedagogy courses, one in earth/space and the other in life science (see Table 4–1). Interns are expected to incorporate any appropriate content and pedagogy into this internship. Thus, they often choose to write their own lessons in a sequence that they decide as opposed to following the county curriculum.

The Narrative Structure

What follows are interns' written responses to the final exam, presented in Figure 4.2. Although the interns did provide weekly written reflections after each teaching episode, the final exam is intended to be summative, incorporating any and all thoughts on their experiences of being teachers of science in an elementary classroom. The following themes are evident in almost all 11 final reflections and each will be presented using the narratives from the same four interns. These themes are:

- anxiety and issues of concern about teaching science;
- notions of experience and practice, or time on task;
- reflections on the good and the bad; and
- moving forward: ideas and/or responses to quotes in the final exam.

A narrative analysis is conducted, which follows Kohler-Riessman's (2008) assertion that making sense and meaning of a particular passage, understanding why a person acts or reacts in a certain way, or just plain listening to a person's story cannot necessarily be segmented and fractured into small, manageable chunks. Thus, aside from categorizing the narratives into themes, they will be presented as much as a whole as possible.

Anxiety and Issues of Concern About Teaching Science

Katie

Coming into the science internship, I was very nervous about having to teach science to students. I do not feel very comfortable in my science skills and science knowledge, so I did not think I would be able to teach it to students. I also was having extreme anxiety about just being put in the classroom immediately without much instruction at all. Before our first day, all I could think about was how afraid I was of the unknown, and that I would not be able to successfully teach science to these students that I did not even know. I was even more nervous to teach when we were told we had to write 5E lesson plans. I had no idea what these were, and have not even heard of them before entering this class. The only thing that got me through the first day was knowing that everyone else was just as nervous as I was, and that I would have Lacey and Sarah in the classroom with me. (final reflection, Spring 2011)

Lacey

This semester has helped me tremendously with being able to teach science in the elementary classroom. Prior to starting this semester, I was terrified at the thought of teaching science. My apprehension towards teaching science stemmed from the fact that I did not feel very confident about my knowledge of elementary level science concepts. I remembered concepts from previous biology classes and a physical science class, but I was not sure that I knew the content well enough to be able to successfully transfer my knowledge to students. I was also nervous because I did not have any idea how to go about teaching science to children. I became even more nervous when I found out that I would be teaching a whole unit to the class. However, this semester boosted my confidence in regards to my ability to teach science while also preparing me for integrating science into the classroom. (final reflection, Spring 2011)

Jen

I have learned so much this semester about teaching science in an elementary classroom . . . science being a subject that I was not very familiar with. I honestly was very nervous in January when I heard that I would be teaching science lessons from the first day of internship and every week after that. I felt hopeless and unconfident because science was never a favorite subject of mine. I adored English/Reading and I was really good in math, but science was never a subject that I was particularly fond of. I knew coming into Level II that I would need to change my view about science. If I was going to be the best science teacher that I could be, then I would need to learn to enjoy science. Unlike me, who had boring experience learning science in elementary school, I did not want to give that same experience to my future classroom. I viewed teaching science in the elementary classroom as a need and a requirement, and I still hold that view. Science needs to be taught, but enlightened in the younger grades. If children are going to participate in science and love it in high school and college then they will need to be interested when they are younger. I grew up not enjoying science because I did not have a good experience in elementary school. I will take my own testimony to ensure that this does not happen in mine or anyone else's classroom. Science content needs to be emphasized in our elementary schools in order to produce this country's next generation of engineers and scientists. (final reflection, Spring 2011)

Michelle

My outlook on teaching science in the classroom has changed tremendously over the course of the semester. At the beginning of the semester I was so nervous and I had no idea what to expect. Our first class left me confused and worried about what it would be like to work with third graders at Jacksonville Elementary. I did not know what to expect from my mentor teacher and I did not know how to write a lesson using the 5E strategy. Now looking back on the semester, I was being so silly to be so scared. I enjoyed my internship so much and I am so sad that it is over. (final reflection, Spring 2011)

This sequence of narratives is quite telling and is very common among preservice elementary teachers. These interns were nervous about teaching science. Why? The reason generally falls into the realm of content understanding. They believe, and society has reinforced, that the notion that science and scientists are omnipotent; that in order to truly teach science you have to "know" all there is about science and that science is the notion of total objective fact or truth about the world, and that if they do not know this truth, they cannot teach science. As the narratives unfold, you will see changes in the interns' stances or perceptions. Although not everything is "rosy" about teaching science in the elementary classroom, they do come to a realization that it is not only feasible but also necessary and fun.

Notions of Experience and Practice, or Time on Task

The next excerpts show how with practice and experience, or mileage, the interns became more comfortable with teaching science. The term *mileage* comes from my years as a ski teacher. It basically suggests that in order to become a better skier, the students needed to ski, or get mileage, under their feet. The same holds true for these interns. As they gained this experience, they too wondered what the big deal was, beginning to think that the shallow end was "boring."

Katie

Looking back at what I first thought about the science internship, I can't believe that I was so nervous. Teaching science was not even half as bad as

I thought it was going to be. Even if I did not personally know the information I was about teach, I made sure that I educated myself on the concept so that I knew exactly what I was doing when I entered the classroom. I was surprised though, about how much I did know about the matter and science units, I knew more then I thought I did. I felt comfortable in the classroom teaching the students, and was not nervous at all once I got into the teaching aspect.

In the level II program, I really like how the other classes in the program help you to prepare for the science internship. In the physical science class, we did a lot of experiments that can overlap and be used in the science internship. For example, in physical science class, we did many different experiments that help to explain the different types of rocks, and the different layers of the Earth. These experiments could have easily been used in the science internship, especially in the moving mountains unit. Also, I believe that our biology class relates to our science internship as well. Dr. Fred has done many different experiments in class that deal with using microscopes, exploring different animal species, etc. Although these did not particularly apply to the units we had to teach in science internship, these different activities could potentially be used in my future science classroom. I believe that the level II internship has done a great job preparing us future teachers to teach science to students, and was full of great teachers that I enjoyed learning from. (final reflection, Spring 2011)

Lacey

Throughout this semester I found that with each lesson I became more confident about the material that I was teaching. That is not to say that I did not have to do some research about a few of the topics. For example, when teaching about solids, liquids, and gases I did not know how the molecules moved within each state so I had to do research before I began planning my lesson. I also found that when I was in the classroom and actually teaching my lessons I was able to explain the content in ways that would make the most sense to my students. I found that it helped to be able to feed off of what the students and my other intern teachers were saying and doing in order to help me to come up with explanations and answers to the students' questions. (final reflection, Spring 2011)

Jen

There were many times in my science internship where I wanted to repeat them all over again because either they went horrible and I wanted to fix them or they went excellent and I wanted to experience them again. One experience that I remember was when we had the kids experiment with water and soil to demonstrate erosion. This was one the first times we exercised inquiry on our students. We gave them the materials and it was their job to read the directions and figure out how to put the experiment together. It was great to see the children understand how to conduct the experiment without us telling them what to do. I was excited to see them have the chance to observe a model of erosion. As we were debriefing and discussing our observations, the children were able to recognize erosion within the experiment and explain how what they saw symbolized erosion.

Michelle

After trying new things and learning new material, I am pretty confident in my ability to teach science in the elementary level classrooms. I know that there is still a lot that I have to learn about teaching science, but I believe that comes with experience. When preparing for my lessons I had to do a lot of research to re-teach myself the concepts I learned so many years ago. It was interesting to see how I would not remember much about a concept and then once I read a little bit of information, I remembered learning that concept in school. When Kelly and I were planning our rock cycle lesson I remembered how when I was in school we went outside and searched for different types of rocks. After we found the rocks we did specific tests on them to see what kind of rocks they were, tests like: the streak test and the hardness test. Kelly and I chose not to do that activity in our lesson because in our Physical Science class Dr. B taught us that rocks are not classified by physical characteristics, but instead they are classified by how they are formed.

The rock cycle lesson was actually one of my favorite lessons of the semester. Kelly and I decided to try and have the students be as interactive as possible and we did a couple interesting activities. In our Physical Science class we learned about scientific inquiry. We as teachers are not supposed to just give our students the answers, we are there to guide our students and help out if needed but the students are supposed to come up with theories and hypothesis on their own. They then take their ideas and try and confirm those ideas using hands-on experiments and learning. In our rock cycle lesson Kelly and I used a KWL chart, took the students outside to look for rocks, used a book to teach about the different types of rocks and how they are formed, sang a song with the students about the rock cycle, and made an edible sedimentary rock out of saltine crackers and peanut butter. The students loved this lesson; they were very well behaved and stayed involved in every aspect of what we were doing. Even our mentor teacher told us how well we did, he said, 'That was one of the best lessons I have ever seen done by Towson interns.' That made my whole day, probably even my whole semester of teaching worthwhile. (final reflection, Spring 2011)

Reflections on the Good and the Bad

It is important not to paint these experiences as all rosy or to look through the world with rose-colored glasses. The interns had problems in their teaching, and here they express a few of those.

Katie

The students sometimes were extremely crazy, and I think that it takes time to develop your own behavior management skills for the class. The only time we ever got the students to behave properly was when we didn't do group work, or when we bribed them with prizes. I hoped by the end of the internship that the students would start behaving better, but this was not the case. If the teacher left the room at all, they were all extremely talkative and did not follow directions. We had a hard time controlling the students, and sometimes it could be very frustrating, but I tried not to let it get to me. Every teaching experience is going to have its good times and its bad times, but overall I really enjoyed teaching science to the students. (final reflection, Spring 2011)

Lacey

Over this semester, I have faced only minor difficulties when it came to teaching science in the elementary classroom. This semester my classroom management skills were tested and developed. I faced a number of behavior issues in my classroom, so I had to figure out ways to implement classroom management strategies. Even though this is not directly related to teaching science, I found that teaching was difficult when I had many students in the classroom who were misbehaving. My lessons could have gone better had I not had to constantly get the students to stop talking, stay on task, and not be so rowdy. I also found that it was challenging to come up with activities and lessons that were challenging enough for my students but still based on the curriculum. The students in my class were all very intelligent, and many of them seemed to be on a level higher than third grade science. When I was teaching my first few lessons, I found that the students already knew all of the information that I was teaching and the activities were too easy for them. I knew that if I continued to use the activities from the workbook provided, my students were going to be bored and not engaged in learning at all. Therefore, I had to come up with ways to take the concepts that were included in the curriculum but adjust them to meet the needs of my students. Coming up with ways to teach the content to my students on a level that was appropriate for them was a challenge that I was glad to take on. Towards the end of the semester, I actually ended up using a worksheet from a fifth grade science workbook because I thought that it was more appropriate for the intellectual level of my students. When I gave them the worksheet many of the students noticed that it was from a fifth grade book, and they seemed very proud of the fact that they were smart enough to receive a worksheet intended for students two years older than themselves. (final reflection, Spring 2011)

Jen

An experience this semester that I wish went better was probably the Maryland Map activity. After talking about landforms and water features, we were thinking of having the students map out these natural features that are found in Maryland. They would use a map of Maryland to locate the items on the key and place them on a blank map of Maryland. We had no idea what the students' prior knowledge of map interpretation was. We found out that the students did not know how to read an advanced map like the one they had to use. Unexpectedly, we had every student coming up to us claiming that they cannot locate a certain item. We realized that the students would not be able to complete the activity and apply it to the information they learned earlier about natural features. Next time, I would make sure that the students have a good prior knowledge on map interpretation. If they do not, then I would go through the activity with them as a class.

My problems for teaching science have been in figuring out what to teach the students. I struggled a lot with wanting to follow the . . . county curriculum and wanting to change the curriculum. It was difficult because my lessons were not scripted for me, like they kind of are in my math internship. It was as if I was creating my own curriculum: using parts from BCPS but then adding parts from other resources, although, the BCPS curriculum was a helpful guide as far as showing me which direction I need to go in. (final reflection, Spring 2011)

Michelle

With the good there always comes a little bad, and with the bad there is always a learning experience. This semester has also taught me that not every lesson I teach is going to work. I experienced that first hand during one week at . . . but that failure also pushed me a little bit harder for the following week, and the following week was my most successful lesson of the semester. I do not think the lesson failure was anyone's fault in particular, it was more a communication issue. The lesson that did not work well was our lesson on plate boundaries. This did not work as planned because the students did not know how to plot longitude and latitude. I think had we spoken with our mentor teacher about our lesson beforehand he would have been able to give us some feedback and warn us that the students would not understand. I also think it will be easier when it is my classroom because I will know what concepts my students have learned and what concepts they still need to be introduced to. The good part about having a bad lesson is that I am able to learn from it. When reflecting on my lesson I thought about what I could have done differently to make it work better, I also thought about what I would do next time to ensure that the lesson works and the students learn something from it. Acknowledging that I am not perfect and that I can mess up is a big step in being a successful teacher. Everyone messes up, you live, you learn, and you move on from there.

Another thing that this semester has helped me realize is that I need to work on my presentation of material and information. I often found that when students did not understand what I was talking about, I had a hard time thinking of a new way to explain what I was trying to get across. I think that it would benefit me to think about different ways to explain a definition or subject when I am planning the lesson. If I come up with different ways during my planning then I will not have to think on the spot while I am teaching. This would make the process of explaining a lot faster and also keep me from stumbling over my words. I know that time and practice will help me fix this problem and even be able to laugh about it to the students. (final reflection, Spring 2011)

These excerpts relate directly back to the statement by Schubert and Ayers (1992) that the acknowledgment of teachers' desire for experiential learning is worthwhile in education. Regardless of whether teachers are veterans or novices, thoughtful, conscientious teachers *do* reflect seriously on their jobs, and *our* job in teacher education is to provide them the opportunities to analyze, reflect, and then practice.

Moving Forward: Ideas and/or Responses to Quotes in Final Exam

In the following narratives, we see that the interns are not only thinking about the past but also about the future in providing feedback about their experiences. This is reflected in their comments on the quotes on the final exam sheet and also in the way they seem to ask themselves "How will I do this in my classroom?"

Katie

My overall experience with the science internship was a great learning experience and was very enjoyable. I have learned what it takes to run a successful science classroom such as including many hands-on activities. This allows the students to learn on their own through exploring different science concepts, forming ideas, and making claims. Also, by including many different activities, students become engaged in what they're learning, and allows them to have fun while learning at the same time. Behavior management is also key to running a successful classroom. I believe with more time spent in the classroom, it would have been easier to develop my own behavior system with the class, which in turn would have made my lessons run more smoothly. I was sad to leave [this] elementary school, but I'm taking away numerous good experiences that will only benefit my skills and myself in my journey to becoming a science teacher. (final reflection, Spring 2011)

Lacey

My field experiences this semester are what prepared me the most for being able to integrate science into an elementary school classroom. Planning and teaching my lessons for this semester helped me to see the importance of incorporating hands-on activities for the students to be able to be a part of in order to construct their own knowledge about science. I found that my students were the most engaged when they were actively participating in their learning. For example, during the matter unit, one of my lessons featured an oobleck component where the students were each given their own bowl of oobleck and they were instructed to play with it and explore it in order to determine whether it was a solid or a liquid. The students loved this lesson, and every child was so excited to explore the oobleck and get their hands in it. When I reviewed the students' exit tickets from this lesson, I found that they were all able to summarize what they had learned, and I think that the hands-on oobleck activity played a big role in making the students' learning stick.

My other science classes from level 2 also assisted with making me see that hands-on activities should have a large role in the science classroom. In my physical science class this semester, my professor had the class perform experiments or activities during every class session. The activities always related to what we were learning about in class that day, and they always helped me to understand the content better. By performing experiments and doing activities relating to the content that I was learning, I was able to visualize what my professor was talking about, and I was able to relate the concepts to the activities, and vice versa. The activities helped to make my learning more meaningful while also making my learning more concrete. The use of experiments and activities in my physical science class also helped me to construct my own knowledge through exploration before my professor provided an explanation.

My experiences in level 2 have also helped me to realize how important it is to engage the students from the beginning of the lesson and provide a "hook" that will get them excited to learn. From my field experience, I saw firsthand how important it is to get the students excited from the beginning of the lesson. I always tried to start my lessons with something that would get the students intrigued about what we were going to be learning that day. For example, one lesson started with a video about the states of matter, while another lesson started with a classification game using the students in the classroom. My biology class this semester also helped me to realize how important it is to get students hooked on the lesson right away. Professor Fred always brought in materials that got me interested in the topic and wanting to learn more. For example, when we learned about fruits and flowering plants, he brought in a bag full of different fruits that we dissected in order to study their anatomy. He also brought in a live oyster on more than one occasion that served as an engagement for lessons about oysters, water filtration, and mollusks. My experiences this semester have shown me that beginning the lesson with an interesting engagement is critical in order to get the students excited about learning.

I am leaving this semester feeling confident in my ability to teach science. I am also taking a variety of pedagogy skills away from this semester that I can use in my own future science classroom. (final reflection, Spring 2011)

Jen

The best aspects of Level II have definitely been the science internship and the biology and physical science content courses. I have learned many things regarding science content and science teaching strategies/ideas in biology and physical science. In Dr. Fred's class I have gained more knowledge about biology than I have ever thought I could gain. I now have a lot of interesting biology content that I could teach my future class. If I was really intrigued by the information that I learned, I know my children will be too. In physical science, I learned a lot of ideas and experiments that I could include in my science lessons. The activities range from appropriate grade level, to different science topics, to different inquiry levels. I loved how Professor B made us investigate the experiments as if we were elementary school students. I thought that benefitted me because I was able to see how effective the experiment would be by being in a student's shoes. Both of my content courses tied together in my science internship. This was where I could bring the knowledge I gained from biology and the strategies I learned from physical science, and incorporate them into my lesson for my internship. (final reflection, Spring 2011)

Michelle

The article states that elementary school teachers are not receiving adequate preparation to teach science in the classroom, and I disagree with that. I believe that as long as the preparation shows teachers to appreciate math and science and how to teach students to appreciate math and science that we are succeeding in our goal. There are many ways to teach math and science in a fun, interactive, hands-on approach. We just need to make sure teachers are doing that. If I was going to blame anyone for the lack of science appreciation I would not blame the teachers, instead I would point fingers at the state. State tests are focusing more on language and math which leads teachers to focus more on teaching language and math so the students do well on the test. I really enjoyed my science instruction this semester and I would not change it if I had an option. I think I learned a lot about teaching science, and I implemented a lot of what I learned in the classroom and it worked. The students enjoyed what we did and they learned from it, so why would I change it?

I had a wonderful time this semester. I enjoyed all of my classes and especially enjoyed working in the schools. I am so excited to begin my full days teaching, and I will incorporate many of the things I learned this semester into my teaching. Thank you for all of your help, Dr. Blake, I truly learned a lot about science from your course. (final reflection, Spring 2011)

Learning from Narratives

In reading these narratives and reminiscing on Mackenzie's story and my own experiences in teaching skiing and sailing, I am reminded of Wolff-Michael

Roth's 1991 piece on cognitive apprenticeship, in which the author talks about the need for students to practice science under the guidance of an expert, one who models the "pertinent skills as practitioners . . . and coach[es] students in their attempt to handle the practical and conceptual tools" (p. 1). I liken this example to that of a master carpenter and an apprentice: The master does not simply give the apprentice wood, a hammer, a saw, and nails and tell her to build a house. The master shows the apprentice appropriate tool use, models this use, allows the apprentice to practice, critiques the apprentice, and provides continued experiences for the apprentice to hone and assimilate necessary skills in house building. Here too, the interns are apprentices, and in their narratives we see a clear indication of not only their appreciation of the guidance of experts (professors and teachers) but also of the opportunities to practice their skills in the practical reality of the classroom.

As apprentices, the interns comment on how the concurrent content classes greatly enhanced their own understanding, and although maybe not directly related to a specific unit, the methods of content learning helped them as they organized learning for their students. Yes, they make mistakes, but in the reflective process they make plans to correct their conceived "errors" and think of ways to be better at the teaching of science.

In reading the final reflections, I notice that few interns actually responded directly to the main idea presented in the "Slow off the Mark" piece regarding preservice elementary interns' lacking preparation and a knowledge base for teaching math and science. I wonder if their positive experiences during this science internship along with strong support from the elementary school faculty shielded their view on the larger state of science teaching at the elementary level. Was their experience an anomaly and, if so, what can we as science educators do to ensure that this anomaly becomes the norm? Jen comments:

> I somewhat agree with what the text was stating. I do believe that there needs to be a greater emphasis in science in the elementary schools. This includes providing teachers with more training in this area. Even though it means more work, I think that elementary schools should make the effort to have more science learning in the schools and colleges of education should provide more training for their students. The problem is that there is so much focus on reading literacy and math that there is not enough time and money for science, and even social studies learning. I believe that reading and math are still meant to be the focus in education because those are essential to living in society, but science also needs more emphasis. (final reflection, Spring 2011)

Final Thoughts

If science teaching and learning in the elementary classrooms is to come off the "endangered list," then we need to learn from these narratives that the experiences that we provide our interns greatly enhance their conceptions not only of their ability (self-efficacy) but also of their sense of the utility of science as an important everyday endeavor. Simply put, they need to acquire mileage and positive experiences as they become elementary teachers who, by the way, will also be teaching science. As Abby puts it:

> If I had not had the opportunity to teach science each week and explore various strategies with the children, I would not have gained the knowledge I have now about how students can learn science in a meaningful way.
>
> At the end of this experience, I felt as if I was making the decisions that teachers make each day when planning a lesson which has prepared me for using curriculum in the future. The insights that I have gained from being at [this school] will continue with me as I strive to be the best science teacher I can be. (final reflection, Spring 2011)

Reflective Prompts

The following prompts can be used as a springboard for getting interns to think about what it means to learn and teach science. The first four are open-ended prompts to elicit thoughts and beliefs about what it means to teach science. Number five is intended to elicit a list of components that make up good science learning experiences. The key is for interns to think about their own experiences and then analyze these through the lens of becoming a teacher.

1. Science is . . .
2. Teaching is . . .
3. Teaching science is . . .
4. I know when I become a teacher of science when . . .
5. Describe the parts about your science learning experiences that you remember most. Explain why you think you remember these particular experiences.

References

Blake, R. W. Jr. (2004). *An enactment of science: A dynamic balance among curriculum, context, and teacher beliefs*. New York, NY: Peter Lang.

Bruner, J. (1985). Narrative and paradigmatic modes of thought. In Elliot Eisner (Ed.), *Learning and teaching the ways of knowing: Eighty-fourth yearbook of the National Society for the Study of Education: Part II* (pp. 97–115) Chicago, IL: University of Chicago Press.

Bruner, J. (1986). *Actual minds, possible worlds.* Cambridge, MA: Harvard University Press.

Bybee, R. A., Taylor, J. A., Gardner, A., Van Scotter, P., Carlson Powell, J., Westbrook, A., & Landes, N. (2006). *The BSCS 5E Instructional Model: Origins, Effectiveness, and Applications.* Retrieved from Biological Science Curriculum Studies Web site: http://www.bscs.org/pdf/bscs5eexecsummary.pdf

Center for Education Policy. (2008). Instructional time in the elementary schools. A closer look at changes for specific subjects. Washington, DC: Center on Education Policy.

Change the Equation. (2011). Retrieved from http://www.changetheequation.org/

Conderman, G., & Woods, S. C., (Winter 2008). Science instruction: An endangered species. *Kappa Delta Pi Record,* 76–80.

Epstein, D., & Miller, R. T. (2011). *Slow off the mark: Elementary school teachers and the crisis in science, technology, engineering, and math education.* Washington, DC: Center for American Progress.

Karplus, R., & Thier, H. (1967). *A new look at elementary school science.* Chicago, IL: Rand-McNally.

Kohler-Riessman, C. (2008). *Narrative methods for the human sciences.* Thousand Oaks, CA: Sage.

Korthagen, F. J., & Kessels, J. P. (1999). Linking theory and practice: Changing the pedagogy of teacher education. *Educational Researcher, 28*(4), 4–17.

Matthiessen, P. (1978). *The snow leopard.* New York, NY: Viking Press.

Matthiessen, P. (1988). *Men's Lives.* New York, NY: Knopf Doubleday.

National Assessment of Educational Progress. (2011). *Science 2009: National Assessment of Educational Progress at Grades 4, 8, and 12.* Washington, DC.

National Center for Educational Statistics. (2011). *Trends in International Mathematics and Science Study (TIMSS).* Washington, DC: United States Department of Education. Retrieved from http://nces.ed.gov/timss/

National Research Council. (1996). *National Science Education Standards.* Washington, DC: National Academies Press.

National Research Council. (2007). *Taking science to school. Learning and teaching science in grades K-8.* Washington, DC: National Academies Press.

National Science Teachers Association (2002, July). *NSTA position statement: Elementary school science.* Arlington, VA: Author. Retrieved from www.nsta.org/about/positions/elementary.aspx

OECD Programme for International Student Assessment. (2009). *PISA 2009 Results: What Students Know and Can Do: Student Performance in Reading, Mathematics and Science* (Volume I). Retrieved from http://www.oecd.org/document/61/0,3343,en_2649_35845621_46567613_1_1_1_1,00.html

Polkinghorne, D. E. (1988). *Narrative knowing and the human sciences.* Albany, NY: SUNY Press.

Pratt, H. (2007). *Science education's 'overlooked ingredient': Why the path to global competiveness begins in elementary school.* Retrieved from the NSTA Express Web site: http://science.nsta.org/nstaexpress/nstaexpress_2007_10_29_pratt.htm

Pratt, H. (2009). *Testimony to the House Committee on Appropriations Subcommittee on Commerce,*

Justice and Science. Retrieved from http://democrats.appropriations.house.gov/images/
stories/pdf/cjs/Harold_Pratt_03_05_09.pdf

Roth, W.-M. (1991, April). *Aspects of cognitive apprenticeship in science teaching* (ERIC Document
Reproduction Service No. ED 337 350). Paper presented at the annual meeting of the
National Association for Research in Science Teaching, Lake Geneva, WI.

Schaller, G. B. (1993). *The last panda*. Chicago, IL: University of Chicago Press.

Schubert, W. H., & Ayers, W. C. (Eds.). (1992). *Teacher lore: Learning from our own experience*.
New York, NY: Longman.

Strobel, L. (1998). *The case for Christ: A journalist's personal investigation of the evidence for Jesus*.
Grand Rapids, MI: Zondervan.

Note

1. Because these students are considered generalists, I use the phrase "teacher of science" as
opposed to "science teacher." I prefer the former because it implies that science is but one
aspect of the teacher's "load," whereas the latter phrase, often used in by the National
Science Teachers Association, assumes priority in science teaching and thus a breadth of
content knowledge of the topic.

· 5 ·

The Arts in School Counseling Education

HELEN M. GARINGER

The concept of narrative—that is, sharing stories—can be expanded to include the arts: painting, drawing, sculpting, music, dance, and drama. People have always told stories through the arts; the cave paintings of Lascaux tell a story of animals, perhaps linked to religious belief or superstition. This chapter illustrates how graduate students training to be school counselors utilized the arts in a narrative form in teaching select members of their students in their school practicum sites. The graduate students realized that they could use artistic endeavors to engage pupils, convey issues, and provide an alternative to talk therapy. Goodnow (1977) notes that children's drawings reveal much more than what we see on the surface and can be interpreted from a developmental perspective. According to Eisner (cited in Mullins, 2008), art serves as "a language, where the private and personal lives of individual students have a public presence" (p. 82). At the same time, children's drawings tell us about a child's personality, how she thinks and handles problems. Robert Coles (cited in Cohen & Gainer, 1995), a child psychiatrist, says that crayons and paints serve as another language for children:

> Sometimes, actually, they are the only language; an apprehensive, skeptical or badly frightened child has no desire to talk to someone he or she considers strange,

inscrutable, or potentially hurtful. Children, anyway, even with those they know or trust (or yes, love) are often exceedingly reticent, or all too nervously but evasively talkative—unwilling to speak about, commonly, what is not so much "on" their minds as "in" their minds, waiting (it turns out) for a proper expressive occasion. (p. xi)

Coles reinforces the notion that the arts let the child communicate his innermost thoughts.

This chapter's emphasis on using the arts reinforces and exemplifies how important the arts are in education. The famous philosopher and educator John Dewey supported the arts because he believed they were a basic part of the curriculum: According to him, the arts let students develop creativity and their own self-expression as well as an appreciation of the expression of others (Heilig, Cole, & Aguilar, 2010).

Talk therapy defines the counseling profession. Communicating through other means, such as the arts, is not usual practice for therapeutic intervention with adolescents and adults. Play therapy and art therapy, more commonly used with young children, require specialized training and practice. However, these techniques can be used with individuals and groups of any age. Education programs for school counselors, mental health professionals, and regular and special education teachers could benefit from using the arts to engage and students, particularly those who are at risk for failure.

Arts as Narrative

It is unfortunate that the arts have suffered due to the recent emphasis on high-stakes testing. This is a problem. The arts allow students to expand their perceptions of the world and provide an alternative way to view reality (American Arts Alliance, 2006; Berliner, 2009). Therefore, art in the curriculum needs to be valued. The arts can enhance teaching methods and counseling techniques because artistic methods offer additional opportunities to explore problem solving and different modes of thinking.

From a broader perspective, one of the challenges when working in schools is how to get teachers and counselors to use the arts in a narrative capacity. Educators need to learn that valuable connections can be made in untraditional ways between areas of student interest and traditional subject matter. Mullins (2008) shares an example of a preservice teacher who did not understand the purpose of the arts. This graduate student who was teaching first graders wanted to know more about an education class and its focus for the term and "did not understand how art could possibly be important to children learning to read and write" (p. 74). It is hard to imagine children's books without pictures. It seems that this young woman did not make the connection between the visual world of children and the didactic part of her instruction. The learning progression toward reading usually starts with symbols, and moves to letters, and then to words. This is reinforced when adults read picture books to toddlers, pointing at an object such as a tree and read the word for it, and vice versa.

Establishing the belief that the arts can be used to direct students to share their thoughts and tell their stories, as well as to engage them in subjects that they might otherwise dismiss, will allow them to take the arts seriously and commit to the work. Student teachers and counselors know that educational techniques are ever changing to meet the various demands placed on them, including with students who have learning disabilities, emotional problems, and diverse ethnic and cultural backgrounds. The challenge confronting educators working with resistant students who are not engaged in school is overcoming negativity and failure. How much or little imagination and creativity a student possesses does not matter. Encouraging a student to try something new is the challenge. As Thomas and Mulvey (2008) suggest, "As students exercise their imaginative capacities, they gain access to new perceptions and possibilities of human experience" (p. 244). Thus, students who are at risk because they perform well below grade level are given an opportunity to improve. Tapping into personal issues that interfere with their learning processes is essential to breaking down barriers. And one way to do this can be through individual narratives expressed through the arts. Maxine Greene (1995) writes that "the role of imagination is not to resolve, not to point the way, not to improve. It is to awaken, to disclose the ordinarily unseen, unheard, and unexpected" (p. 28). When students have this opportunity to express themselves artistically, how will their overall learning and attitude toward school improve? The arts present a unique set of approaches to problem solving. As Thomas and Mulvey put it:

> Students' encounters with the arts facilitate active learning, risk taking, and greater capacity in approaching difficult concepts and problems. . . .The use of visual arts, creative writing, and performance has helped us to create unique learning experiences and has afforded deeper investment and understanding of questions and concerns encountered in the classroom and in our students' and our community work. (p. 248)

In a variety of counseling practicum sites in school settings, five graduate students used arts as narratives with their pupils as an alternative to talk therapy. Each of the graduate students shares her story of allowing the children or adolescents to express their feelings through the arts from a first-person perspective, thus creating a narrative within a narrative. This technique seemed to be a more effective intervention than talk therapy alone, as well as an interesting way to learn more about each pupil. The graduate students' anecdotes that follow illustrate that the arts as narrative can be used as a means of expression in counseling sessions.

Art as Narratives in Counseling

At our university, all first-year students in the counseling master's program are required to obtain over 200 hours of practicum experience. At least half of this time must be spent providing direct service, including individual and group counseling. To fulfill this prerequisite, I chose to spend eight hours a week interning at a public high school in the suburban Northeast.

Alicia

During my time interning at the school, I met a number of bright and interesting youth. One student who really stood out to me was a 14-year-old freshman named Marie. The lead counselor referred her to me for individual treatment, and I began working with her weekly. Marie is an intelligent, gregarious and mature teenager. She is an excellent student who takes pride in never getting below a 96. More often than not, Marie is cheerful, smiling and ready to engage whoever is in the room.

Despite her infectiously positive attitude, Marie has faced a number of challenges in her life. For years, she has struggled with a syndrome that causes her to become ill when subjected to drastic temperature changes. Simply taking a shower in the morning can make her sick. Doctors have run a number of diagnostic tests but have been unable to identify a cause for the illness. There is no cure for the disorder, and treatment options are limited.

As a result of this infirmity, Marie occasionally misses school. When her peers see that she is given flexible deadlines and allowed to make up work, they become frustrated by what they call "preferential treatment." They accuse her of using her illness to avoid assignments and tests. Thus, Marie's sickness fosters resentment in her classmates, causing her to feel distant from them. She has told me that their finger-pointing and ridicule makes her feel judged and misunderstood.

In addition to being ostracized for her health issues, Marie faces criticism for her passionate involvement in musical theater. She is a talented singer and actress whose abilities have not gone unrecognized. She often gets the lead in school plays and has won a number of state and national competitions. Instead of waiting for opportunities to fall into her lap, she ambitiously pursues her dream. She takes lessons from renowned singing coaches, auditions frequently, and has earned wonderful opportunities. Marie told me that her classmates react to these triumphs by labeling her as arrogant. They talk behind her back and accuse her of thinking she's better than they are. She has often felt betrayed by peers who, instead of being supportive and proud, show contempt and jealousy. She finds it particularly hurtful when people she considered friends join others in disparaging her.

Though Marie tries hard not to let the ridicule upset her, the sadness and frustration are sometimes evident. As an adolescent attempting to find her place and struggling with an undiagnosed illness, it is difficult for her to feel that she doesn't fit in. Because she doesn't get along with most people in her class, she finds herself associating with students who are either younger or older than she is. As a result, Marie feels that she has a loose network of acquaintances as opposed to a cohesive set of close friends. She wishes that she could relate to people her age.

Adding to her sense of loneliness is the fact that she is the youngest in her family and her siblings are six to eight years her senior. Marie found it particularly difficult when her brothers and sisters went away to college, essentially leaving her behind. Because she does not have a secure group of friends, Marie relies predominantly on her family for support. They are the few people in life that she feels she can rely on. These feelings of dependence cultivate much anxiety in Marie. She is terrified that something will happen to her family and is constantly worrying about their safety. She likes to know where they are at all times and becomes very anxious if she cannot predict when her family members will return home from work or school.

Marie uses our counseling sessions to alleviate some of these stresses, but mostly vents about specific situations. If she is facing drama with a friend, feeling anxious about a family member, or experiencing academic stress, it is therapeutic for her to speak to me. But when it comes to her deeper and more persistent feelings of loneliness and rejection, she is less willing to open up verbally. In the early stages of therapy, Marie rarely articulated her emotions surrounding these issues. She spoke about experiences with a level of detachment that underplayed her emotional response to the events. When I learned about Marie's penchant for musical theater, I hoped this art form would provide a window into her deeper sentiments. It wasn't until I implemented the arts in therapy that I got the fuller picture of what Marie was enduring.

When engaging in musical theater, Marie enjoys portraying deep characters facing the trials of reality. She can relate to these roles because she has had to overcome a number of challenges in her own life. Marie connects particularly well with stories that involve teenage angst and the desire to find true friends. She is much less attracted to fairytales and dreamy fantasies because she has trouble connecting such plays to her personal life.

Marie told me that singing in musicals is cathartic. She puts her own story into the songs and allows her genuine emotions to shine through. In order to connect with pieces, she often allows the melody and lyrics to take her back to specific times in her life. Different songs evoke different feelings from Marie, depending on how they relate to her own experiences. She admits that if a piece of music really resonates with her, it is sometimes difficult for her to control her emotions when performing. She feels that her rendition of a song is unique from that of any other artist because she relates to it in her own way.

One of Marie's favorite musicals to perform is *Les Misérables*. She typically portrays Éponine, one of the most tragic characters in the play. Éponine's character struggles with loneliness and rejection throughout the plot. First, she is dismissed by her parents when her family falls into poverty. Then, she is rejected by the man of her dreams who is in love with her adopted sister. As our sessions continued, I began to see how Marie's struggle to form secure friendships parallels Éponine's feelings of isolation and rejection.

Marie's favorite song to perform in *Les Misérables* is "On My Own." Éponine's character sings this piece while drifting through the streets of Paris alone at night. In the song, Éponine recounts her unreciprocated love for one of the male characters. The title alone seems to resonate with Marie's experiences of being a teenage girl struggling to connect with her peer group. Marie desperately wants to form healthy, fulfilling friendships, but she constantly faces ridicule and betrayal. She even feels abandoned by her siblings, who have transitioned into adulthood and left her behind to work through the tribulations of adolescence. Without a same-age support network, Marie feels as though she is on her own and thus shares some of Éponine's sentiments.

Marie explained to me that she relates most with the opening lines of the song. In this portion of the piece, she connects with the background music, melody, and lyrics to an equal degree. When the song begins, the wind and string instruments create a haunting and penetrating tune that matches the scenario of wandering dark lonely streets while feeling lonely, lost, and afraid. Beneath this somber sound are the whimsical notes of the harp, which bring up subtle feelings of hope and excitement. I began to realize that the affective

component of the musical score parallels the dichotomous nature of Marie's feelings. On the one hand, she feels sad, lonely, and anxious about friendships and
family. On the other hand, she feels excited and optimistic about her ability to
be self-motivated, to overcome challenges, and to attain both academic and
professional success. When we began positing Marie's experiences in the context of "On My Own," I gained a better understanding of the emotional tur-
moil she faces. The connection between the words and Marie's experiences are
even more evident. The opening lyrics of the song are:

> And now I'm all alone again
> Nowhere to turn, no one to go to,
> Without a home, without a friend
> Without a face to say hello to,
> And now the night is near
> Now I can make believe he's here,
> Sometimes I walk alone at night
> When everybody else is sleeping,
> I think of him, and then I'm happy
> With the company I'm keeping,
> The city goes to bed
> And I can live inside my head.

The lines of the song parallel Marie's struggle to find secure, meaningful friendships. Not only is she disconnected from her classmates, but she has trouble
relating to her brothers and sisters who are much older than her. These circumstances match the lyrics' themes surrounding loneliness and isolation. Marie
often feels as though she is "without a friend" and has "no one to go to."
Furthermore, Marie often thinks of what it would be like to have a close group
of true friends. These thoughts are pleasant, and, as the song suggests, she is
happy to "live inside her head" when thinking optimistically. The extent of
Marie's loneliness was not clear to me until we began fleshing out her connection to the song.

When Marie performs this piece, certain lines are sung at a rapid pace, con-
veying feelings of desperation. Other lines are sung with a slow deliberateness
that seems to portray self-reflection. When Marie sings the parts that address
being alone and not having people to turn to, a sadness permeates her delivery. It is evident that she connects with the words she is singing. Marie admitted to me that sometimes she begins to cry during these parts of the
performance. However, when she sings about the joys of thinking positively, a
smile tugs at the corners of her mouth; she is connecting with feelings of hope-

fulness in those moments. Her performance helped me understand her emotional reactions to both the loneliness and optimism she faces in life.

When Marie finishes singing this portion of the song, she tells me that the experience felt cathartic. There is the sense that she feels some relief. However, while singing provides an emotional release, Marie admitted that she would be very reluctant to discuss the personal hardships she connects with "On My Own." In other words, she was not willing to talk about the internal experiences that she relates to the song. This confirmed that musical theater provides an outlet for her inmost feelings that verbal communication does not.

Watching Marie perform "On My Own" was very moving for me. There is a vulnerability when she sings, and it is clear that her genuine emotions are shining through. The sadness, loneliness, uncertainty, anxiousness, optimism, and hopefulness that surround her health issues, friendship troubles, family circumstances, and personal successes are all displayed when she performs. She is connecting not only with the music, but with her audience. There were times when I got goose bumps because her emotion was so palpable.

Notably, I was unable to access these feelings when using talk therapy with Marie. As I explained previously, Marie presents as very cheerful and positive when engaging in conversation. Even when she is explaining some of the difficult challenges she faces, there is a detachment from the negative emotions that surround the issues. Furthermore, because she is in early adolescence, Marie has trouble articulating some of her deeper thoughts and feelings. During our counseling sessions, I had to use a lot of reflective listening to uncover what was going on below the surface.

From my experiences with her, it seems Marie is more willing to express painful emotions through musical theater than she is through verbal communication. When speaking to me, she maintains a very positive affect and is reluctant to reveal her vulnerabilities. However, when singing, I noticed Marie is not afraid to be exposed and often uses her connection to the song as a way to release emotions that surround different events in her life. As a counselor, I felt a stronger therapeutic connection to Marie when she sang than when we spoke in the guidance office. In essence, Marie as Éponine had more to "say" than Marie the high school student.

Working with this client has shown me how powerful the arts can be as a mode of therapeutic expression. Musical theater was able to tap into Marie's innermost emotions in ways that talk therapy could not. While my client was comfortable discussing specific events, she was less able to verbalize her struggles with sadness and loneliness. Using the arts as a counseling tool allowed me

to obtain a window into Marie's feelings and gain a more substantive understanding of her personal experience. As a result, I am much more cognizant of
using the arts to benefit future clients. Early in the therapeutic process I plan
to engage with clients about the role of art in their lives. If I sense that it can
provide an outlet, I will incorporate it into therapy accordingly.

Debby

I am what is often referred to as a "nontraditional student." After almost two
decades raising my three sons, I returned to graduate school in the summer of
2010 to pursue a master's degree in School and Mental Health Counseling. As
a requirement for the degree, I undertook a one-day-a-week practicum in an
urban K–8 school in the northeastern part of the United States. Several years
prior to returning to school I developed an interest in beads, taught myself the
necessary techniques, and started a small beaded jewelry business. I loved the
colors, the textures, and the creativity involved in jewelry design. When I began
my counseling program I wondered about ways to incorporate this art form into
therapeutic work with clients.

As part of the practicum, I led a small group for seventh-grade girls. Each
of the three participants had a health issue that affected her food choices. Rose
and Jane, who are cousins, both had diabetes. Mary had eczema and some associated problems with her liver. The idea for the group emerged in late fall, when
the sixth-grade teacher, who knows the girls well, approached the school counselor about creating a group for them: she felt they would benefit from the
opportunity to explore their health and food issues together. The school counselor, in turn, asked me to run the group. The plan was to meet weekly, but the
public school schedule and a series of snow days resulted in every-other-week
meetings.

In mid-December, before winter break, the sixth-grade teacher and I conducted a preliminary meeting with the girls. We told the girls that we were considering forming the group and wanted to confirm their interest. Each girl said
that she would like to participate. Despite their expression of interest, however,
the first two sessions of the group were challenging—for me as a new group
leader, and, I believe, for the girls as well.

Although the girls had seen me around school for several months, and
even interacted with me occasionally in the classroom, I was only nominally
familiar to them. Our first meeting took place in the sixth-grade classroom
and included the teacher, who had proposed the idea for the group. The student teacher assigned to the sixth-grade class ended up participating as well.

We did introductory exercises, recognized safe space, and began to get acquainted.

I was surprised by the girls' extreme reticence; I was also frustrated with my own lack of preparation. Because the girls had opted to participate I expected them to be more forthcoming. I had thought that each of the girls had a solid understanding of her disease, and that they would be inspired to talk about the challenges of eating healthfully. But I quickly learned that we would first need to devote significant time to trust building.

During this first session I shared my interest in beading with the girls and wore a magnetic and crystal bracelet I had created. I did this both to let the girls learn something about me and to see whether they had sufficient interest in beading for us to incorporate this art form into our sessions. I didn't yet know precisely how I would do this, but my firm belief in using creative approaches in conjunction with talk therapy convinced me that it was worth exploring.

After the first session, my supervisor and I strategized about making adjustments the next time the girls and I met. We decided to eliminate other adults from the group, so the girls would know who was the leader, and to find a different space. Later sessions were held in the counselor's office, where I had to rearrange the furniture before and after each meeting.

During our second session the girls were still reserved, although they spoke a bit more than before. Rose and Jane ate their lunches, but Mary seemed to have no interest in her food. We talked more about confidentiality, ground rules, and the qualities of a good leader and of good group members. The girls answered the questions I posed, and we even talked in slightly greater depth about an issue or two. Rose and Mary mostly just giggled.

At the end of the session, I took out a tin of beads to let the girls examine and talk about them, as I pondered how best to use them therapeutically. Jane and Mary explored the beads and said that they were looking forward to working with them, but Rose said explicitly said that she was not interested.

When I prepared the counselor's office for our third session a couple of weeks later, I set up trays of beads along with elastic, scissors and plates on which to work. I did not know who would participate, or when, but I hoped that having the opportunity to work with the beads might affect the atmosphere as well as the outcome of our gathering.

As I walked with Rose, Jane and Mary from the lunchroom to our meeting, I told them they could use the beads whenever they wanted during the session. From the time the girls settled down at the table, the beads were a focus of their attention. Mary, Jane and Rose spent the hour eating lunch, participating in our discussion, and making bracelets. Although Mary had eaten nearly nothing during our first two sessions, she ate her entire lunch.

We began the session with check-in time and then moved on to a question-naire I had prepared to give some structure to the session. The girls were not only able to concentrate on each of the questionnaire items while creating their bracelets, they also expounded on their responses, asked questions, and shared bits of information. Rose even dug through her binder to find a document she wanted us to see, a packet that revealed to me that she did, in fact, know more and have access to more information about diabetes than she let on in our first session.

I was impressed, and I was relieved that we had reached a new level of trust and comfort. I believe that giving the girls the opportunity to be creative, to keep their hands busy with small and beautiful beads, and to do something fun were all key factors in the phenomenal shift in our little group. The beads and the chance to create jewelry did not detract from our work together, but enhanced it.

I was fascinated by the differences in the bracelets that the girls created. Rose, who had earlier rejected the very thought of working with beads, made two bracelets. The first, a series of identically shaped spheres in clear, blue, and green hues, reinforced Rose's self-declared preference for order in her life. The second, an apparently random ordering of multi-colored seed beads, seemed a branch from this inclination for organization. Jane sorted through to find beads with texture—small raised bumps, squiggly lines or layers of glass—just right for a young woman who presents a strong veneer as well as depths of sen-sitivity. Jane found so many beads she loved that we all had a good laugh when we saw how big her bracelet had become. Since she very much wanted to wear her bracelet, Jane painstakingly chose which beads to remove to make it fit. Finally, Mary produced a highly designed bracelet that reflected both her delicate frame and her delicate personality: rows of deep blue seed beads inter-rupted by an occasional larger red bead, each of which was unique.

As our session time drew to a close, all three girls begged to stay. I agreed to an extra 15 minutes, which I knew their schedules would allow. As they fin-ished their beading, the girls continued to talk, to ask questions, and to inter-act, and we discussed a plan for our next session. I offered the girls the option to conduct computer research on diabetes and eczema, a task in which they had previously expressed interest or to continue with talking and beading. After our session that day, it came as no surprise to me that they chose beading.

Over the course of our time together, I have reiterated to the girls that although we initially came together with a focus on their personal health and food, I am open to any of their thoughts or concerns. In our third week, the girls did talk more about themselves and shared feelings that were not always specifically related to their diseases. For instance, Rose said that she does not feel comfortable talking to anyone about diabetes because, she told us, she does not like to talk to people in general. Mary revealed that she does not like to talk to anyone about eczema because she thinks her skin disgusts everyone, including her doctors. Furthermore, she does not want to learn more because she is scared of what she might find out. Throughout this session, Jane displayed more of her calm demeanor while also sharing her excitement about getting a puppy for her upcoming birthday. She is not worried about her diabetes, but she also told us that she is unsure whether she is comfortable discussing her health.

Overall, I was pleased, even amazed, by the shift in the energy of our third session. The openness the girls displayed seems to validate my belief that creative endeavors are not a distraction in group therapy, but rather a way to become grounded and focused. Concentrating on the craft and sharing a pleasurable activity let the girls engage in meaningful introspection and grow more comfortable together.

Using art in conjunction with talk therapy can open pathways of understanding within individuals and avenues of communication among group members. Letting the girls work with beads and make bracelets made a significant difference in the growth of our group. Though the girls did not initially open up to me, when they were able to be creative and talk simultaneously, remarkable changes occurred. Using the arts allowed the girls not only to share more easily with me and with one another, but also to have a finished product of which they were proud. Based on this experience of combining bead craft and conversation with young teenage girls, I hope to find more ways to use art and talking together to increase comfort and communication in group therapy.

Allyson

The school where I completed my counseling practicum is progressive and encourages active learning. This approach is often described as experiential. The students take part in lessons both in the school building and outdoors; for example, one day per week during the warmer months, students have science lessons in a natural setting. Another feature of this school is the structure of the classrooms. Kindergarten, third, and sixth grades are independent sections. First and second, fourth and fifth, and seventh and eighth are combined. These grades are organized in a large, open space, which has replaced the typical classroom in this school. Some of the lessons take place within the specific grade level, while others combine students from various grades.

The school places significant emphasis on participation in and education through the arts. As a private school, it has access to resources and forms of funding that public schools often lack. In addition to the regular art specials offered to each grade during the week, this school gives students access to clubs such as drama, dance and chorus. They can participate in the culinary arts. Sometimes, school-wide events include many forms of artistic expression, with a meal prepared by all students in the school and performances from several grades. Often, parents of students volunteer to assist with these events or develop afterschool programs in their area of expertise.

Andrew, the student with whom I worked regularly, was in a fourth and fifth grade classroom; he was 10 years old and in the fourth grade. Within the past few years, the school had taken a proactive approach to developing healthy social skills. Some of the students in grades four and above had not benefited from this focus. His teachers and parents explained to me that Andrew was one of these students. For this reason, he began to use the counseling services offered through school. Generally, the school psychologist meets with the family and discusses possible options for outside resources. However, because I was a practicum student, the family and my supervisor agreed to let me work with Andrew. We met both individually and in a group. Speaking with an adult in a safe atmosphere seemed to help Andrew, but I also saw the need for him to interact with peers in the group. His attitude was almost completely different in each environment. Individually, he was polite and relatively quiet, while with his classmates, he was dominant, often disruptive. For example, he frequently had conflicts with one of the other boys in his class. During group sessions, they often made violent threats to each other, such as "I'm going to punch you" or "I'll throw this chair at you." Although nothing serious took place in our meetings, they were experiencing trouble in their daily interactions at school. Their teachers described this class as a "young" group of boys, referring to their immature behavior for their age.

In addition to his aggression in the classroom, Andrew's parents were troubled by his behavior at home. His father acknowledged that the family had a challenging schedule, which prevented the entire group from seeing each other regularly; the family rarely enjoyed a nightly dinner together. His mother worked full time and often got home after the children (Andrew and his younger sister, Margo) went to sleep. Andrew's father was the primary caregiver, but he also ran his own business. He worked from home but often had meetings or other important events to attend. The parents also hosted fundraising events in their home. Andrew and his sister were regularly left at home with a babysitter or in after school care at their school. I asked Andrew how often he and Margo had a babysitter at their house. He responded, "A lot." When I asked him to clarify, he said, "At least once a week."

When you meet Andrew for the first time, he seems to be a polite, respectful child. Though he does use proper manners, always saying "please" and "thank you," he seems to know exactly what to say in order to manipulate the situation in his favor. From conversations with his parents, I learned that he preferred to spend time alone either reading or drawing. Often, he did not respond when asked to perform a task during his "free time" at home. He became so absorbed in his activity that he ignored those around him. This behavior affected his eating and sleeping habits, as he rarely stopped what he was doing to listen to his parents' requests. After being told repeatedly to go to sleep, Andrew often stayed awake, working on an art project or reading quietly.

Andrew and I had several conversations about the fact that he wished his parents were home more often. He also told me that he called his father by his first name and his mother "mom." When I asked why, he explained that he wanted to make his dad angry, but not his mom. Based on his frustration regarding the absence of both parents, I thought this distinction was interesting, especially since he sees his father more often. One possible reason for this attitude may be that his father is the main disciplinarian in the family, while his mother generally spends time doing fun activities with the children.

Andrew's parents also mentioned that they received calls from his teachers on occasion regarding his behavior in school. His refusal to respond when addressed or to acknowledge requests seemed to carry over into the academic setting. I noticed this in our group work. I would ask Andrew repeatedly to stop doing something and listen, and he would simply ignore me. Not until I walked over to him and made eye contact would he consider what I was asking him to do.

In Andrew's art, the emotions that came into play most often were anger, frustration, and violence. He came to school every day with an art project he called "battle materials." This was not a typical drawing. Basically, Andrew had made at least 50 small cutouts of people and weapons that could be used in a battle that happens at school. He was meticulous in his design and care of these parts, and he spent a significant amount of time at home drawing, cutting, and taping these pieces into what he envisions. When I asked about them, he became defensive and put them away as quickly as possible. He kept them in a plastic bag and carried them around with him.

Because I saw Andrew's sister at school as well, I had the opportunity to ask her about her brother's project. Margo, a kindergartener, respected the components of the "battle" to the degree that she never touched or moved them when they were set up at home. Her attitude reinforced the importance of this form of artistic expression for Andrew. As she answered my questions, I could see that Margo understood this to be a serious activity.

Initially, I was concerned that a fourth-grade student took such pride in a seemingly violent project. But I learned that these "battles" are common at the school in several grades. The students in younger grades brought larger toys to school, which caused an obvious distraction in the classroom, and the teachers were able to stop these "battles" before they began. However, small paper pieces such as Andrew's were easier to hide.

Andrew assured me that this was simply a fun activity between him and his classmates. What confused me was that Andrew seemed to be a sweet, kind-hearted child at his core. I saw the angry side of him come out in his participation in these games with his classmates. I wondered whether this behavior was due to peer pressure or whether Andrew genuinely enjoyed the "game."

This caused me to explore more positive ways for Andrew to express his emotions. I believe the relationship he and I formed through our work together was one example of this change. The fact that I saw him regularly at school, whether in a group session or individually, helped him open up to me, and I noticed that he began to respond to me more quickly. He also became significantly more friendly, and we had conversations about what he likes to do, his family life, and other school-related topics. As our relationship grew, I noticed his connection to his "battle pieces" diminish. Andrew came to school without them on several occasions. When he did bring them, he did not seem nearly as protective. Perhaps he did not feel such a strong emotional attachment to this game. My hope is that it became just that: a simple game.

Another example of Andrew's artistic expression took place early in our work together. I asked him to draw a picture of himself in one of our group meetings. Andrew chose to use a red pen. I found this rather odd. There were markers, colored pencils, and crayons from which to choose. Some of his classmates would argue excitedly over different colors. This did not seem to be a consideration for Andrew. It took him a long time to begin to draw his picture. When he did, it consisted of harsh, straight lines, which made up his body and clothes. I could tell from looking at the drawing and casually observing it as he drew, that he put a tremendous amount of pressure on the pen to make the lines on the page. His head was a small, insignificant part of the drawing. I wondered if this demonstrated a sense of insecurity.

Because he struggled with social skills, I found it to be difficult to encourage him to express what he had created, but it was evident from his art that anger and frustration were major components of his life. His choice of the red pen and style of drawing showed this from the start, and his work on his war project and aggressive behavior toward his classmates confirmed my observation.

As a practicum student with a focus on counseling, viewing Andrew's artistic work gave me tremendous insight into the issues with which Andrew was struggling. Without the drawings and "battle pieces," I would have needed more time to come to realize that Andrew may have had violent tendencies. Otherwise, Andrew appeared to be a polite student who was simply frustrated with some of his peers. This does not seem abnormal for a fourth-grade boy.

As we continued to work together, Andrew began to open up to me, sharing his experiences, thoughts, and opinions on various topics. It seemed that he appreciated this opportunity to express himself without having to simply talk to an adult. The combination of an art activity (one that he chose) and the formation of a trusting relationship was beneficial to Andrew.

Bridget

Jessie is an eight-year-old, third-grade Chinese girl in a public school. The school is in an area where a large number of residents are recent immigrants. It has a diverse population of students, and 50% of them come from families that speak Chinese.

Jessie's teacher referred her to CSAP (Comprehensive Student Assistance Process) because she was not doing well in either math or reading. She looked depressed in the classroom and seemed uninterested in interacting with teachers or peers. Since I could speak Jessie's language, the school counselor asked me to work with her. I asked Jessie if we could have a little talk. She refused but agreed to come at another time. I went to pick her up two days later, and she suggested that we go to the library. There, she picked up the book *Corduroy*, which talks about a lonely toy bear in a store who is eventually brought home by a girl who loves him as he is. After telling me the story in her own words, she picked up a crayon box on the table and started drawing. In the following weeks, she told her stories through drawings.

Except for courses related to child development taken in graduate school, I had no previous exposure to using art in therapy. In order to better equip myself to work with Jessie, I gave myself a crash course, seeking help from my practicum advisor and reading books about art therapy. It was amazing that the drawings brought Jessie and me closer and a strong therapeutic relationship grew between us.

Classroom Avoidance: I was surprised at first that Jessie liked to spend time with me. According to her teachers, she was a depressed child who did not enjoy being with strangers. At first, Jessie did not talk much about what was happening in her life. I thought she was comfortable with me partly because I also came from China, and I could speak both English and Chinese with her during the sessions. When she grew more and more reluctant to go back to class after every session, I suggested that she draw a picture about her classroom.

This is the only black-and-white picture that Jessie drew during our sessions. She drew it with pencils and was not interested in coloring it with crayons. In the picture, eight students are sitting in a classroom in two rows. Jessie puts herself in the first row under the direct attention of the teacher but in the corner of the classroom, where she maintains a geographical distance from other students. Students in the second row are looking at her with big smiling faces, while Jessie looks upset. All the figures in the picture are relatively small, and the students are not tall enough to sit in the chairs, so they stand on them.

It is clear that the classroom is not very attractive for Jessie. It looks like a colorless place where she feels lonely and under pressure. The tiny human figures indicate that she feels a sense of powerlessness and helplessness. But she is the only one who is not happy in the classroom. We can interpret the smiles on the faces of other students who look at her either as encouragement or as ridicule. But since Jessie appears to be very unhappy, those looks probably suggest ridicule from peers. At the same time, as she is sitting in the front row, it is a reasonable assumption that Jessie experiences some level of discomfort and feelings of being exposed because the teacher is watching her.

We talked about the picture, and Jessie indicated that she did not like the classroom because she could not fully understand what the teacher was saying. Jessie's native language is Chinese, and she said she did not like to speak English. She had trouble following the teacher's instructions in math classes, too. She felt she had no one to turn to when she had difficulty solving a math problem because of her limited language ability.

Before Jessie drew this picture, I had little idea of how she felt about her classroom experience, since she didn't seem ready to talk about it. The drawing gave me a glimpse of her emotions toward the classroom. Jessie usually likes to use colors in her drawings, and I believe she had very good reasons for drawing such a lifeless picture to portray her school life. This drawing was so vivid that it immediately evoked a deeper empathic understanding in me toward Jessie. I asked myself what it was like to be Jessie: sitting in a corner, being put on the spot to speak a language she is not good at, not understanding well what's going on in the classroom and facing ridicule from peers. It was as if I was in the classroom with her, and I felt her pain. I also felt trusted because she regarded me as someone she could relate to and was willing to share her story with me via her drawings.

Peer Relationship: Jessie drew this picture when we were trying to explore her peer relations. There are two girls in the picture. One is wearing Jessie's favorite color, pink, and the other is wearing orange. The two girls are wearing dresses of the same style. They stand very close to each other, but they are not looking at each other directly. In fact, they are facing different directions as they talk, and Jessie puts a colorless flower between them. The girl in orange is holding a bill in her hand. She appears to be very happy about the money she has.

My impression is that this picture is more about peer pressure than about friendship. Since Jessie usually uses pink to portray herself, it is safe to assume that she is the pink girl with no money in her hand. The two girls are not looking at each other in conversation, indicating that they are not really close. And the pale flower between them signifies their pale relationship. It looks as if the orange girl is bragging about the money she has, which makes Jessie feel bad about herself.

It was great that Jessie liked to offer descriptions of her pictures while drawing. She talked about her father and how she liked it that he gave her pocket money to buy snacks. She said she was trying to save the money so that when she had $100, she could buy whatever she wanted. However, her father was not around that much, and therefore saving up to $100 seemed impossible to her. She also revealed her unpleasant interaction with students in her after-school tutoring class. A girl named Brittany was deliberately distancing her, and the other students favored Brittany.

This picture offered me a chance to take a better look not only at her interaction with peers but also at what was happening at her home and how it affected her performance at school. It aroused my interest in learning more about Jessie's home environment. From the bits and pieces that Jessie told me as she was drawing, I found out that her father might be working very hard in order to support the family and, therefore, didn't have much quality time with

Jessie. It is worth noting that an eight-year-old was so concerned about saving money, which indicated that she was feeling the pressure of not being financially secure, and this might have had something to do with the financial struggle her parents were experiencing. Also, Jessie was not comfortable interacting with Brittany, who obviously had more pocket money than she did. The pale flower between them not only described their poor relationship but also Jessie's feelings toward the relationship.

This drawing aroused my curiosity, and my head was full of questions. What did $100 mean to Jessie? What would Jessie do if she had the money? With regard to Brittany, was she sad or jealous? How did their relationship affect her interaction with other students? I was surprised that none of her teachers could answer these questions. This led me to propose that we should have a meeting with Jessie's parents.

Home Environment: Most of the time, Jessie preferred not to talk in detail about herself or her family. Even when she talked, the pieces of information she provided sometimes contradicted those provided by her mother. Therefore, I decided to ask Jessie to draw a picture of her home to get a clearer view of what it was like.

To my surprise, Jessie had tremendous difficulty drawing the picture. She tried three times and finally finished one. It is not an ordinary picture of a home. It is only a square with some curtains on the top, and, astonishingly, Jessie is standing outside of it. Jessie uses three colors on herself but none on the square beside her.

I was struck by an overwhelming sense of loneliness the moment I saw the picture. Two interpretations might fit here. The square could represent Jessie's concept of "home," and there is nobody and nothing in it that makes her feel cozy and warm. Or it could also be the window in her room, next to which Jessie might usually stand, feeling lost and empty.

As we discussed the picture, Jessie told me that she had two baby sisters, a two-year-old and a one-year-old, who could not talk much. I asked her whom she talked to when she was sad, she responded that there was no one to talk to and she usually played with her little sisters. She said her parents were busy.

My observation was that Jessie really needed someone she could communicate her feelings to. Her parents did not speak English and could not help her with schoolwork. They were also busy with work and two newborn babies. With all the attention her parents might give to her baby sisters, Jessie probably felt that she was not loved as much as before but was unable to articulate what she was going through internally.

As our sessions went on, Jessie revealed to me that her parents and two little sisters had gone back to China and would stay for several months before coming back to the States. She lived in the apartment by herself, with her grandparents in the same building.

I was shocked. I told the school about Jessie's situation, and the counselor intervened to tell her grandparents that Jessie should not be left alone in her apartment. After this session, I found it not so hard to imagine why Jessie had difficulty drawing a picture of her home. She was very lonely there. But the good news was that she became increasingly interested in talking about her experiences and feelings with me. It was as if Jessie was gradually able to say what was on her mind without relying on drawings. If the ultimate purpose of art therapy was to end it someday, then Jessie and I were ready to embrace that day very soon.

My experience with Jessie definitely enriched my professional life. It offered me a new lens to look through when working with children as well as adults. Successful counseling relies a lot on the expressiveness of spoken language, but working with Jessie taught me that art could be just as effective, if not more so, in eliciting feelings. I looked through one window at a child's life and was touched so deeply that our relationship changed fundamentally.

Art is a tool to encourage verbal expression, too. Sometimes children use art to shield their vulnerability, and when they feel safe enough to be vulnerable, they do not have to hide behind that shield anymore. I loved Jessie's drawings, but months later, the moment she walked into my office and said she just needed to talk was magical and sacred to me.

Leslie

My field practicum site was a charter high school and one of the first of its kind. Originally meant to be a residential treatment facility, this day school was created to meet the needs of foster children and children within the Department of Human Services (DHS). With the constant changes and relocations that foster children must endure, the school allows for some consistency in their lives; they are bused in from as far as an hour away. The students, who are predominantly African American, are referred to the school through DHS and come from a variety of backgrounds. Their current situations vary: some have been reunited with their parents; some live with another family member, and some live with a foster family.

As a result of their rough and unstable background, the students are unable to perform at the level expected of 15 to 20 year olds. Their reading and math skills are far below what is grade appropriate, generally ranging from a second-grade to fourth-grade level; nor are they proficient in reading and math according to their School Assessment test scores. As a result of the non-traditional nature of the school, much was still needed in the way of program development. There was no set behavioral and mental health model by which to assist students in need.

I spent my first few weeks at the school assisting in the classroom. This gave me the opportunity to observe students socially, academically, and individually. Overall, the students are rambunctious and often rude and confrontational. They incessantly discuss drugs, sex, and violence; this behavior appeared to serve as a defense mechanism for coping with their difficult lives. To keep their attention for any extended period of time was incredibly challenging. Their lack of motivation was amplified by their feelings of shame and embarrassment when they were unable to complete simple tasks and assignments. The students were obviously aware that they were not performing at the level expected of someone their age. Necessary disciplinary action had also hampered their ability to succeed. They cursed constantly, fought frequently, and showed a continuous lack of respect toward adults in general. Without a sense of order and consequences, such behaviors would drastically increase; at the same time, the students regularly missed school due to suspension.

The student I worked with was a 20-year-old African American male, whom I will refer to as Tom. Tom had a slightly withdrawn and quiet personality. Unlike most of his classmates, he regularly attempted to complete his assignments and avoided disrupting class. He often appeared lethargic, resting his head on the table for extended periods of time. Tom was friendly with many students but did not appear to have a core social circle. Occasionally Tom would ask for help, a rare occurrence at this school because many students view it as a sign of weakness. Although he tried hard, his reading and math abilities were on a third grade level.

Tom had a rough past, both physically and emotionally. He was born prematurely, weighing less than two pounds. The first year of his life was spent in the hospital. Tom was diagnosed with "failure to thrive," as well as a chronic lung disease. At the age of eight, he was hit by a car, which resulted in traumatic brain injury and a femoral fracture. Consequently, he was hospitalized for more than a year. At the age of twelve, DHS removed him from his mother's home because of her drug use as well as neglect, as Tom had not been attending school. For the next two years, he and his younger sister lived in a different city with their aunt. When Tom turned fourteen, he decided he wanted to move back to his hometown. He was separated from his sister and placed in a verbally abusive alcoholic's home where he stayed for only two weeks. Tom ran away to his mother's house, and she promptly returned him to DHS. His second foster family was, Tom said, the best. He was reunited with his sister and given clothes, food, and spending money. After only six months, he and his sister were transferred to another foster home, where, sadly, the woman tried to physically abuse them; consequently, they ran away. For the next two years, from the ages of 16 to 18, Tom and his sister were hiding from DHS and living at a friend's house.

The most appalling aspect of the six years of his life leading up to his 18th birthday is that he did not enroll in or attend school at all. He could not explain why DHS allowed this to happen. When he turned 18, he signed out of DHS and returned to his mother's home. When I worked with him, Tom was at a lower academic level as a result of his school attendance in the past. He had a mild learning disability; however, his previous health problems no longer affected him.

Over six sessions, Tom slowly told me his life story. As he had done many times, he explained the facts with little emotion. His teachers had noted a vast change in his behavior, both in attendance and focus. After finding out that he was not far from being eligible to graduate, Tom stopped skipping school and getting high on marijuana quite as much. When I probed a little deeper into the feelings behind his troubled past, Tom appeared indifferent and smiled. My questions often elicited an apathetic response coupled with a smile: "I don't know," "I don't care."

In preparation for this narrative art therapy project I explained to Tom that there was nothing in particular he was supposed to draw. I suggested two drawings, something that brings him joy or pride, and something that represents a struggle in his life. Tom took his time to think about what he wanted to draw beginning with his struggles, and carefully began scribbling with a pencil. He first drew a semi-two-dimensional closed book. He colored it a light brown and shaded the edges with his pencil for dimension. The title was "books." Tom explained that the book represents his trouble in school, particularly reading. While school performance is a common concern, what struck me the most was how he connected these insufficiencies to his "real world" success. Tom was concerned about more than getting a good grade. Without a higher reading comprehension level, he had been unable to get a job; struggling with even reading and responding to an application. Unlike many students in the school, Tom wanted to work and be a responsible member of society. He was acutely aware of his extremely low ability level, which caused him much distress.

Next to the book, Tom drew a picture of a stick-figure girl and wrote "girls calling me ugly." The girl's body was green, with a yellow face. Her hair was like two upside down tear drops on either side of her head, the color of burnt orange. Tom drew vacant dots for her eyes and nose and a neutral line for her mouth, with one side slightly curled up as though she were smirking. I believe that the picture of the girl was a reflection of his self-esteem. Although he is an attractive young man, he claimed that "girls calling me ugly" is a source of struggle in his life. It is also interesting to note that the girl he drew appeared to be Caucasian; possibly acknowledging his struggle and marginalization as an African American youth in our mainstream white culture.

What was most curious to me was his choice of "struggles." Not fifteen minutes before he began drawing, Tom told me that his mother might have cancer and was going into surgery the next day. When we discussed his drawings and what they meant to him, I eventually asked whether those were in fact the most significant struggles in his life. His response didn't change so I mentioned his mother's surgery and asked whether he was worried or nervous. With a shrug he said no, without emotion. It wasn't until the end of our sessions together that I noticed his pattern of coping. Tom acknowledges the struggles in his life over which he has a moderate amount of control, and he remains as numb as possible to those over which he does not.

On the "joy or pride" paper, Tom drew a computer screen and keyboard. The keyboard was shaded with orange crayon, and the screen was shaded red with a blue outline. At the top of the screen, Tom wrote "www.facebook.com," and in the bottom left corner he drew a green money symbol. Tom explained that the things that bring him joy in his life are "playing on the computer with Facebook and money." I believe that this picture is an appropriate expression of his lack of a positive social outlet. Facebook substitutes as his "friends" and keeps him connected to a social network. Money is a central concern. Tom, and most youth in his situation, focus on physical presentation, as it is one of the only things in his life he can control. Money is the means to nice clothes, shoes, and cellphone; symbols of status in his social circle. The concept of "pride" was never addressed, as he was able to effectively avoid any such conversation.

Tom spent much of his free time smoking marijuana with friends. When I asked on multiple occasions what he likes to do, what he is interested in, the answer was always "nothing really" or "just playing on the computer." Tom has no role models, no encouragement, and no job to keep him occupied. It appears that he is effectively self-medicating to deal with the stress in his life. Although he appeared to be genuinely honest, our definition of certain things vastly differed. The first time I asked whether he used drugs, the answer was no, because he doesn't consider marijuana a drug. He told me that, as a result of watching his mother do drugs, he would never do them. In that same breath he told me he was hospitalized with an overdose of Percocet "because I didn't have any weed." Tom reported that he had not taken Percocet since that incident two years earlier, which I believe to be true.

Tom has been let down by almost every adult in his life. When asked who the most important person in his life was, he said no one except his mom, "but only because she gave birth to me." Most everything he says is very neutral, which is most likely a defense mechanism. If he doesn't have strong feelings about something or someone, then he can't get hurt or disappointed. Although he appeared comfortable and open with me from the beginning, it wasn't until our final session that he acknowledged ever being emotionally upset about things in his life. Talking about watching his mother do drugs in front of him, Tom said that it made him want to cry. With my assistance, we explored what makes him a good person, along with what aspects of himself he wants to work on. Initially, this was quite difficult, as he couldn't come up with positive characteristics about himself. In the end, he was able to articulate his positive attributes, as well as his desire to work on his mood swings and self-esteem. I felt that this was a tremendous step in the right direction. How many people in his life have told him what a good person he is, and all the things he is capable of? It wasn't until our final session that Tom disclosed to me that he would be the first person in his family to graduate from high school. This is a huge source of pride for him, something that enables him to look to the future in a positive light.

Drawing and doodling in class was something of a stress reliever for Tom. Although his free drawing did not necessarily display anything in particular, it was something that came with ease and provided an outlet for his frustrations. Tom was forced to grow up at a young age, never having the chance to experience a true childhood. As an adult, he did not have the capability to express himself through the use of writing. The drawings that he did for me facilitated a deeper discussion of his life and unique perspectives. Unable to appropriately articulate, Tom used to sit with his thoughts in an effort to better explain them.

Narrative art brings a different dynamic into a therapeutic relationship. For young children, it is essentially the most efficient means of communication. The same can be said for Tom, who is developmentally equivalent to a child. Serving as a type of "ice-breaker," narrative art therapy is an easy-to-use and adaptable tool that puts the client at ease. For many people, "therapy" can be

an unknown and intimidating endeavor, and art serves as a relaxing and concrete therapeutic task, increasing the comfort level of both client and clinician.
Art can also be used to initiate verbal discussion and give the clinician insight
into the meaning behind the client's words. I could not fully comprehend
what Tom has gone through, but art gave me a deeper understanding than his
words ever could.

Conclusion

The success that five graduate counseling students experienced with the arts
is only one example of how the arts can effectively be used as narrative in a
school setting with individuals and groups. The graduate students and their
pupils alike benefited from their experiences. The graduate students learned
through actual experience that there are effective ways to communicate and
build relationships without words. It is unfortunate that these methods are not
included in most counseling training programs, but they are essential to becoming and being an effective school counselor.

Alicia studied both piano and flute, but she reports that her studies interfere with her ability to practice and play. Her student used singing to convey
her personal frustrations. The words from a song in Les Misérables related to her
own feelings, making the artistic connection even stronger. Marie indicated to
Alicia that her physical illness and her alienation from her so-called friends
made her feel like an outsider, but music was her salvation. Through her musical gift, she was able to find fulfillment as she struggled with peer issues and worried about her physical health.

Debby, a practicing artist, who designs and makes jewelry, used her talents
while working with a difficult group of girls. She automatically turned to what
she knows and loves, beading, which was a natural, easy fit with her group. The
activity allowed the girls to delight in their achievements, have meaningful discussions during group time, and create wearable art. Most likely, the students
were able to sense Debby's comfort and passion about her work and thus follow her lead, quieting down and focusing on their task as they conversed.

Ally has musical talent and numerous professional accomplishments. She
has studied voice and taken lessons for years. Her student Andrew made paper
sculptures. That she and Andrew express themselves using different art forms
did not seem to be significant. She easily related to what he was doing artistically. In interpreting Andrew's creations, she saw that he released his aggres-

sion and negativity not only through his behavior but through his world of paper figures as well.

Bridget studied piano beginning at the age of five, but since moving to the US from Shanghai as a graduate student, she has had no opportunity to practice or play. Her student, Jessie, an eight-year-old Chinese girl, was depressed. Jessie's parents took her two baby sisters with them and returned home to China for two months, leaving her in the care of relatives. Jessie drew three pictures for Bridget. The most moving image was her representation of her room, which revealed her depression and isolation. In it, Jessie depicts herself standing alone in a room adjacent to a window. At eight, her developmental abilities prevented her from articulating her emotional response to the feelings of abandonment by her parents that she was experiencing. But her visual narrative displayed her raw feelings. What must it feel like to be alone in a large room with nothing in it?

Only Leslie does not participate in expressive arts. Her subject, Tom, draws and doodles all the time. Tom has had the most challenging life of all the graduate students studied. He is also the oldest. Because his background lacked so many aspects—security, attachment, and love—he seems to have suffered the most. It is unfortunate that Tom was heavily dependent on marijuana in his daily functioning. Leslie noted that drawing is something he does to relax. Perhaps drawing and doodling was what he did in his various chaotic foster homes. Leslie would encourage him to continue with his drawing and reinforce the necessity of trying to reduce his drug use.

The ease with which these students were able to use the arts as narrative in their therapeutic sessions reinforces the necessity for more training directed toward using the arts in counselor education programs and for regular education teachers as well. Regular education teachers could benefit by having this additional resource available to them to engage some challenging students. For example, a student from one of my studies claimed to have been an excellent handball player who was failing in his academic subjects. If his physics and math teachers knew of this talent, they might have been able to devise some specific lessons to address his interests, such as the helping him figure out the angle of the ball and the speed of the trajectory that enabled him to overcome opponents. A history or English assignment could have had him research and write about the origins of early ball sports. Instead, this senior was contemplating dropping out of school since his grades were so low and graduation was questionable. Another failing student was obsessed with rock music. There is no reason why assignments could not have asked about the origins of such music, which instruments are the most popular, and how they came to be. Or about sound waves and hearing. Or about the influence music has on people. Personal attention should be shown to students coupled with creative approaches to capture their interests, and devising lessons from a different perspective should simply be part of teacher training. Engaged students are rarely disciplinary problems.

Tapping into the latent or obvious talents of students can bring meaning and fulfillment in the lives of children, adolescents, and even adults. The arts should not be restricted or limited to only those students deemed in need of help. The arts are much more than a resource or an outlet for troubled youth; they enhance the counseling experience and counseling techniques, enabling the expression of feelings. The arts benefit all who are involved.

Reflection Question

On a final note, the arts take many forms within our lives, some more apparent than others. Reflect on your own work and life, considering how you might have approached a situation differently had you been more creative in your solution. Can you take this new thought and apply it to another situation for a more successful outcome? Aristotle said, "The aim of art is to represent not the outward appearance of things, but their inward significance."

Reflection Questions/Arts Exercises

1. Either you or a friend should select three different types of musical pieces (no longer than three minutes), such as jazz, classical, rock, Latin music, or other. Listen to each selection and as you hear it, write or draw whatever comes to your mind. What does the music evoke in you? Notice the differences in your reactions to each type of music and in how you interpreted each piece. Did you notice any inhibitions within yourself or were you able to freely express yourself in verse, random words, lines, or images for each type of music?

2. This activity is best done in a small group circle. Have one volunteer or two walk back and forth in front of the others as the others observe. Then, ask for two volunteers to mimic the walking style they just observed. Reflect on how carefully they notice nuances and subtleties of others' walks. This could be repeated with

any form of gestures that people make and observe.

3. Trace your hand on a piece of paper. Using colored pencils or thin colored makers, draw and/or write things about yourself, such as your favorite color, sport, or activities you enjoy, within each finger. If you are working in a group, exchange "handshakes" and learn whether or not you share similarities, differences, likes, and dislikes.

Author's Note

I would like to thank my incredible students who made this chapter possible, Alicia Hayes, Debby Michelman, Ally Parker, Leslie Sitkoff, and Bridget Zhang. Without their contributions, this experience would not have been possible. Each one of these counseling students has shown creativity and dedication to the field, and touched the lives of their students at their practicum sites as well as mine. Thank you.

References

American Arts Alliance. (2006). *Arts Education: Creating student success in school, work and life.* Retrieved from the Michigan Art Education Association Web site: http://www .miarted.org/data/masterdata/uploadedfiles/file/ UPLOADEDFORMS/studentsuccess.pdf

Berliner, D.C. (2009, June). *Rational response to high-stake testing and the special case of narrowing the curriculum.* Paper presented at the International Conference on Redesigning Pedagogy, National Institute of Education, Nanyang Technological University, Singapore.

Cohen, E. P., & Gainer, R. S. (1995). *Art: Another language for learning* (3rd ed.). Portsmouth, NH: Heinemann.

Goodnow, J. (1977). *Children's drawings.* Cambridge, MA: Harvard University Press

Greene, M. (1995). *Releasing the imagination: Essays on education, the arts, and social change.* San Francisco, CA: Jossey-Bass.

Heilig, J. V., Cole, H., & Aguilar, A. (2010). From Dewey to No Child Left Behind: The evolution and devolution of public arts education. *Arts Education Policy Review, 111*, 136–145.

Mullins, H. (2008). At the crossroads of preservice teacher education, NAEA, and Terry Barrett: Exploring Metaphors of Meaning, Narratives of Hope. *Curriculum and Teaching Dialogue, 10*(1/2), 73–86.

Thomas, E., & Mulvey, A. (2008). Using the arts in teaching and learning: Building student capacity for community-based work in health psychology. *Journal of Health Psychology 13*(2), 238–249.

· 6 ·

Digital Narratives by Digital Natives

Online Inquiry and Reflective Practices in a Third Space

SANDRA SCHAMROTH ABRAMS

Introduction

Twenty-first century technologies and virtual spaces provide educators and students dynamic opportunities to construct personal and collective narratives. Technology has provided new media through which in-service and pre-service educators can tell their stories (Clandinin & Connelly, 1995) and reflect upon their practices, enabling them to consider alternative ideas as a means to improve pedagogy. According to Beldarrain (2006), in this way, digital spaces and tools have "change[d] the roles of learners as well as instructors. The added control and interaction provided to learners using technology tools may help tap into a student's expertise, and promote collaboration through peer-to-peer mentoring, teamwork, and other strategies" (pp. 143–144). The virtual world, therefore, offers an environment that can enhance reflective practices, inspire interactive feedback, and engender effective teaching.

Wedding technology and reflection to stimulate student participation and critical thinking, I incorporated an online discussion forum into my university classroom; here, students posted concurrent responses while convening in the room. The six preservice undergraduates enrolled in my required adolescent education course, Language Acquisition and Literacy, composed digital reflective narratives, underscoring the promises of a protean third space in which personal and academic experiences would converge. Figure 6.1 showcases a typical online forum conversation. The initial post, located in the center box, is by Marcie, followed by one by Phillip, then one by Cynthia (name shown in the top left corner), who is responding to both Phillip and Marcie. This image shows an interactive, threaded reflection among students (all names are pseudonyms), revealing insights into their personal scholarship, pedagogy, and practice.

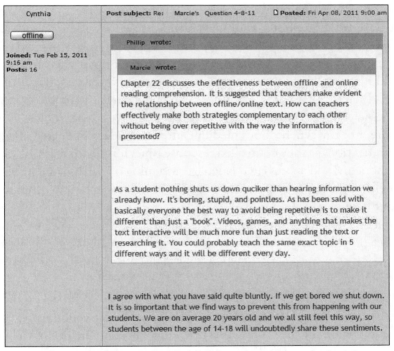

Figure 6.1 Marcie, Phillip, and Cynthia conversing on the forum.
The centermost box is the initial post.

The conversation among Marcie, Phillip, and Cynthia occurred on a virtual discussion site (forum) in real time (synchronous). Though my class and I utilized the synchronous virtual forum during face-to-face sessions, we also visited the site when outside the classroom (remotely) during real-time class hours. On the forum, the written conversations were reminiscent of free writing; students posted, viewed, and immediately responded to each other's ideas. Having access to other students' feedback contributed to an organic narrative that continued to take shape as students added related posts and/or threads about their learning experiences and their pedagogical stances.

Unlike typical online learning, this forum usually took place around a square table in the university classroom, with the preservice educators typing on their laptops as they sat alongside their classmates and professor (me), also contributing to student responses. In other words, we were simultaneously present in a shared physical and virtual space (the classroom and the forum), which created a unique opportunity for students to explore and develop their thoughts in an online venue, scaffolding the in-class conversation that followed the virtual session. Given the physical academic setting; the instructions for posting how, why, or what questions; and the students' presence in a professor-created and -operated forum, the students' responses adhered to the "rules and expectations about writing and storytelling, literary conventions, rhetorical strategies, and ideas of what is interesting or important to readers and listeners" (Maynes, Pierce, & Laslett, 2008, p. 70). No doubt, the academic context and guidelines may have constrained the students' narratives. Nonetheless, the virtual context of the synchronous medium afforded students a degree of agency in their reflection, as they controlled response time, font modification, and the use of emoticons and abbreviated language, assuming ownership of a space that, as Danielle explains, "allows me to more freely express myself without worrying about how correct I sound."

Danielle's sentiment suggests that the students may have viewed the online forum as akin to other virtual spaces, such as cell phone texts, social networking sites, or instant messages, in which digital discourse does not seem subject to grammatical evaluation (Crystal, 2006; Turner, 2009; Turner, Katic, Abrams & Donovan, 2011) and there is "freedom from regulated orthographic and spelling conventions" (Plester, Wood & Joshi, 2009, p. 147). However, the length and breadth of the forum posts resembled blog entries rather than chat or text messages, and the students seemed to associate the space with both social and academic discourse. In addition, the connection of the forum to an academic setting, the discussion of required reading, and the adherence to forum rules (e.g., the requirement that each student must participate and respond to at least one other classmate) would indicate that the forum was, indeed, an academic space. This duality suggests that the forum created an alternate "third space" (Bhabha, 1994; Moje et al., 2004; Soja, 1996) that enabled students to explore "translations" and developments of self and pedagogy (Cook-Sather, 2001, p. 16). The third space was an evolving shared environment that capitalized on the confluence of social and academic elements and granted students a degree of freedom to safely and collaboratively contemplate teaching and learning.

Knowledge Landscapes and Translations in a Third Space

Narratives simultaneously constructed in a shared virtual and real environment complicate what Clandinin and Connelly (2000) acknowledge as the personal/social, temporal, and contextual elements of the "three-dimensional narrative inquiry space" (p. 50). The features of the online environment (e.g., the context or space) that provide students selectivity and agency also introduce a depth to the space in which the narrative exists; they seem to offer a new topography for knowledge landscapes that shape practice (Clandinin & Connelly, 1995) that may not exist in real-world (interview, field note) interpretive spaces. Online communication involves *Discourses*, as defined by Gee (2008, 2011), or socioculturally situated doing-being-valuing combinations, that privilege the user's agency; in fact, in most online spaces, one may post images, thoughts, videos, and sounds that reflect authorial power and the reification of ideas and/or experiences. Online text is viewed by the author before submission, and, as opposed to interview data that are spoken and not seen by the participant, there is a metalevel of review and perhaps analysis before the student presses the Submit button. Further, the action of making a response "public" suggests that there is agency in the act of posting, in that the student determines when to submit the information and then is physically responsible for clicking the virtual button. In so doing, knowledge landscapes include an understanding of virtual worlds and Discourses, and there is a sense of ownership and control that may not exist within academic or professional landscapes (Clandinin & Connelly, 1995).

In many ways, the landscape changes because the synchronous virtual forum creates a third space (Bhabha, 1994; Moje et al., 2004; Soja, 1996) in which students can access and reflect upon their personal and social experiences and integrate their academic and personal/online Discourses. In a third space, students build upon their funds of knowledge (Cavazos-Kotte, 2005; Moll, Amanti, Neff & Gonzalez, 1992; Rowsell, 2006) or "historically accumulated and culturally developed bodies of knowledge and skills" (Moll et al., 1992, p. 133), and the third space becomes a "different or alternative" domain in which home and academic Discourses "merge" (Moje et al., 2004, p. 41). However, a third space is more than a combination of experiences; as Soja (1996) suggests, "It does not derive simply from an additive combination of its binary antecedents, but rather from a disordering, deconstruction, and tentative reconstitution of their presumed totalization producing an open alternative that is both similar and strikingly different" (p. 61). In the third space, convention is disrupted to create reception to change and/or the expansion of ideas; it is a dimension in which students

- begin to share their experiences,
- find commonalities among their responses,
- learn from each other, and
- reconsider and improve their pedagogy and practice.

This alternate safe space that is shaped by its inhabitants allows genuine reflective narratives and discussions to burgeon, creating an environment necessary for personal and professional development. As Palmer (1998) explains:

> If we want to grow as teachers—we must do something alien to academic culture: we must talk to each other about our inner lives—risky stuff in a profession that fears the personal and seeks safety in the technical, the distant, the abstract. (p. 12)

Soja suggests that important to the concept of the third space is that, despite its acceptance of new ideas and directions, there is a "certain practical continuity of knowledge production that is an antidote to the hyperrelativism and 'anything goes' philosophy often associated with such radical epistemological openness" (1996, p. 61). This boundary is essential especially in a reflective third space, as there is a maintenance of foundational constructs and/or theoretical concepts that ground ideas for practice in the understanding of child development and ethical and effective pedagogy.

The reflective third space of the synchronous forum offered opportunities for students to reconstruct the topography of their knowledge landscapes for communicating about teaching and personal experience. The integration of academic and online Discourses generated an environment that was both constrained by academic requirements and evaluation and indulged by the uninhibited and sometimes flippant nature of virtual communication. At times, elements of threaded discussions or proclamations related to third-space postings extended into the classroom, and I was privy to the level of intrinsic motivation inherent in voiced exclamations, such as Katherine's, "Wait! I have to post something!" The desire, immediacy, and control in Katherine's statement reveal how important she perceived her materialized reflection to be.

Her contribution was an essential piece of the forum narrative and synchronous community, thus underscoring "social presence as a prerequisite to establishing an online learning community where students can collaborate" (Beldarrain, 2006, p. 149).

The students' participation in this online learning community played a large role in their "translation" or "re-render[ing]" (Cook-Sather, 2001) of self to accommodate the teaching realm and the culture of classrooms in which they have opportunities to student teach. In this third space, not only did they share their experiences but they also learned from those of others, and this whole-class online interaction fostered a learning community that may be absent in other virtual synchronous courses (Wang & Reeves, 2007). In other words, postings exist within the interactive community and not as isolated obligatory responses, and an overall social narrative contributes to epistemological and methodological shifts. As Phillip explains, "I feel like the forum is effective because we talk about our experiences and hear the opinions of our classmates. We can also learn other methods to use from our classmates."

Creating the Third Space for Reflective Narratives: Establishing the Forum

The majority of the preservice educators enrolled in my course were in their third year of their undergraduate career, specializing in adolescent education in one of three main concentrations: math, history, or English. The synchronous virtual forum the students and I utilized during select class sessions helped to support rich face-to-face discussions involved in 21st century literacy practices, cross-disciplinary methods, and teaching with/without new media in high school classrooms with a range of technological resources available. The forum, therefore, became an alternate space outside the high school and university classrooms. Further, this virtual environment that we frequented in synchronous (real-time) scenarios was primarily conducted in the physical classroom but occasionally from distant locations.

Though I had experience utilizing WebCT Blackboard and wiki sites, such as pbworks, I searched for a simple space (e.g., with limited icons and easy navigation) that would enable all the students to view each others' posts simultaneously, embed the original post in the responses in a clear fashion, and not limit the amount of text in the discussion boxes and/or threads. I found open source (legal and free) forum software that I hosted on my personal server, and the infrastructure for the forum was predesigned and ready for immediate use/formatting, and, because I hosted the site, I had complete control over the site and could ensure a high level of privacy (certainly higher than if I looked to an outside host that could archive my class's information). Students signed on to the site with a self-selected username and password, which I did not have access to, and, with administrator authorization (my approval), they gained entrance to their class's forum. The level of security was of upmost importance to me because I wanted to foster a safe (as safe as possible) and user-friendly environment that would lend itself to introspection, freedom of expression, and genuine collaboration.

Digital Natives and Their Narratives in a Third Space

Digital communication in the 21st century is a pervasive activity, and "millennials, those aged 18–33, remain more likely to access the internet wirelessly with a laptop or mobile phone . . . surpass[ing] their elders online" with their use of various tools, such as social networking sites, instant messages, blogs, and virtual worlds (Zickuhr, 2010). Kress (1997) suggests that for most millennials, "life on the screen is an everyday, natural practice—they know no other way of being" (p. 167). Many millennials, teenagers, and younger generations are viewed as digital natives (Prensky, 2001, 2006) because they have grown up in a digitally ensconced world and have seamlessly developed knowledge and skills that inform their interaction with and understanding of multimodal texts. Therefore, inhabiting online spaces and participating in digital discourse are part of personal, social, and academic/professional living for this generation, and digital communication has cultural currency because, as Taylor and Harper (2003) suggest, it may "embody that which is special to the owner" (p. 273), and it can "cement" social relationships (p. 268). In other words, as Domokos (2007) points out, digital communication is "an important part of the new narrative culture based on electronic literacy" (p. 50).

Although digital natives (Prensky, 2001, 2006) may only know a technologically rich world and as a result have greater facility with and negotiation of virtual interaction, such facility does not automatically beget reflection. Social networking sites (e.g., Twitter, Facebook) may detail minute-by-minute postings that provide a blueprint of one's day or one's feelings, but many posts on these sites do not necessarily generate a written response. As a result, digital natives may grow accustomed to online communication that is disproportionately self-dominated. Such "single tellership" is bereft of multifaceted reflection and varied perceptions (Ware, 2006, p. 46). However, in virtual environments, such as asynchronous online spaces where nonconcurrent contributions are expected and promoted, as with some blogs or online classrooms/blackboards, Burniske (cited in Grisham & Wolsey, 2006) points out the setting "allows the writer/speaker to compose statements in the absence of an audience. The 'turn taking' here does not allow for interruptions, which means each participant has an opportunity to speak without pause, inspiring declamations as well as dialogues" (pp. 651–652). The same held true for my class's synchronous online forum, where Cynthia felt that there was "no domination of discussions," and Phillip explained that one could "get your words and your thoughts out there; it's not like the conversation's changed and you think, 'Oh, never mind.'"

Although students benefited from the affordances of uninterrupted discourse, the synchronous class forum, coupled with the physical academic setting and parameters, reminded them that it was a collaborative online environment, and "shared tellership" enabled them to participate in what Ware (2006) refers to as "co-telling the narrative. They challenge[d] a fact here and there, ask[ed] questions, and elaborate[d] on parts of the story" (p. 46). The shared tellership may have come easily for some, like Marcie, who felt that the forum was "second nature" because "we're used to it . . . IM, text messages." Given the forum's academic setting and the presence of the professor-as-moderator, the genre differs from that of personal/social texting and instant messaging; nonetheless, the forum posts and the interactive environment empowered student-driven online discussions and, as is evident in the opening example (Figure 6.1), this seemed to nurture the class's development of threaded narratives and shared telling experiences of their past, present, and future pedagogical ideals.

The narrative third space represents a combination of students' personal/social and academic realms, and the evaluative overtones of academic standards and assessment carried over into the alternate space. In this sense, digital natives needed to negotiate their "funds of knowledge" for both the online and in-class experience; there remained the tension between situated digital and traditional practices, with assessment possibly the culprit of any student's seemingly contrived responses. Though most students viewed the online forum as "less stressful" or "informal," there were mandatory components (e.g., minimum number of posts, required responses) used to initiate student online interaction. This formality may have fueled students' academic anxieties, as I found students asking me to verify if their participation was satisfactory, thus reinforcing that the third space was not entirely a social space. Even though posts were ungraded, academic Discourses and evaluative overtones, which seemed to stem from forum requirements and students' schemata for school, seeped into the third space.

Reflecting in the Third Space:
The Academic Space

Given that the forum created a third space for communication and reflection, there was an extraordinary duality between my online supervision and students' seemingly autonomous postings; students appeared to speak openly and freely, yet they admittedly noted their awareness of the school-related context. On the forum, Phillip explains that he was genuine in his postings, but that his responses were tailored to the academic environment: "I personally didn't change my answers or how I talked out of uneasiness about you reading it. It's not like I was going to curse or talk dirty or anything like that."

Phillip expected that the virtual space demanded decorum similar to that of the physical classroom. Likewise, Marcie notes her cognizance of my presence:

> I think that knowing you are reading our posts changes our language in how we post our questions and responses. This is a positive aspect because we are going to have to learn how to compose online criteria such as emails to our coworkers, principles [sic], parents, etc [sic] so it is important that we have a schema for this specific online behavior.

Marcie's vocabulary and tone suggest that, even in a personal response, she was focused on revealing scholarship, as though she has been accustomed to academic spaces being spaces of judgment.

It is possible that the third space may have had instructional or evaluative overtones because the forum was a tool I had created and overseen, *and* because we primarily used it in our physical classroom. However, during our April 8th synchronous forum discussion, which took place solely in the virtual environment (e.g., synchronous distance learning), I asked students what they thought about my presence online, and they indicated that they saw me as a "facilitator," one "involved" in their learning. Phillip thought that the forum discussions resembled a "conversation between peers," with me included as a peer being that he did not perceive me as "a rule with an iron fist kind of teacher." Likewise, Danielle explains that

> if I weren't online, her answers might be a little but [sic] more relaxed, meaning maybe not grammatically correct or using a different style of writing like that I would use in a text. I do feel like this is a conversation among peer [sic] because even when you do give us feedback its [sic] like it is coming from a peer in the respect that it is only mean [sic] to help us and to give us an avenue to explore new ideas.

Despite the students' seeming comfort with the space as one free from tyranny (and grammatical or lexical judgment), they still perceived the forum as an academic space that demanded that they adhere to specific standards, such as following directions and using respectful diction. The students also seemed aware that they were corresponding on a professor-run site in which they were accountable for their words. As Phillip candidly responds, "You're [sic] interjection provides us with more questions to think about and you should do it because, well you're the teacher and this is your forum." Though I had hoped the students would recognize the third space as mine as well as theirs (aspects of their posts did suggest a degree of ownership), Phillip's comment highlights how the forum's ownership was ultimately seen as mine, a fact underscored by my administrative role in granting students access to the forum and activating their accounts.

Gravitating toward the traditional teacher-as-authority construct even in an environment that was supposed to be shared and primarily student driven, the students seemed to find comfort in my presence online because I could validate that what they were doing was "right." Using pink font (a form of ownership of expression), Katherine explains that, "You being online had no affect [sic] on my posts, if any it made me aware of how many times I responded to my classmates. I hope I did well!" In a virtual dimension that students acknowledged as "informal," or a "free space where I can be myself rather than worring [sic] about being the 'good student' and writing about what I think the teacher would like the reflection to look [sic]", my presence, nonetheless, seemed to signal assessment. The forum posts may not have demanded the formal writing of the reflection papers that students were required to submit throughout the semester, but posting, itself, had become imbued with evaluative overtones, and each of the six students at some point during the semester had contacted me; Katherine, for example, asked me to confirm that she had met the required number of posts. The students appeared hyper-vigilant of the idea that their posts represented their participation, and, though their writing wasn't being graded, their presence online contributed to their overall grade. In other words, the digital narratives in the third space were constrained by students' overriding concerns of professorial evaluation and yet admittedly informal and natural or, as Marcie put it, "second nature."

Immersion in the Third Space

Perhaps the forum discussions developed simply because students were conscious of the post requirements, or perhaps they developed because the students were fully immersed in forum writing. In either case, the students were amazed how quickly time passed when writing online. Within 27 minutes of our in-class

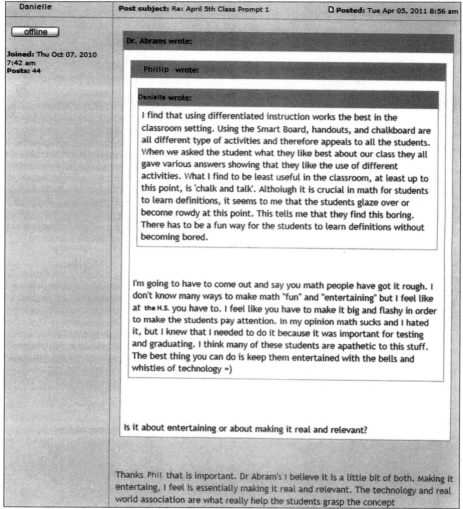

Figure 6.2 A forum conversation among Phillip, Danielle, and me.
The centermost box is the initial post.

forum writing on April 5th, students created a total of 33 posts. This number does not include my 16 contributions intended to help students clarify their points. As seen in Figure 6.2, a screen shot of the forum posting (modified only to obscure identifying information), the students began by engaging in their own discussion about differentiated instruction (the center box, Danielle, is the initial post). Phillip's response to Danielle is casual and personal ("in my opinion math sucks and I hated it"), and student-to-student discourse appears less formal than the student-to-teacher interaction, as is evident in Danielle's final posting (at the bottom). Though the students perceived my online role to be similar to that of a peer's, they couched their comments with references to educational theory and/or concepts we has discussed in class, thereby suggesting that although the third space may have been situationally informal or formal, the students' narratives had a pedagogical focus and a reflective tone. As a result of interacting with their classmates and with me on the forum, the students may have been exploring what Cook-Sather (2001) refers to as a "new version of a text or self, [which] carries inextricably woven within it all previous versions and readings" (p. 18). In other words, in the turn taking, peer feedback, and self-expression, students were able to explore their roles as current students and future educators in a flexible third space that continually accommodated and reconciled the confluence of individual expression and academic boundaries.

For the April 8th distant but synchronous forum experience (conducted outside the classroom but during class hours), the six students were required to post eight times (an initial post, a response to each classmate's post, and a follow-up response). Instead of the required 48 posts, the students created 61 posts, which primarily were student-to-student discussions; however, I contributed 12 times (not counted as part of the 61 posts), which might have prompted students to write more in response to my thoughts. Though I was concerned that my presence might have been intrusive, Jane's sentiments suggest that my participation in the forum was an indication of my interest in their education:

> I wouldn't answer differently if you weren't online but, your presence shows that you are actually reading what we are saying that you are not just on vacation somewhere or in a meeting. Your [sic] involved with our conversation so it is like a class.

This final statement leaves me questioning if the students would perceive the online conversation as something other than "like a class" if I were not present. Would the forum discussions feel unregulated, as many Facebook and Twitter accounts do, even though there is an "other" overseeing and archiving material?

The students' feedback suggests that comfort in the third space may be more individualistic, thereby reinforcing that it is not a fixed entity and further complicating the notion that it may be shaped and/or accessed in different ways by different students. In looking at Figures 6.2 and 6.3, Phillip tended to assume a casual tone, integrating colloquialisms (e.g., "math sucks," Figure 6.2) or abbreviated language ("lol," Figure 6.3), suggesting that the academically designed and operated forum did indeed allow students to draw upon their own experiences and expressions that situated the discussions *and* introduced a social element to the third space. In other words, the students seemed to negotiate the academic nature of the space and discussion topics to include personal reflection and social conventions of digital practice. Their conversations appeared to have impacted the topography of their learning landscapes as the academic setting became infused with digital and personal Discourses and literacies and the third space accommodated and nurtured individualized learning and growth.

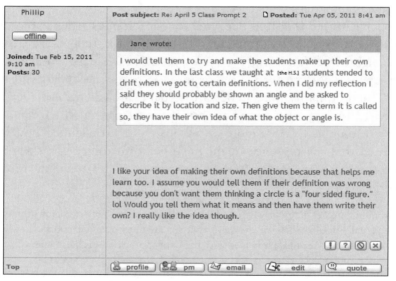

Figure 6.3 A forum conversation between Jane (initial post) and Phillip.

Reflecting in the Third Space:
Individual and Collective Digital Narratives

The synchronous forum enabled students' voices to resonate both individually and collectively. Though each student's forum post helped to develop his ongoing reflective narrative, it also contributed to a larger narrative—that of a class of preservice educators exploring their previous and current classroom experiences and their thoughts for future practice. As Figures 6.1 through 6.4 reveal, the students' reflections had a symbiotic nature; they advanced their thinking about education and practice through the online interaction and shared tellership (Ware, 2006), building upon social interaction to achieve new understandings.

The topography of the students' knowledge landscapes for teaching and learning, therefore, seemed to be transformed perhaps through the adoption and acceptance of collaborative techniques. The discussion between Jane and Marcie in Figure 6.4 reveals how they co-constructed a narrative about their joint experience by creating a wiki page in my class and how that translated into their understanding of teaching and learning and prompted ideas for future practice. What seems evident is the organic nature of their conversation. Though both girls were online (and, in this instance, not sitting in the same room), the absence of a visual audience did not seem to impact the social nature of the conversation. Marcie noted the confidence she developed for collaborative work, using an emoticon as a signal of her friendly and cooperative experience with Jane. Further, Marcie's expression suggests that she was able to move between formal, academic discussion and casual, social gestures and understand that there was a place for both in the third space.

In terms of the collective narrative, the forum conversations provided multiple perspectives on a topic, thereby suggesting that shared tellership (Ware, 2006) creates a narrative that supports future educators "thinking about the world together" (Palmer, 1998, p. 61) and establishing and maintaining a third space culture that hinges on connected experiences and honest yet supportive feedback. In this sense, the narrative third space was one that I was able to, as Palmer (1998) describes it, "co-create with [my students] a content in which all of us can teach and learn" (p. 72). Therefore, despite the evaluative connotation of my presence, the forum offered an alternate joint space and reflective environment for the convergence of personal and academic contemplation.

Figure 6.4 A forum conversation between Jane (initial post) and Marcie.

Digital Narratives and Synchronous Spaces: What This Means for Teacher Education

The creation of the forum led to an unconventional and mutable setting in which students could simultaneously engage in narrative reflection, enabling them to respond to each other in real time, receive immediate feedback, and partake in a community event. The forum may have carried academic implications (students were required to post on it), but it also enabled them to draw on their personal experiences in an environment that existed because of collaborative ownership. Unlike the physical classroom that has inevitable structures that confine bodies and/or position students (Ford, 2003), the online forum enabled students to control the manner of their presence. As is evident in the examples in this chapter, students could modify the font, monitor their own responses (because they had to write and submit them), and offer ideas that might not have followed the current of the undulating discussion threads. Further, unlike in a physical space, there was joint ownership of the forum, and the students appeared to feel safe in expressing their thoughts, questioning each other, and disagreeing with me. There seemed to be an honesty that existed in their posts, perhaps because they appeared in the third space and/or because they were accustomed to writing thoughts online.

The Collaborative Experience

In exploring the role of the forum in preservice education, educators should consider the ways in which a synchronous forum can nurture the development of students' individual narratives and the collective narrative; through reflection and communication in the third space, students can develop critical thinking and explore pedagogical perspectives, innovations, and applications. Unlike in an online space that may have uncontested, unidirectional posts, and unlike in teacher-dominated classrooms in which students can succeed without having to interact, my class's forum was successful because of the interplay among students; the students' codependence on their colleagues for interaction and feedback and their shared participation in virtual and real environments fostered a responsibility to be present and active forum contributors. In the following passage, Katherine explains how the forum offered her access to her classmates' thoughts and how the collaborative experience in the third space demonstrated how student-driven classrooms can fuel multifaceted learning:

> The reason why I like this site is that I can see the responses to my classmates. I like what [sic] my classmates have to response [sic] to my ideas and reflections. I like the back and forth because it makes me think of new ideas that I havent [sic] thought of. This adds examples to one of the main concepts that I have learned through my experiences as an educator: students not only learn from the teacher, they learn from one another. . . . This is why I feel that students should constantly work together on things because it making [sic] for learning not only a fun experience but a rewarding experience.

Together, the students learned from each other, and their reflective posts suggest that the topography of their knowledge landscapes shifted as their concepts of teaching shifted. As indicated in Katherine's response, the act of reading other classmates' posts and writing discussion threads and/or responses to them helped to facilitate a meta-reflection that might not have been achieved if the students had written a formal paper. The act of crafting discussions and hearing feedback in real time is part of the digital narrative structure that seems akin to face-to-face conversations about teaching that enable students to "do what we must do if we are to help each other grow as teachers: speak openly and honestly about our struggles as well as our successes" (Palmer, 1998, p. 146). However, although the students' screen names identified their ownership of their posts, there remains a proprietary distance from the post because the responses are written, not spoken. In other words, there is time to formulate ideas in writing, and this spatial component allows for additional perhaps incidental reflection. Further, because students can read each other's entries, they have time to contemplate the discussion threads. The forum entries were not perfunctory gestures of participation; the iterative posts signified ownership of thought and responsibility to the forum community. There was an interdependence among the students and a mutual student–teacher dependence that fostered community (Palmer, 1998) in the virtual third space and supported an ongoing narrative that reveals how students rethought the trajectory of their own teaching and learning.

Contemplating the Third Space Narrative in Education

In considering a widespread use of a synchronous forum in a physical classroom, I look beyond the issues of technology and resources to contemplate the creation of the third space. We know that the act of writing on a forum in a face-to-face, real-time situation provided students an alternate approach to writing and communicating, but there is still the question of any long-term effects that such interaction may have on students' ability to reflect; specifically, we might ask how their forum experiences impact the longevity of their openness both to sharing reflections with others and to receiving peer feedback. In their first years of teaching, will students search for professional online forums, such as the asynchronous National Council of Teachers of English (NCTE) Forum Digest? Will they be able to establish and maintain a running interactive digital narrative about teaching? The dynamics of my class's virtual forum stemmed from a third space that integrated the personal and the academic and enabled a necessary open-mindedness that fostered collaborative and personal growth. Important to consider, however, is the role of physical presence: How, if at all, might reflection change when students sit beside those they are communicating with online? Or, how might the absence of the physical body impact the comfort, community, and responsibility of a virtual third space, like the one that my students inhabited? Finally, with online learning, class sizes are usually larger than the six students who enrolled in my class. At what point does a class get too large for students to read and respond to each other's work without it becoming an unwieldy and perhaps ineffective experience?

The narratives the students generated in the forum indicate a sense of free-dom, ownership, and personal and collaborative agency. Though they may have carried their evaluative perceptions of teaching into the forum, the students were able to explore alternate ideas for pedagogy and practice *because* they entered a shared third space that was neither classroom nor chat-room. The forum was its own entity for which the students seemed to establish their own cultural register, and the third space narrative, therefore, represented an empow-erment of student-driven learning.

Reflective Questions

1. How would you define being a teacher and teaching in the 21st century?
2. Continuing your response to the above question:
   • What affordances and limitations exist?
   • How might personal and community narratives be included in these definitions?
   • How does a third space fit into your pedagogical vision?
3. To what extent has online writing (e.g., e-mail, text messaging, social-networking posts, blogging) helped you to reconsider your pedagogy? Your practice?
4. How has the hyper-connectivity of the Internet (the availability of browsing among linked Web sites) contributed to your under-standing of meaning? Of teaching? Of reflecting?
5. In light of social networking and personal narratives effecting social and political revolutions (vis-à-vis the uprisings in Egypt, Syria, and Libya), what role do virtual narratives play:
   • in your development as a teacher? A learner? A citizen? A crit-ical thinker?
   • in your students' development as learners? Citizens? Critical thinkers?
   • in the reshaping of knowledge landscapes?
6. What are the global implications of an online third space and narrative inquiry?

Afterword

The open-source (legal and free) forum software I utilized was offered by the phpbb Web site, and I hosted the forum on my personal server. For those who are looking to utilize phpbb software (or a forum similar to it) and who do not have a personal server to host the site, there are options:

- Purchase space from a hosting provider (ranging from $4 to $7 per month) On the phpbb Web site, there is a link to providers (http://www.phpbb.com/hosting/). A popular site Blue Host (http://www.bluehost.com/) offers a one-click installation of phpbb forum software. This seems to be the most user-friendly option. However, the phpbb site lists eight possible hosting providers, and most have an installation of phpbb forum software as part of the package.
- Blackboard 9.1 (C.E. 8) Forum, the most recent version of Blackboard (9.1), which only recently became available, seems to offer a forum that is very similar to the one I used. (In fact, I wouldn't be surprised if Blackboard runs a modified version of the phpbb software.) If your institution offers you access to Blackboard, *I would recommend this option* because
  - ~ it is available to you free of charge (no hosting fees),
  - ~ you will be able to get support through your IT department (which is key), and
  - ~ the forum most likely will be configured for your class, as you are creating a discussion board forum through the specific Blackboard class site. If the forum requires additional configuration in order for you to add students to the discussion forum or adjust the privacy settings, then your IT department will be able to assist you.

An Important Note When Using the Forum

Posting and responding to a topic on the forum are completed by clicking the New Topic or Post Reply buttons. To create an embedded thread (including the original post as its own entity/box when you respond so that the connection between the posts is evident):

- Press the Quote button located on the far right (Figure 6.5).
  - ~ You will be directed to a page that looks like Figure 6.6, (I have modified the response field for generic instructional purposes).
  - ~ It is important to keep the initial post and the information therein available.

- Enter your response underneath the quoted material.
- If you choose to add color, highlight the section or word(s) you would like to place in color, and then select the color.
- Adding an emoticon is as simple as clicking on any one of the emoticons available on the left-hand side of the page.
- When you are ready to post your response, just press the Submit button. Note that if you do not receive confirmation that your response is posted, you may need to press the Submit button once more.

Figure 6.5 The tool bar located at bottom of each forum post.
Choose the Quote button to create an embedded thread.

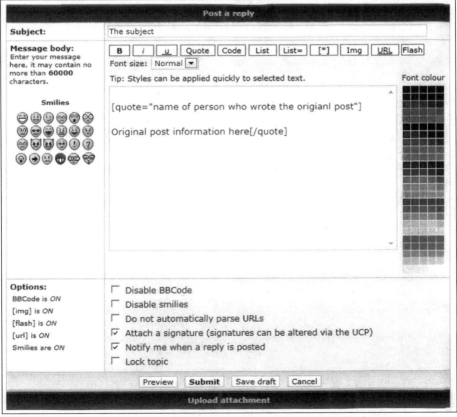

Figure 6.6 An example of the response field for an embedded post.
Enter the response underneath the quoted material.

References

Bhabha, H. K. (1994). *The location of culture*. New York, NY: Routledge.

Beldarrain, Y. (2006). Distance education trends: Integrating new technologies to foster student interaction and collaboration. *Distance Education, 27*(2), 139–153.

Cavazos-Kotte, S. (2005). Tuned out but turned on: Boys' (dis)engaged reading in and out of school. *Journal of Adolescent & Adult Literacy, 49*(3), 180–184.

Clandinin, D. J., & Connelly, F. M. (1995). *Teachers' professional knowledge landscapes*. New York, NY: Teachers College Press.

Clandinin, D. J., & Connelly, F. M. (2000). *Narrative inquiry: Experience and story in qualitative research*. San Francisco, CA: Jossey-Bass.

Cook-Sather, A. (2001). Translating themselves: Becoming a teacher through text and talk. In C. M. Clark (Ed.), *Talking Shop: Authentic Conversation and Teacher Learning* (pp. 16–39). New York, NY: Teachers College Press.

Crystal, D. (2006). *Language and the Internet* (2nd ed.). New York, NY: Cambridge University Press.

Domokos, M. (2007). Folklore and mobile communication. *Fabula, 48*(1/2), 50–59.

Ford, M. (2003). Unveiling technologies of power in classroom organization practice. *Educational Foundations, 17*(2), 5–27.

Gee, J. P. (2008). *Social linguistics and literacies: Ideology in discourses* (3rd ed.). New York, NY: Routledge.

Gee, J. P. (2011). *An introduction to discourse analysis: Theory and method* (3rd ed.). New York, NY: Routledge.

Grisham, D. L., & Wolsey, T. D. (2006). Recentering the middle school classroom as a vibrant learning community: Students, literacy, and technology intersect. *Journal of Adolescent & Adult Literacy, 49*(8), 648–660.

Kress, G. (1997). *Before writing: Rethinking paths to literacy*. London, United Kingdom: Routledge.

Maynes, M. J., Pierce, J. L., & Laslett, B. (2008). *Telling stories: The use of personal narratives in the social sciences and history*. Ithaca, NY: Cornell University Press.

Moje, E. B., Ciechanowski, K. M., Kramer, K., Ellis, L., Carrillo, R., & Collazo, T. (2004). Working toward third space in content area literacy: An examination of everyday funds of knowledge and discourse. *Reading Research Quarterly, 39*(1), 38–70.

Moll, L. C., Amanti, C., Neff, D., & Gonzalez, N. (1992). Funds of knowledge for teaching: Using a qualitative approach to connect homes and classrooms. *Theory into Practice, 31*(2), 132–141.

Palmer, P. J. (1998). *The courage to teach*. San Francisco, CA: Jossey-Bass.

Plester, B., Wood, C., & Joshi, P. (2009). Exploring the relationship between children's knowledge of text message abbreviations and school literacy outcomes. *The British Psychological Society, 27*, 145–161.

Prensky, M. (2001). *Digital game-based learning*. New York, NY: McGraw-Hill.

Prensky, M. (2006). *Don't bother me, Mom—I'm learning!* St. Paul, MN: Paragon House.

Rowsell, J. (2006). *Family literacy experiences: Creating reading and writing opportunities that support classroom learning*. Markham, Ontario: Pembroke.

Soja, E. W. (1996). *Thirdspace: Journeys to Los Angeles and other real-and-imagined places*. Malden,

MA: Blackwell.

Taylor, A. S., & Harper, R. (2003). The gift of *gab*? A design oriented sociology of young people's use of mobiles. *Computer Supported Cooperative Work, 12*, 267–296.

Turner, K. T. (2009). Flipping the switch: Code-switching from text speak to Standard English. *English Journal*, 98, 60–65.

Turner, K. T. (2011). Digitalk: Community, convention, and self-expression. In S. S. Abrams & J. Rowsell (Eds.), *Rethinking identity and literacy education in the 21st century, 110*(1), 263–282.

Turner, K. H., Katic, E., Abrams, S. S., & Donovan, J. (2011, April). *Digitalk: The digital writing of adolescents*. Paper presented at the American Educational Research Association Annual Meeting, New Orleans, LA.

Wang, C., & Reeves, T. C. (2007). Synchronous online learning experiences: The perspectives of international students from Taiwan. *Educational Media International, 44*(4), 339–356.

Ware, P. D. (2006). From sharing time to showtime! Valuing diverse venues for storytelling in technology-rich classrooms. *Language Arts, 84*(1), 45–54.

Zickuhr, K. (2010, December 16). *Generations 2010*. Retrieved from the Pew Internet & American Life Project Web site: http://pewinternet.org/Reports/2010/Generations-2010/Overview.aspx

· 7 ·

Learning with Middle-Grade Students

Narrative Inquiry and Reader Response in the Classroom

MARY BETH SCHAEFER

Welcome to my seventh-grade English language arts (ELA) classroom. Follow me into the room. Notice two walls completely covered with 82 ELA standards. Look out the window. You see buildings—lots of them. Most of the windows on the lower floors are barred. There is a bodega across the street where teachers run to get candy, soda, a quick sandwich, or cigarettes. Open the window. Listen to the honking, the screech of airplanes preparing for landing, and the sounds of Spanish, Urdu, and Mandarin mixing with English. Notice the yellow buses chugging up to the front of the school to discharge most of the 1,200 students from 70 different ethnic groups who attend this school: By law, this middle school is academically and ethnically diverse.

Close the window and turn. Can you hear the thirty seventh-grade students lined up outside of the classroom? Are you nervous? I am. I haven't taught in several years. I'm a teacher-researcher in this seventh-grade class. Will they like me? Will I understand them? Will they get my humor? Look out the high windows that face the hall—you can see their faces and heads popping up, trying to peek in. We'd better let them in—they're starting to hit each other. Now open the door and smile, but watch out for the students and their backpacks as they shoot past, yelling for their favorite seat. Okay, I'm ready now. Would you please leave us? Don't forget to close the door behind you. I promise to write and let you know how my year goes.

This is the story of what happened while you were gone.

After telling the class that I did not like them . . . in rows . . . they laughed with me and helped me put all of the desks into groups of four. Gradually we developed a routine: Daily lessons usually began with a five-minute discussion about assignments and activities or shared reflections/interpretations of the events of the previous day. A mini lesson and whole class discussion then ensued, and a 15–20 minute group activity sometimes followed—but often our whole-class conversations were just too interesting to stop, or we had to begin class with unfinished group work. Students were especially interested in how I interpreted their thoughts, actions, or Reader-Response journals from the day before. I talked about the stories they told in their journals and shared the literary understandings that I thought they were developing. These conversations helped me understand how I, as a teacher and researcher of thirty diverse seventh-grade students, could use narrative inquiry to help myself and my students understand and deepen their responses to literature.

Narrative Inquiry: The Window to Reader Response

Narrative engages us in learning about life (Bateson, 1989), and narrative inquiries teach us about life in and out of the classroom (Chan, 2006; Clandinin & Connelly, 2000; Coulter, Michael & Poynor, 2007; Moss, 2004; Schaafsma, Pagnucci, Wallace & Stock, 2007). An interesting narrative gives the reader what Schaafsma and Vinz (2007) describe as "a door to open and walk through" (p. 277), so that "stories lived and told educate the self and others" (Clandinin & Connelly, 2000, p. xxvi). Yet, to understand *how* stories gain the power to accomplish the "living" and "educating" that Clandinin and Connelly speak of, we must look at how readers respond to what they read. In this chapter, I argue that helping students understand, appreciate and extend their responses to narratives helps deepen their "literary knowing" (Blake, 1995).

Using narrative inquiry helped me look closely at my seventh grade students' responses to literature and examine the stories they told about their self-selected novels. Narrative inquiry countered what Bakhtin (1981) claimed of interpretation, that "a whole series of phenomena remained beyond its conceptual horizon" (p. 269). By encouraging students to write about the stories they read and then asking them to examine the way they analyzed and produced understandings about literature, an unexpected phenomenon emerged on the conceptual horizon of my classroom. The phenomenon was a tension between what students understood to be the way to build their own reading skills in order to do well on state tests (through discrete-reading skill learning) and what *I* knew about how to develop deeper understanding and learning (through inquiry into their own and others' responses to literature). The students and I examined this tension that underpinned our classroom experiences (Atkinson, 2010), and together we discovered the complexities of our classroom teaching and learning (Barone, 2010).

To make salient the tensions and affordances of narrative inquiry in the classroom, I will first describe the general ways that inquiry was used in the classroom and then illustrate the experiences of one student in the classroom at a particular time in the trajectory of stories about schools. As Clandinin, Murphy, Huber, & Orr (2010) point out, these stories are "increasingly driven by standardized achievement plotlines" (p. 82), and in this chapter, that plotline becomes an unexpected subtext for understanding one student's response to literature in the context of an urban ELA classroom situated in a "data-driven" school.

In the classroom featured in this chapter, I was not only the teacher but also the "narrator/researcher who is the medium for storying the research journey and the understandings that emerge along the way" (Gordon, McKibbin, Vasudevan, & Vinz, 2007, p. 327). I wrote daily field notes, analytical memos, and personal reflections. I conducted open-ended interviews, analyzed Reader-Response journals and students' stories, and taped/transcribed classroom discussions. Following Clandinin and Connelly (2000), my notes were filled with details of place, thoughts about time, and ongoing reflections. The reflections were attentive to the idea that in narrative inquiry, I am also under study and an integral part of the inquiry itself (Clandinin et al., 2010). As patterns of literary understanding emerged from conceptualization and classification of codes, I used the comparative method (Charmaz, 2000) to make emerging theories and patterns denser and then shared my interpretations with students. In this way, we co-constructed knowledge through words and stories. Through inquiry into my own and my students' shared experiences, I tried to improve my pedagogy (Conle, 2003) and by extension, my students' experiences of literacy in the classroom. As Clandinin and Connelly (2000) explain, "These narrative beginnings of our own livings, tellings, retellings and relivings help us deal with questions of who we are in the field and who we are in the texts that we write"

(p. 70). By seeing their thoughts and words honored daily, students knew they were active participants and an integral, powerful part of that text.

Reader Response in the Classroom

More than any other mode of communication, I used the Reader Response journal to activate students' interest in reading for pleasure and generate deep responses to literature. I also used the journal as a way to ask students to try to understand themselves or probe more deeply into a particular story's elements or structure. Becky Atkinson (2010) convincingly argues that "the relational and transactive character of the reader-response relationship across narrative inquiry texts and their readers makes it possible to examine the contextual and discursive influences . . ." (p. 92). Positioning works of literature as potential sources of inspiration and creation also positions students as active constructors of meaning and learning. This position contrasts sharply with the passive stance students assume as they are, in Blake's (1992) words, "trained to 'find' the received meanings of poems" (p. 17). We have known for many years that an active, inquiring child is a learning child (Dewey, 1933/1986), and privileging students' responses to literature in the classroom places them in this active, inquisitive position.

Early in the year, I taught my seventh-grade students two frameworks for understanding their own and others' responses to literature: Louise Rosenblatt's (1978) *Transactional Theory* and Judith Langer's (1995) *Envisionments*. These conceptual frameworks gave students the lenses and words to understand, explore, and articulate what was going on as they transacted with and responded to literature; the framework placed the student-as-reader in the position of actively producing and generating knowledge (Fish, 1980; Rosenblatt, 1978).

When students borrow language from Langer to describe their experiences of "being in a text" and "moving in the moments of the story" they essentially describe what theorists call a tension between the world of the text and the world of the reader (Benton, 1992; Holland, 1975; Iser, 1978; Langer, 1995; Rosenblatt, 1978). This tension provides part of the fruitful site for narrative inquiry, because as the reader responds, he or she also re-creates the story; the reader is invited to, in Iser's (1978) words, "live with the characters and experience their activities" (p. 192). Langer (1995) describes this kind of interactive experience as an "envisionment," which she defines as "text-worlds in the mind . . . [a] dynamic set of related ideas, images, questions, disagreements, anticipations, arguments and hunches that fill the mind during every reading, writing, speaking, or other experience when one gains, expresses, and shares thoughts and understandings" (p. 9). The significance of Langer's conception of stances became important to me when I began trying to analyze and describe what my students were doing and saying in their Reader-Response journals (Table 7.1).

Table 7.1 Description of Langer's (1995) Envisionments

ENVISIONMENT	Reader's Activity
A. Being out of the Text and Stepping Into an Envisionment	The reader makes sense of the text in terms of her own knowledge and experience.
B. Being in the Text and Moving Through an Envisionment	The reader uses personal and textual knowledge to build meaning and understanding of the whole work.
C. Stepping out of the Text and Rethinking What One Knows About It	The reader reflects on his feelings toward the book and the larger issues raised by the story.
D. Stepping out of the Text and Objectifying the Experience of It	The reader assumes the critic's gaze; she disengages from the text and talks about it analytically.
ADDITIONAL ENVISIONMENT* **that emerged from research into** **students' Reader Response journals**	
E. Stepping out and Reflecting on One's Reading Self	Through active inquiry into her responses to literature, the reader demonstrates a deep understanding of herself as a reader.

*The "additional stance" was added following analysis of how my students responded to literature in their Reader Response journals.

Langer's stances are important because they help us to see ways in which students actively create meaning from literature. They also give us ways to see, as teachers, where our students may be having difficulty with books. For example, if a student has trouble "stepping into" an envisionment, it may be worth sitting down with the student and exploring *why*: Is the plot line boring to him? Perhaps the vocabulary is unfamiliar or the story's syntax too complex. During this conversation, students become the expert on their reading skills and explain what they need in order to "enter" into a book. Once the student has a text that she can enter, the active meaning making, in all of the stances, can occur. In some cases, certainly with my middle-grade students, permission to enter the text and take an aesthetic stance toward reading must be clearly articulated. In this era of high-stakes testing, many of our students have been well schooled in passively reading for meaning. The active student reader, on the other hand, creates meaning and builds knowledge of literacy. Rosenblatt's (1978) work helps us understand *how* this active meaning making occurs.

Rosenblatt (1978, 1993) describes two distinct stances that a reader takes when he picks up a text: On one end of the continuum, Rosenblatt plots the "efferent" stance, a position the reader assumes when she wants to "carry away" something from the reading, usually in the form of directions or information. On the other end is the "aesthetic" stance, a position the reader assumes when he is paying attention to the way his feelings, ideas, and emotions are aroused by the text (see Figure 7.1).

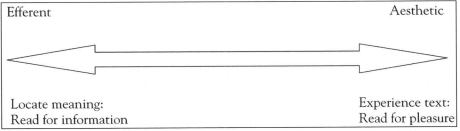

Figure 7.1. Continuum of Readers' Stances based on Rosenblatt's Transaction Theory

Rosenblatt's (1978, 1993) concept of transaction is crucial to understanding our students as active readers. In contrast to viewing texts as works whose meaning can be "found" through rational analysis (Blake, 1992), in a transaction, the reader is part of what is read; thus, the literary work, or what Rosenblatt calls the "poem," is an event that occurs when the reader reads, forging a relationship among the reader, text, and poem. In a transaction, the reader selects the aspects of meaning she will attend to during a reading. A more aesthetic stance will yield a "lived-through" experience, and a more efferent stance will focus on information that may be retained. Whereas Rosenblatt explores the internal dialectics of the reader and text, narrative inquiry opens up this vision of the reader and the text to include the experience of reading, telling, and retelling in the context of a classroom. Narrative inquiry gives us the opportunity to understand ways that the experience of the "particular world of the reader" (Rosenblatt, 1978, p. 11) enters the particular world of the classroom. Just as I invited you to enter the physical space of my classroom, I now invite you to enter two stories, first the larger story of how my students initially rejected Reader Response and then the story of one student who embraced it.

Standards Versus Feelings: A Tension in the Continuum of Readers' Stances

Before teaching this class, I had visions of engaging my students in reflective, exploratory, and engaging conversations about literature, life, and learning. It is difficult, however, to engage in meaningful conversations in 43 minutes. Also, there were standards to teach to and tests to prepare for. It was against this backdrop of competition for time and content that I struggled to engage students in conversations about reading. Every day, I reflected on my practice in my journal, and the next day I shared my interpretations and assumptions with my class. For example, when my ongoing analysis of classroom transcripts revealed that about half of my most highly engaging classes (as measured by student participation) were classes on teaching discrete reading skills and strategies, I was horrified. When I took this finding back to the class, they explained that the emerging pattern made perfect sense. There was a high-stakes state reading exam they had to take in April. Doing well on that test meant getting into a good high school, so they were deeply invested in acquiring the "skills" needed to do well on that test.

In a classroom conversation, "Edie," an African American student who longed to go to a "really good high school," explained this further when she suggested that perhaps my emphasis on responding to literature (what she called "feelings") was not as important as the standards. According to Edie:

> Maybe they [the people who create standards] are worried about our future. You know what I'm saying, like they know they're going to have to teach these things to you first and then later on you can go and say how you feel and everything like that. 'Cause you're going to need to know how to do whatever they say you have to teach us. That's probably what we're going to need to know when we grow up. So that's what you need to teach us first and get that out of the way and then you can teach us how you feel, you know, cause that's not really gonna help you when you're 21 and you're in college whatever, and trying to earn a degree. That's not gonna help you—how you feel about a book [laughs], but, but, you know what I'm saying. (classroom conversation, March 13)

Edie's words help illustrate the central tension in our classroom: Her idea of our first needing to deal with "what you need to teach us" translates into skill learning. Her idea that only after that, "you can teach us how you feel" is her way of letting me know she does not believe that her understanding of her own responses to literature were helping her learn. So I taught students discrete reading skills at their own insistence and continued to push their thinking with whole-class literature and through the writing they did with self-selected novels.

Based on the idea that skills were boring, I tried extra hard to make what I thought was intolerable palatable. I often apologized to my students before introducing a skill or strategy that I thought would bore or irritate them. One thing I constantly relied on was participation: I felt if students could come up with their own meanings, definitions, and examples for the skills and vocabulary from the state reading tests, the concepts would be more relevant and memorable. I cannot ignore the possibility that my approach to the teaching of reading skills may have contributed to its status as a source of engagement. For example, in one of our last classes together, I asked students to write an evaluation of my teaching, and nearly all of them wrote that my class was "fun." In a whole-class conversation, I asked them what that meant. My question was, "No, that's not what I mean. I mean, what did you mean by fun?"

Maggy answered:

> You didn't give us a textbook and tell us to see a certain page. We did hands-on projects, so like we got a chance to, like, when we did the poems, we didn't just like look at other poems, we made our own poems and that's like, why it was fun, because we actually participated in the stuff that we were learning. (classroom conversation, June 21)

Intrigued with the idea of student engagement with reading skills, I continually took this idea back to students for discussion. I wanted us to co-construct an understanding of what I thought of as an odd finding. But I also used their Reader-Response journals as critical places for developing reading and self-knowledge. It was interesting and gratifying to see how Edie's ideas about the relevance of "feelings" changed by the end of the school year. According to her:

> Like, I like . . . the journal, since I'm writing how I felt about it, I think then it makes me understand the book more and understand how I was feeling, and I understood what I was talking about, how I felt about the book and everything. I think that's why it helped me become a better reader.

My question in reply was, "So you started to understand your own response to what you were reading, and you wrote it down and then you were able to look at it and see how you were responding?" Edie answered:

> Yeah, I think. Yeah. Like, you said the [way you taught us to take tests] and that helped 'cause if I don't want to read it, I still do it, that helped me in other subjects, 'cause in science it's boring . . . but I read it and stuff.(interview, June 4)

I was interested to see that many students were drawing from their emerging self-knowledge of reading to directly help in their enjoyment and understanding of self-selected literature and then using this as a strategy to do better on their state reading exams. The remainder of this chapter will focus on the story of one student who moved consciously and purposefully through Langer's envisionments and with ease and increasing awareness up and down Rosenblatt's continuum.

Reader Response Journals: Mary's Story

Mary interested me as a student who embraced the tension that undergirded our classroom experiences: She used the "reading skills" acquired in ELA class to enhance her pleasure reading and responses to literature. Mary, a vivacious, outgoing Asian American girl, filled every inch of every page in the 100-sheet black-marble composition book that was her reading journal. She often illustrated her words with characters from various anime clips and manga books. Although she preferred to handwrite her responses to self-selected literature, sometimes she would e-mail them to me, but she always printed out our correspondence and pasted it into the pages in her journal, which was extraordinarily rich not only for its length but also for the quality of the journal entries. She enjoyed responding to my questions and loved to write long letters to me about the books she was reading and her involvement with them. In one response to me, she writes:

> Ms. Schaefer, when I write in my journal, it's like talking or communicating to the characters. I feel as if the characters will pop right out the book at night and read my journal and take my advice or read my thoughts about them or actions they made. That's why my entries are always so long; I feel that books have powers that fairies have. (Reader Response journal, March 12)

Mary describes how she uses her feelings as she reads to help her understand the characters and their motives. She becomes a more sympathetic reader "because I've been in a car accident and I know how bad life can be" (personal interview, June 10). This car accident left physical, emotional, and cognitive scars on Mary. She was hospitalized for months and endured operations that left her unable to eat, much less attend school. Mary describes her sixth-grade experience as a disaster. She did not do well on her state tests. Her report card was average, which was unacceptable to Mary, who continually compared herself to her older high-achieving sister. Her sister had earned a place at one of the best high schools in New York City. Mary wanted to go there too, but the school looked closely at report card averages and state tests. Now in the seventh grade, Mary needed to score in the top 2% on her state reading exam and achieve a minimum grade of 92 in every subject area. She was highly motivated to learn, and her Reader Response journal demonstrateed a unique synthesis of reading skills and Reader Response theory:

> Well, I have a few [state reading] test strategies. My first strategy is to stay calm, not be nervous, and relax. Without this, I can't think!!! My second strategy, is to read and examine stories and poems slowly, understanding it, knowing the characters, and getting "into" it. It may seem like a waste of time, but it isn't. Once you do this, you instead save time. After reading the questions and the possible answers, something immediately pops up in my head, like "Nissa's Place is the best title, because she can't find out the place in which she belongs!" My final strategy, is to put myself in the characters' spot, making myself encounter those events that they encountered, so I can feel their feelings, the mood and their tone of speaking. These strategies may seem corny and funny, but they actually help me! (Mary, April 8)

Mary pulls from efferent and aesthetic stances to help her create the best conditions to understand and answer the reading test questions. She uses similar strategies as she reads for pleasure:

> Are you wondering why I suddenly am reading the end of the book? Well this is what I've decided to do: Read the beginning of the book, Analyze the characters' actions and personality. After that, read the end of the book. Think about how the beginning may have influenced the end, and how the characters' personality may have influenced it. Finally, as you read through the book, find how these events lead to the resolution of the book, cause and effect. (Mary, Reader Response journal, May 29)

Although Mary often expressed feelings of fear and anxiety in the days leading up to the state reading test, she was very happy afterward and confided in me that she thought she did well. Her hunch was correct: When I met her early the next year as an eighth grader, the first thing she said after squealing Hello was that she had just found out that she scored in the top two percent of students taking the reading test. Later that year, she e-mailed me with the news that she had gained admission into the high school of her choice. How did this happen? What stories did Mary read, and what can we learn through her inquiry?

Using Langer's four descriptions of envisionments helps illustrate Mary's rich responses. It also helps us see how she goes beyond the framework to develop even more complex and high-level Reader Responses.

1) *Being out and stepping into an envisionment.* In this stance, the reader is trying to make sense of the text in terms of her own knowledge and experience. Mary spends little time in this stance, except with one book that she attempts to read towards the end of the year, *The Trojan War.* She has a hard time "entering" into the action of that story. To help herself, she asks questions and tries to develop an envisionment:

> Today I continued to read that book relating to the Trojan War. One thing I don't get is this: Aphrodite promised Helen, queen of Sparta, to Paris if he gave her the golden apple, right? Wouldn't that mean that Paris would have no trouble to getting and keeping her? (Reader Response journal, May 10)

I help Mary answer some of the questions here, but her disinterest in the book continues. Although with my assistance she follows the plot of the story, she still has trouble "stepping into" an envisionment and tries to figure out why:

> It's not that fun to go "in" the book this time. I don't like going into a place where there's destruction, violence and dead bodies lying around with blood. Ew-ee! I'll just stay "out" and analyze the gods, goddesses, and characters' actions, since I find it more fun. (Mary, Reader Response journal, May 14)

Mary understands that the setting of *The Trojan War* is not the kind of environment that she prefers to "enter." Although she does not say so, I think it is partly her inability to establish a relationship with one of the characters that eventually causes her to put the book down. Establishing relationships with main characters and entering into their situations with empathy and sympathy is a key feature of Mary's reading, and nowhere is this reading strategy more evident than in the next stance.

2) *Being in and moving through an envisionment.* A reader in this stance is "in" the text-world of the story. The reader uses her personal and textual knowledge to build meaning and understanding of the whole work. Mary thinks about her place in the story, what it feels like to be "there," and what she thinks about her experience. The following passage from Mary's reading journal shows the easy dance she does between the efferent and aesthetic stance while "moving

through" an envisionment. She writes here about Mary, Queen of Scots and eventually chooses this name to represent herself in this research:

> She keeps on moaning and groaning about that she has to practice ballet. Wouldn't that be a privilege? Learning gracefulness, dance, and many other aspects. She thinks of it like torture. Now I really think she's a spoiled child! Don't you? But I don't completely blame her I don't either. She doesn't have a lot of freedom. I think that if she grew up in the United States or in a country with democracy, that she would be a different person. But I feel sad and sorry today for Mary [Queen of Scots]. One of her dear best friends might die! She tried to save Mary's dog and fell in ice, and is unconscious. Boy how would I feel if my best friend might be dying? I'll feel extremely horrible and would rather die for him/her. Luckily, she woke and is recovering. A happy ending to this adventure! (Reader Response journal, June 3)

Mary thinks about the privileges of the main character, Mary, Queen of Scots and decides that the queen is being ungrateful for her many advantages. Mary muses that perhaps this queen would have been a different person had she grown up in a democratic environment. In her reflection, Mary comes to deeper realizations of the kinds of events that shape characters, both real and historic. In this way, Mary's reading is efferent. On the other hand, Mary searches out ways to establish relationships with her characters and frequently refers to books and characters as "friends." She establishes a relationship with Mary, Queen of Scots, and shows, by feeling "sad and sorry" for her, that she is "living through" the experience of the story. In this way, Mary's reading experience may be characterized as aesthetic. She explores her feelings further, wondering how she herself would feel if her "best friend might be dying." Her reading of the same chapter of the same book balances between the efferent and aesthetic stances (see Figure 7.1). Most of Mary's responses follow this efferent/aesthetic pattern, finding a balance between being in and out of reading and between thinking and feeling with and about the main characters. Some of these experiences lead her to "rethink" several critical issues raised by the story, a strategy described in Langer's third stance.

3) *Stepping out and rethinking what one knows.* In this world, the first two stances have already been accomplished, and the reader brings the experience of the text world into her repertoire of knowledge and experience. In this stance the reader reflects on her feelings towards the book and larger issues raised by the story. When Mary carries away a new thought or a reconsiders a previously held opinion, it is usually after she has "lived through" a particularly dramatic event in the book. Sometimes these events lead her to a new appre-

ciation for her life, including her family, friends and privileges. Others lead her
to think about world issues, including the holocaust, war, race, and democracy.

Mary's willingness to explore more challenging books combined with a
determination to address and answer some of my more difficult questions
helped her explore her own reading and world views more fully than most of
my other students:

> Today Nissa goes back to Harper, and starts making her library. It goes smoothly, with
> people donating bookshelves, books, chairs to the furniture, until the issue of separat-
> ing colored people from whites comes up. Nissa doesn't know what to do. She has black
> friends, and she doesn't want to be racist, hurting their feelings. But if she doesn't sep-
> arate them, whites will start quarreling with Nissa, and maybe close her library. If I were
> in Nissa's situation I would just open my library, without separating blacks and whites.
> According to the constitution, slavery was abolished in 1865, civil rights were guar-
> anteed to them in 1868, and they were given voting rights in 1870. Therefore, they're
> equal. Whites have no right to be racist. I wouldn't care if my fellow neighbors started
> quarreling with me, because the constitution can protect me. (I'll stick my nose up in
> the air after they leave, filled with pride!) (Reader Response journal, April 30)

Mary feels for Nissa's dilemma. Nissa is trying to set up a library during the time
of the Great Depression, and Mary has just found out that there was segrega-
tion during that time. When she talks about what she would do if she were in
Nissa's situation, her first thoughts are logical and informed, based on consti-
tutional law. Her second assertion that "whites have no right to be racist" is
based on law and on personal feeling—again showing evidence of the balance
in her thinking that is so evident in her reading. With the law supporting and
"protecting" her legal and ethical position, she feels that she would be able to
handle any disputes or arguments that might arise. This concern with finding
support for her own opinions and criticisms is abundantly evident in her
responses located in Langer's fourth and final stance.

4) *Stepping out and objectifying the experience.* In this stance, the reader
assumes the critic's gaze; he disengages from the text and talks about it analyt-
ically. The reader compares the text to other works or examines the characters'
lives or social situation. Mary tries to "step out" to understand her aesthetic
experiences after describing a particularly vivid "lived-through" experience. The
efferent reading of the same text leads her to analyze and critique characters,
story elements, and text frames as follows:

> This book has been able to keep my interest for a few reasons. First of all, this book
> talks about real-life situations, which are both funny and interesting at the same time.
> Next, this book mainly talks about friendship, which is always part of life, including

mine. Finally, I seem to participate in Jennifer's exciting adventures, and almost being her friend. . . . I wonder how it feels to be a king and queen! By reading the description, the gym, where they held this event, was very beautiful in my imagination. (Reader Response journal, November 20)

Mary's efferent stance is shown in its full force here, as she brings away her aesthetic experiences from the text in order to guide her analytic thinking about textual elements. Although perhaps unsophisticated by formal critical standards, Mary's analysis nonetheless demonstrates her ability to detach and think through her experience with the book. She analyzes why the book has been able to hold her interest and cites interesting plot situations, realistic situations, and the theme of friendship. She also points to the author's descriptive abilities, which allows her to imagine a particular event as "very beautiful." Later, in other responses, I ask her to be more specific. Below, for example, is what she wrote after I asked her to state explicitly the descriptions that captured her imagination:

> Oh yeah! I forgot! There's another reason why I said Tituba was proud, and that's because of a sentence in the book. "She was short compared to John, but she held herself so erect that she looked taller than she really was." This sentence meant that although Tituba's height was smaller than John's, her self-esteem, importance and pride made her height increase. (Reader Response journal, January 4)

Mary's ability to move between the efferent and aesthetic stances allows for a more full analysis of story elements: Her experience at each end of the continuum informs the other. This drawing on both sides gives her a balanced view of the text in a way that helps her critique story elements and gives her the distance to see, in ways that most of my students could not, the way texts work.

In Langer's framework (see Table 7.1), there is no description for what happens to a reader's understanding of herself after fully engaging in a reading experience. Mary's extraordinary participation in responding to literature offers another reading stance. In keeping with Langer's framework, I will call it "stepping out and reflecting on one's reading self."

5) *Stepping out and reflecting on one's reading self.* In this stance, Mary shows how she is led to a deeper understanding of her "reading self." This self-awareness is evident in one of the last letters she wrote to me in her journal:

> This is the best language arts class I've ever attended. I learned so many things about reading, literature, life, and the world from you. Most importantly, I feel like I actually understand myself and the world in another way. (You've met your teaching goal!) And that's all I can say. (Reader Response journal, June 4)

Although in this passage Mary credits me with what she's learned about reading, literature, and life, it is her own willingness to take up my admittedly challenging questions that leads her to a place at which she realizes that she
understands herself "and the world in another way." She trusts me enough to
believe that reflecting on her own reading and trying to understand her own
Reader Responses and strategies will ultimately help her think and learn. The
following response that I received from Mary shows that she examines her taste
in literature and from that examination develops unique reading strategies
and skills. In this passage, we can see the actual co-construction of our understanding:

> Ms. Schaefer, remember when you said, "When you move 'in' the story, you are with
> the characters: when you move 'out' of the story, you analyze the characters' actions,
> the plot of the story, the morals or purpose of the story, and your own attitude towards
> it"? I was pretty impressed by how you put my actions into words . . . I find this state-
> ment very precise. When I go through a door to go to the magical and fantastic world
> of books, I like to participate with the characters, because I do like to experience the
> wonderful and tragic events they encounter, and because I like to be their friends.
> When I'm finished reading, also known to you as going "out" of the book, I like to
> examine the characters' actions, saying whether it was a good move or not, the main
> story development (also known as the plot), the morals or lessons I learned, and the
> point (purpose) of the story. I finally express my feelings, opinions, or moods, after read-
> ing a book. I also want to tell you that I am in and out of the story at the same time.
> It may seem difficult to you, but it isn't! All you have to do, is imagine yourself with
> the characters when you read and that'll transfer you to the world where your charac-
> ters live. When you want to come back out, it's like waking up from a little nap. (Reader
> Response journal, March 12)

Mary resonates with my analysis of her reading and suggests that she appreciates how I "put [her] actions into words." She uses my description as a jump-
ing-off point for elaboration. She compares being "in" the story to going
"through a door." Mary describes her aesthetic transaction with texts after she
has gone through this door as participating "with" characters and claims their
experiences as her own. She regards characters as friends and in this friendship
she enjoys participation in the life of the characters. In this way, Mary talks
about her taste in literature and her preferred mode of participation. She talks
in a general way about the kinds of textual elements, plot, characterization, story
purpose, and kinds of story development that affect her "feelings, opinions, and
mood." The more analytical participation, however, occurs "after reading a
book," when Mary's efferent stance becomes more pronounced.

When she talks about being "in and out of the story at the same time," I believe Mary is showing that she understands the kind of balanced reading that Rosenblatt's continuum (see Figure 7.1) helps conceptualize. She talks about how this in/out stance might be "difficult" to understand and tries to explain her approach to reading. As she discusses her own reading experiences, she also begins to talk about her own developing reading skills and strategies. She then broadens her self-analysis of her participation in literature to look at her preferred reading strategies: She recommends that you "imagine yourself with the characters" and "that'll transfer you to the world where your characters live." In this new world, Mary learns to reflect on herself and develop self-understanding. She draws moral lessons from some of the stories she reads and talks about how she would "never make the mistakes" and choices that characters in historically "true" situations make:

> I always try to understand the type of experiences and events I read in a book. For example, when I read a book called *After the War*, I understood the type of experience and event I was reading about, which was warfare, relating to World War II. I know that I understand my interaction with books, because while I'm interplaying and interacting with the book, I'm learning and understanding about the morals of the book, and lessons from the book. I also seem to understand how I'm influenced and how it has effected [sic] me, because I would never make mistakes that characters did in the story again. (Reader Response journal, March 12)

Mary uses distance from the book to contemplate its story and think about why it held her interest. Her interest in historical fiction is crucial to her attempts to "understand the type of experiences and events" that she reads about. This is a kind of efferent and aesthetic stance: It is efferent in the sense that Mary reads with a purpose—to understand the mistakes made in history so that she "would never make mistakes that characters did" and aesthetic in the sense of her deep "interaction" with the book. Both stances combine to lead Mary to a deeper understanding of her reading and of herself. The following excerpt from her journal illustrates my probing questions and Mary's responsive self-reflection:

> Dear Ms. Schaefer, Remember when you asked me whether or not wisdom was the best gift one can have? I feel that it's one of the best gifts one can have, since everything you do in life is involved with wisdom. But I feel that the best gift of all is your family and friends. Your family and friends are the ones that love you, care about you, and support you in life. Without them, life is almost meaningless! (since wisdom can't exactly love and care about you!) Do you think the same way that I do? (Reader Response journal, May 28)

I respond to this comment in her journal as follows:

> Dear Mary, Yes, I think you're right, but I think you're right about *you* and *your* situation. I think of other kids who are a LOT less fortunate than I was as a kid, kids who don't have caring parents and good friends, and in their cases I think wisdom is more important, since through wisdom perhaps they will have a better future than their parents. I'm thinking specifically of one girl in my mom's class who told her yesterday that she was terrified, that her father had tried to kill her mother. My mom was devastated ....Imagine living with parents who fight, beat and threaten! It's only my opinion of course, but for this little girl I imagine that wisdom would be the better gift. Reader Response journal, May 31)

My attempts to have Mary consider other points of views resulted in this response from her:

> Remember that wisdom issue I was talking about? Well, after reading your response back to me, I've come up with this: Family and wisdom and friends=most important things in life. With these 3 aspects, we'll live happily. The reason I put wisdom in the middle is because your family and friends revolve around wisdom, making decisions that may affect you. What do you think this time? Reader Response journal, June 3)

It is clear that our conversation in this journal has moved away from the book that prompted it. From exploring the emerging nature of her own literacy, Mary now moves into an exploration of herself, trying to understand the nature of what was important in her life and those of others and demonstrating a renewed appreciation for her privileges and gifts.

Constructing a Professional Stance

The process of narrative inquiry creates many opportunities for educators to understand students. The narrative interpreter gathers students' thoughts and stories and constructs knowledge in a transparent way. Students see their voices honored as their words are placed at the center of inquiry. In my classroom, I honored their desire for discrete skill development while offering them an alternative. Over time, as students' trust in me grew so too did the depth of their responses to literature. By placing the tension between what students thought they needed in order to become better readers and what I knew they needed in order to become better, more thoughtful readers into the center of classroom learning, students felt respected, honored, and powerful. Students learned reading theories and felt proud that they understood and used these concepts. Narrative inquiry changed everything about the nature of power and learning in our classroom. The shared experience also profoundly changed the ways I viewed students and their learning. By placing their needs and desires at the center of this inquiry, we all excelled. Knowing and experiencing this has transformed and renewed my professional teaching stance as a secondary ELA teacher.

Reflective Questions

1. Do you read for pleasure? Why or why not? How will you encourage students in your class to read for their own enjoyment?
2. How might you use Reader Response in your classroom?
3. How would you address Edie's desire to learn reading skills?
4. Where would you plot your own reading on Rosenblatt's continuum between efferent and aesthetic stances? What kinds of texts push you to one end more than another? How might you use the continuum in your classroom?
5. How might you use being a reflective reader yourself to help your students to develop literary knowledge and understanding?

References

Atkinson, B. (2010). Teachers responding to narrative inquiry: An approach to narrative inquiry criticism. *The Journal of Educational Research, 103*(2), 91–103.

Bakhtin, M. M. (1981). *The dialogic imagination: Four essays* (C. Emerson & M. Holquist, Trans.). Austin: University of Texas Press.

Barone, T. (2010). Commonalities and variegations: Notes on the maturations of the field of narrative research. *The Journal of Educational Research, 103*(2), 149–154.

Bateson, M. C. (1989). *Composing a life.* New York, NY: Plume.

Benton, M. (1992). *Secondary worlds: Literature teaching and the visual arts.* Buckingham, United Kingdom: Open University Press.

Blake, R. W. (1992). Poets on poetry: The morality of poetry. *English Journal, 81*(1), 16–20.

Blake, R. W. (1995, November). *From literature based reading to reader response in the elementary school classroom.* Paper presented at the Annual Meeting of the National Council of Teachers of English, San Diego, CA.

Chan, E. (2006). Teacher experiences of culture in the curriculum. *Journal of Curriculum Studies, 38*(2), 161–176.

Charmaz, K. (2000). Grounded theory: Objectivist and constructivist methods. In N. K. Denzin & Y. S. Lincoln (Eds.), *Handbook of qualitative research* (2nd ed., pp. 509–535). Thousand Oaks, CA: Sage.

Clandinin, D. J., & Connelly, F. M. (2000). *Narrative inquiry: Experience and story in qualitative research*. San Francisco, CA: Jossey-Bass.

Clandinin, D. J., Murphy, S. M., Huber, J., & Orr, A. M. (2010). Negotiating narrative inquiries: Living in a tension-filled midst. *The Journal of Educational Research, 103*(2), 81–91.

Conle, C. (2003). An anatomy of narrative curricula. *Educational Researcher 32*(3), 3–15.

Coulter, C., Michael, C., & Poynor, L. (2007). Storytelling as pedagogy: An unexpected outcome of narrative inquiry. *Curriculum Inquiry 37*(2), 103–122.

Dewey, J. (1986). How we think: A restatement of the educative process. In J. A. Boydston (Ed). *John Dewey: The later works, 1925–1953* (Vol. 8l, pp. 105–352). Carbondale: Southern Illinois University Press. (Original work published 1933).

Fish, S. (1980). *Is there a text in this class? The authority of interpretive communities*. Cambridge, MA: Harvard University Press.

Gordon, E., McKibbin, K., Vasudevan, L. & Vinz, R. (2007). Writing out of the unexpected: Narrative inquiry and the weight of small moments. *English Education, 39*(4), 326–351.

Holland, N. (1975). *5 readers reading*. New Haven, CT: Yale University Press.

Iser, W. (1978). *The act of reading: A theory of aesthetic response*. Baltimore, MD: The Johns Hopkins University Press.

Langer, J. A. (1995). *Envisioning literature: Literary understanding and literature instruction*. New York, NY: Teachers College Press.

Moss, G. (2004). Provisions of trustworthiness in critical narrative research: Bridging intersubjectivity and fidelity. *The Qualitative Report, 9*(2), 359–373.

Rosenblatt, L. (1978). *The reader, the text, the poem: The transactional theory of the literary work*. Carbondale: Southern Illinois University Press.

Rosenblatt, L. (1993). The transactional theory: Against dualisms. *College English, 55*(4), 377–386.

Schaafsma, D., Pagnucci, G. S., Wallace, R. M., & Stock, P. L. (2007). Composing storied ground: Four generations of narrative inquiry. *English Education, 39*(4), 282–305.

Schaafsma, D., & Vinz, R. (2007). Composing narratives for inquiry. *English Education, 39*(4), 277–281.

Strauss, A., & Corbin, J. (1998). *Basics of qualitative research: Techniques and procedures for developing grounded theory* (2nd ed.). Thousand Oaks, CA: Sage.

· 8 ·

Critical Incidents in Social Foundations

Reflecting on Theory, Connecting to Practice

JULIE H. CARTER

This book has thus far made a case for the power that teacher stories possess in helping new teachers (re)imagine their work as both powerful and transformative. This chapter explores one example of the use of story, or in specific critical incidents, as a pedagogical tool for teacher identity development in a social foundations of education (SFE) course. *Critical Incidents*, defined here as decisive moments in teachers' educational biographies, are utilized as a lens through which to interpret how teacher candidates use stories to locate themselves both within and against educational institutions and to position themselves within larger sociological and political communities of practice. The chapter also posits SFE courses as spaces in which teacher candidates can identify and problematize their values and perspectives on teaching as they carry them forward into their practice.

Theoretical Framework

As other authors in this volume have explored, narratives are a powerful reflective tool in helping new teachers revisit their own stories in purposeful and meaningful ways as they consider the bigger questions of our field (i.e., those that are involved in building classroom communities, testing versus curriculum, teaching for social justice). Reflective practice is a relatively pervasive and accepted framework in teacher education (Schön,1983, 1987, 1991; Bushnell & Henry, 2003; Tripp, 1993; Greene, 1978), most significantly marked by Donald Schön's (1983) work *The Reflective Practitioner*, in which he distinguishes "reflection-in-action" as vital to the practice of teaching, among other professions (p. 62). Part of his conceptualization includes a discussion of the potential that a new or novel way of thinking about an event can have on future practice. In Schön's framework, action need not occur in the moment and, in fact, may not come quickly at all. He writes, "[Action] is bounded by the 'action present,' the zone of time in which action can still make a difference to the situation" (p. 62). Schön gives examples of various professional contexts in which actions or decisions may stretch over weeks, months, or even years. Based on the assumption that teachers continue to learn and to act on their learning over the span of their career, Schön's action present turns out to be lifelong for a teacher.

This notion of time is particularly pertinent within the context of preservice education, as the distance between "reflection" and "in-action," may be significant. The time between these two states spans at least the time it takes for preservice teachers to be placed in-service in a school. However, reflection-in-action is not necessarily enough to transform the problems of everyday practice without the aid of new information. As David Tripp (1993) posits, reflection tends to be informed by the particular worldview of the person doing the reflecting. The reflection, therefore, tends to be circular, in that the lens through which experiences get interpreted is already informed by values and judgments that make sense to the interpreter (p. 12). Tripp, therefore, suggests that in order to "develop our professional judgement, we have to move beyond our everyday, 'working' way of looking at things" (p. 12). Further, Maxine Greene (1978) reminds us that moving beyond a situation requires looking back, an acknowledgment that "we identify ourselves by means of memory." In the process of engaging in memory, "looking back, [and] recapturing their stories, teachers can recover their own standpoints on the social world" (p. 33). If we are to use narratives to help teachers situate themselves within larger communities of practice, then these idiosyncratic stories, or personal "touchstones" (Strong-Wilson, 2008), must be shared and negotiated. Greene notes that in sharing these stories with others, "[teachers] may be able to multiply the perspectives through which they look upon the realities of teaching" (p. 33). It seems particularly important, then, that teachers make connections backward,

and then forward, in order to excavate the ground on which they make pedagogical decisions of method and practice.

Teresa Strong-Wilson (2008) writes about her work with in-service teachers, helping them to "bring memory forward" as they discuss their uses of children's literature. Through writing personal narratives about favorite children's
stories, teachers grappled with the memories of stories about national identity
told and retold to them from childhood. The narratives helped teachers deal
with the contradictions those stories once placed against indigenous people's
perspectives on that same national identity. Exploring their personal attachments to romantic notions of national identity helped them make better pedagogical choices about the literature they offered their students (p. 150).

Not only can narratives be used to make such methodological decisions,
they also fit nicely into theoretical courses in which candidates explore expert
voices and research about teaching as they consider the choices those new voices present for their practice. Theoretical courses, specifically those in SFE, that
harness reflection through narratives (i.e., critical incidents, reflective journals,
autobiography, reading responses) can bridge the real and imagined gap that
exists for new teachers between what is learned during their preparation for
teaching and what is experienced in the practice of it (Bushnell & Henry, 2003;
Murrow, 2006; Burgum & Bridge, 1997; Carter, 2008; Butin, 2004). When personal narratives are written around and through newly acquired understandings
about teaching and learning, critical education moments in candidates' own
lives are cast in a new light and have great potential for reframing the work of
teaching. Sonia Murrow (2006), for example, finds that when undergraduate
students are asked to "dialogue" with social foundations texts, they can and do
develop an "authentic theory-and-practice-based" philosophy of education
that may allow them to enact critical pedagogy in real classrooms, which might
include "advocacy for their students and schools" (p. 54). In this way, reflections-in-action (Schön, 1983) break circular reflective patterns (Tripp, 1993)
to reflect new philosophically based decisions for future practice. Critical incidents that require candidates to reflect on their personal educational history in
light of newly acquired educational theories allow what Tripp calls an "analysis of our problematic" or the opportunity to scrutinize our values and judgments
in making pedagogical decisions.

Schools of education are under increasing scrutiny regarding the linkages
between preservice coursework and classroom efficacy. Critics argue that "too
many teachers are unprepared for the classroom, though they may have more
education credentials than ever before" (Otterman, 2011, p. ED 24). Various

studies and policy reports both within and outside of social foundations circles have indicated that new teachers see their coursework as only marginally important to the work of teaching (U.S. Department of Education, 2002; Public Agenda, 2000; boyd, Grossman, Lankford, Loeb, & Wyckoff, 2006; Haberman, 1987) As Tripp (1993) indicates, "The professional education of teachers has to take much more into account how educational theories are individually perceived, mediated and reconstructed by practitioners" (p. 17). Several issues in preservice classwork become salient in ensuring that students are able to translate their coursework into action: First, students' preservice reflective experiences must result in a set of philosophically based principles about teaching and learning. These principles might either reinforce previously held beliefs and values or be critically revised in light of new theoretical understandings. Second, students must have experience in translating philosophical principles into action plans for classroom practice (what Schön [1983] called reflection-in-action). Last, even if these plans are not relevant to their actual students, teachers must have become proficient in the skill of reflection-in-action as to use it in novel and emergent situations. I argue here that the use of critical incidents in social foundations coursework can not only help preservice teachers become more aware of the problems of everyday teaching, but, through exegesis, allow them to question these practices, or problematize them in ways that allow for more questions about professional decision making and professional identity itself.

Context and Organization of the Social Foundations of Education Course

The graduate social foundations of education (SFE) course takes place at a career change program at a private university in New York City. The course is meant to facilitate student inquiry into the historical, sociological, and political contexts of teaching and learning, developing the articulation of a personal philosophy of education. The summer section from which these data are culled was an online version of the full-semester SFE course, which is organized around professional standards established by the Council for Social Foundations for teacher certification. It is a required course in a 42-credit sequence leading to certification and a master's degree. Throughout the course, teacher candidates engage in narrative responses to primary sources and to educational research articles with political, social, and historical themes. The 13 graduate education student participants (a mix of practicing and preservice teachers) represent diverse backgrounds—urban, suburban, white, black, Caribbean, and Catholic and public school educated, all headed into both Catholic and public school settings. Readings are the focal point of all course activity in that they form the basis of assignments and inquiry-based classroom activities. Each week, students read several primary-source readings, which may include research articles, biographical works, or educational theory. Authors include, but are not limited to, John Dewey, George Counts, Maxine Seller, Alfie Kohn, William Ayers, Lisa Delpit, Patrick Finn, Gloria Ladson-Billings, Ray Rist, Vito Perrone, and Audre Lorde. In-class student-driven discussions form the basis of group activities that apply the authors' ideas to the current context and the work of teachers. After a final reading by Lorde (1982), in which the author shares a critical incident memory from her schooling, students are asked to describe their own critical incident. The assignment asks students to "write about a moment from your own schooling experience which was memorable or meaningful to you." After explaining the incident in detail, they are asked to make connections to themes in the course that resonate with them. Lorde's chapter includes the following themes:

- alienation,
- discrimination,
- being a child with special needs,
- being black in school,
- being a child of immigrants,
- the home-school connection, and
- tracking.

The broad range of themes in the work allows students the opportunity for cross analysis with other course readings, and to make complex and individualized connections to their own critical educational moments. For example, students connected their stories to Vito Perrone's *Teacher with a Heart: Reflections on Leonard Covello and Community*, a biography about renowned principal Leonard Covello; Gloria Ladson-Billings article "Your Blues Ain't Like Mine," in which the author explicates the experience of being an African American academic, and to Jean Anyon's study about social class and schooling described by Patrick Finn (1999) in his book *Literacy with an Attitude*.

Findings

For the purposes of this chapter, because the analyses are more vital than the stories themselves, I will summarize the nature of the student stories. Students chose a range of critical education incidents that spanned from kindergarten through grade school and college, and recalled memories of teachers—positive, negative, and neutral. About half of stories ($n = 6$) were negative, recalling teachers who had said mean things to them, had low expectations of them, or demonstrated biased behaviors. The other half ($n = 7$) reported positive or neutral educational experiences, with particular emphases on teachers who "saw something in me." Based on the limited number of cases ($n = 13$), it was not possible to distinguish if stories followed any particular racial or gendered patterns, although there is ample research that indicates that students of color and immigrants endured lower expectations, both within and outside lower quality schools (Orfield, n.d.).

Students reflected on their stories in various ways that allowed them to rethink these memories as iterations of current educational struggles and issues. I found that three trends emerge in their analyses: First, they used their stories to locate themselves either within or against educational institutions. The extent to which they felt they succeeded at school is an example of this finding. Second, they used their stories to find resonance with communities of practice, such as those whom they consider caring practitioners or those who resist the pressure of standardized testing. The last, and most predominant, trend involves candidates using their stories to envision their own futures as agents of change, using their own experiences as a model for ways to advocate for children and engage in socially just teaching practices.

Critical Incidents Help Locate Candidates Within and Against Institutions

The reflections show that in stories in which candidates decribe themselves within institutions, they reinterpreted their challenges in schools in a way they had not at the time of the experience. Yolanda, an Hispanic student who never considered the quality of her education until she transferred from public to private school, draws a connection to Jean Anyon's (as reported by Finn, 1999) findings about disparities in socioeconomic class, falling under the initial theme of students locating themselves within institutions. Yolanda describes her struggle for achievement in private school and the revelation that she feared being "average," which marred her educational path for some time:

> I think the issue that can be related to my critical incident is the disparity between public school and private school. The struggle that I had trying to keep up with the other students is indicative of the achievement gap between the haves and the have nots. I think my experiences reflect Anyon's study of different socioeconomic classes being taught differently. In public school, my ability to memorize the facts that I knew teachers thought were important made me a star student in that environment. I could not do this in the private school environment, students were responsible for their own achievement. . . . In college I think fear of being average caused me to sabotage myself. I went to several different schools. I even dropped out for a while. . . .

Yolanda sees her public school as poor preparation for the elite institution into which she went. Her use of Anyon's work helps redefine her struggles from personal failures into a larger and systemic issue—class stratification. Yolanda was not aware of schooling inequities as a student; however new information has revealed not only their existence but her place in them. A second iteration of this first theme involves candidates locating themselves against institutions. Examples of this are student experiences retold in ways that confirm suspicions about schooling inequalities. Lisa, a biracial girl who grew up in New York City, chose a critical incident about a teacher who mistook her for another child of color who misbehaved:

> Looking back on the incident, I feel that Mrs. D. may have had some preconceived notions that led her to believe that because I was bi-racial I would misbehave in class. Perhaps this is why she could so easily confuse me with another child who had behavioral problems. Another theory is that her beliefs about my race led her to treat me as though I wasn't worth the time and effort it would take to remember my name. Mrs. D.'s treatment of me caused me to intensely dislike school to the point that I dreaded going.

Although is likely that Lisa may have been aware of racial bias in school as a biracial child and that teachers may have had "beliefs about [her] race," when she begins to grapple with the manner in which beliefs get translated into actions of bias, she is only positing speculative theories about what may have been the case. She uses her newfound knowledge of the linkages between race and teacher expectations gathered from her social foundations course to do this intellectual work.

Critical Incidents Help Candidates Locate Themselves Within Communities of Practice

Students also use critical incidents to position themselves within larger socio-logical and political communities of practice. In this theme, students identify favorite teachers or role models who have informed their thinking about their future work. Jackie, for example, writes about a male teacher who prevented her from doing a sports assignment because she was a girl. Reading Vito Perrone's reflective biography of Leonard Covello allowed her to locate herself among master teachers to whom she aspires to emulate rather than the teachers she actually had. As she describes:

> This incident has really helped me understand the issues that are present in schools that can hinder a child's learning. I can't help but think about Perrone's novel. Perrone truly describes what it means to be a teacher and how to be that teacher that truly makes a positive change in a person's life. Because of the readings and my reflections, I now know the kind of teacher I want to be and the kind of teacher I don't want be. I will be that teacher who has an open heart to all her students. I will hold no stereo-types and do my best to get to know each individual child. Ultimately, I want to be that teacher that the students talk about twenty years from now about how much of a difference I made on their lives. My dream is to one day be that teacher.

Writing about her critical incident and reading Perrone (1988) allowed Jackie to connect specific issues of gender equity to equity issues writ large. Gender discrimination, she realizes, is part of a set of practices that deny the individ-uality of children in favor of stereotypes. In this case, Jackie uses Leonard Covello's life example to "look back" and "discover her own standpoint" (Greene, 1978, p. 33).

In the next example, Abigail uses Lorde's (1982) story of suffering through unreasonable standards as a child to posit that Lorde would not have thrived under today's educational conditions. She uses her newfound understanding of the No Child Left Behind (NCLB) policy to forward this analysis, writing:

> Under the NCLB Act the disabled and the underprivileged are promised provision for the tests they are required to take. If these provisions are not being fulfilled however would Lorde survive under this Act? Like Lorde, I would be greatly affected by the NCLB Act because the school I went to in Queens is targeted by this Act. Currently in the schools children are taught with the "scientific research-based approach" and the teachers have to focus more on the test than ever.

Abigail connects the unreasonable expectations that Lorde experienced as a legally blind child to the experiences of children in schools with inadequate funding to fulfill the provisions of NCLB with respect to special-needs students. She believes a child like Lorde today would be no better off than Lorde was 50 years before NCLB was enacted. Having understood how students use their stories to situate themselves within larger communities of practice, it is easy to see how they translate these ideas to reimagine their work as social justice teachers.

Critical Incidents Help Candidates Re-imagine Acts of Social Justice

Anne's experience as a white student in an Afrocentric high school classroom left an enduring mark on her biography. Here, she re-imagines the mixed feelings about her politically conscious African American teacher as a powerful outsider's experience:

> I'm emerging from the experience of writing this paper fairly troubled by my own racial baggage and the real anger I feel toward a teacher who I know took her work seriously and strove to be the very best she could be. Intellectually I have endless generosity for this woman, yet emotionally I still have a lump in my throat (and I actually teared up at one point in writing this). I am amazed by the way that I still carry this early educational experience as baggage (I guess that is the nature of a "critical" incident) and I now know that it is a part of what I need to keep digging into as I go about the important work of teaching.

Later, Anne indicates that the experience of writing a critical incident has awaked a compassion for the marginalized outsider, that is, for her white male students, who tend to reclaim the center when conversations of inequality arise in her classroom:

> One thing in particular that this exploration has awakened in me is a new compassion and empathy for my male students who, when I teach a unit on gender, insist that their lives are hard too and that it is really tough to be a boy in America today. This is a position that I would not have previously had much patience for. Similarly, before writing this paper I would have said that white people crying racism just need to get over it.

Already critical about white privilege, Anne's experience "looking back" at a time when she felt marginalized aroused a patience in her for allowing students the developmental time they need to critically analyze gender relations.

This cross-cutting analysis is good example of the range of connections that can be made when we allow students the space to mine their own lives for philosophically based reflections-in-action. In a similar theme, Annette, a child of Polish immigrants, watched her mother "take on menial jobs" due to her limited grasp of English. As she describes her mother: "She refrained from expressing her own knowledge because she was not confident in her English-speaking abilities and in her own knowledge. I, too, adopted this behavior in my schooling." This shyness allowed Annette to see that others were also marginalized at school, an issue she now sees as a matter of injustice. As she explains:

> My public school teachers did not have dispositions towards social justice. On the contrary, they treated their non-white students differently and, via their Euro-centric curriculums and racist attitudes, provided white students with easier and better opportunities to succeed. My teachers also treated me, a quiet student, differently by not acknowledging my good work and by not providing me with an alternate means of showing my abilities. This, I believe, would have had a negative impact on my education were it not for other teachers like Mrs. R and, for Audre Lorde, the personal motivation and confidence she had. Mrs. R's dispositions definitely acted for and toward social justice. As stated before, she truly believed in the potential of every student, and she acted in a way that gave all students an opportunity to share their knowledge and abilities. She would not even allow quietness or shyness to limit her students. In fact, through her dispositions, she helped me to overcome my shyness and gain confidence in myself.

Through her critical incident, Annette demonstrates her fluency with social justice education practices. She identifies both prohibitive and prescriptive examples of social justice in teaching. Again we see a cross-cutting analysis involving social justice, as it relates to the ways that teachers deal with difference, in this case race and language ability.

Connected to Annette's example are others in which candidates begin to articulate the moral dimensions of the work. Ethan, for example, explores the moral implications of teachers' work in light of his critical incident and his readings:

> I said on an earlier posting that it was the "teacher's moral responsibility to teach in an unbiased, socially justified way." In application to Audre Lorde's and to my experiences I think it's fair to say that some aspect of our teacher's responsibility in each case was not fulfilled. The question remains, though: Is this violating their moral responsibility? This is a strong statement, but in some ways I think it holds. If we look at school as a system that stratifies society, then any holding back on the part of the

teacher would seem to, in turn, create an unfair society. Students shouldn't have to prove themselves worthy of a great education, as Lorde or myself did. They should simply be worthy of a great education by their very presence.

Ethan's acknowledgment of the moral dimensions of the work of teaching connects an individualistic act (moral responsibility) to systemic conditions (a stratified society). Similar to Yolanda above, Ethan's personal struggle gets transformed into a common struggle for equity that upends the notion of individual merit into a condition in which all children are, by nature, worthy.

The thematic excerpts presented here show that storytelling can be used as a pedagogical tool in social foundations courses to help candidates locate themselves within the field of education. The narratives also allowed students to imagine philosophically based and socially just plans and practices and to juxtapose those to their own lived experiences. The themes presented here are not all inclusive, but those critical incidents reexamined through the SFE literature become decisive moments in one's educational biography and can allow candidates to locate themselves both within and against educational institutions and within larger sociological and political communities of practice. Rehewn as educational stories, their power and utility for new teachers cannot be underestimated. In the next section, I share some reflective questions that seek to help pre- and in-service educators think about how critical incidents have the potential to help candidates become better teachers.

Encouraging Reflective Analysis

If we are to make a case for the importance of reflection and analysis by using critical incidents with teacher candidates, it is constructive to first ask foundational questions regarding the use and purpose of personal stories in education. The questions below are keyed to teacher educators interested in getting teachers thinking and analyzing their own experiences and how these processes may (or may not) impact their own practice of teaching.

Questions to Consider in Using Critical Incidents with Pre-service and In-Service Candidates

What is the place of personal story in teacher education?

Michael Apple (2006) among others (Meier & Wood, 2004; Selwyn, 2006; Sunderman, Kim, & Orfield, 2005) have linked NCLB's (as have been taken up by Race To The Top) commitment to closing achievement inequities directly to the "instrumentalization" of teaching and avoidance of course content that highlight issues of race and class inequities. When candidates share personal stories of education, regardless of their racial, social class, or gendered identity, these stories tend to shed light on moments of struggle and triumph. New teachers must do this work to reconnect to how it feels to struggle and persevere if they are to avoid those experiences occurring in the future for their students. Making space for personal stories in the teacher education curriculum is vital to developing this reflective practice. Reflecting on their own experiences as learners ensures that these experiences will be translated into reflection-in-action, with which teachers can create powerful learning experiences for their students.

Why couple autobiographical critical incidents with "theoretical course readings"?

Teacher education has come under ever-increasing scrutiny internally, via national accreditation efforts, and become externally based on a concerted push for alternative routes to certification. It has become more important than ever to be able demonstrate what new teachers learn from and do with their coursework (Carter, 2008). This is particularly true for theoretical coursework. The 2000 report by Public Agenda (funded by the Open Society Institute and the Thomas B. Fordham Foundation), "A Sense of Calling: Who Teaches and Why," for example, reported that teachers see their teacher education coursework as far too theoretical to be helpful in the work of teaching. However, when we create opportunities for teachers to tell us how they use theory to inform their developing understandings and their work, we learn "what prospective teachers actually do with what they learn in teacher preparation coursework" (Cochran-Smith, 2004, p. 163). The use of critical incidents coupled with educational theory allows teacher educators to unearth these connections in candidate's own words.

What kinds of critical incidents have the greatest potential to connect theory and practice?

When we ask students to look back on their own educational biographies and choose the moments that were meaningful to them, we cannot predict what they will discover about themselves. However, the fact that they make the choice to do this reflection ensures the potential for deep exploration. In SFE coursework, the reflection on and discourse with readings are essential to both understanding and using the wisdom that master teachers and researchers have to offer. If we are thoughtful about providing readings and research that align with the professional standards in our respective fields, the connections students make have the potential to be transformative for future practice. Whereas policy makers and even new teacher education students often search for formulaic answers to questions of practice, hoping there is one "proven" method to solve the challenges of classroom life, the experience of mining one's own life experience for critical educational moments, and translating those into pedagogical plans, reveals that there are as many answers to the "problems" of teaching as there are teachers. This is the true potential of the theory-practice paradigm.

References

Anyon, J, (1980). Social class and the hidden curriculum of work. *Journal of Education, 162*(1), 67–92.

Anyon, J. (2005). *Radical possibilities: Public policy, urban education, and a new social movement*. New York, NY: Routledge.

Apple, Michael.)2006). *Education the 'right' way: Markets, standards, god, and inequality*. New York: Routledge.

Ayers, W. (1995). *To become a teacher: Making a difference in children's lives*. New York, NY: Teachers College Press.

boyd, d., Grossman, P., Lankford, H., Loeb, S., & Wyckoff, J. (2006). How changes in entry requirements alter the teacher workforce and affect student achievement. *Education, Finance & Policy, 1*(2). Retrieved from http://www.teacherpolicyresearch.org/portals/1/ pdfs/ how_changes_in_entry_requirements_alter_the_teacher_workforce.pdf

Burgum, M., & Bridge, C. (1997). Using critical incidents in professional education to develop skills of reflection and critical thinking. In R. Pospisil & L. Willcoxson (Eds.), *Learning Through Teaching: Proceedings of the Sixth Annual Teaching Learning Forum, Perth, Australia*, 58–61. Retrieved from http://otl.curtin.edu.au/tlf/tlf1997/burgum.html

Bushnell, M., & Henry, S. E. (2003). The role of reflection in epistemological change: Autobiography in teacher education. *Educational Studies, 34*(1), 38–61.

Butin, D. W. (2004, July 24). The foundations of preparing teachers: Are education schools really "intellectually barren" and ideological? *Teachers College Record*, Retrieved from http://www.tcrecord.org/content.asp?contentid=11349

Carter, J. (2008). On the path to becoming "highly qualified": New teachers talk about the relevancy of social foundations. *Educational Studies, 44*(3), 222–246.

Cochran-Smith, M. (Ed). (2004). *Walking the road: Race, diversity and social justice in teacher education.* New York, NY: Teachers College Press

Counts, G. (1978). Dare the school build a new social order? In Marvin Lazerson (Ed), *American education in the 21st century: A documentary history* (pp. 98–99). New York, NY: Teachers College Press.

Delpit, L. (1996). *Other people's children: Cultural conflict in the classroom.* New York, NY: New Press.

Dewey, John. 1959. My Pedagogic Creed. In Alan Sadovnik, Peter Cookson & Susan Semel (Eds.). 2005. *Exploring education: An introduction to the foundations of education.* Pp. 202–205. Boston: Pearson/Allyn & Bacon.

Farkas, S., Johnson, J., & Foleno, T. (2000). *A sense of calling: Who teaches and why: A report from public agenda* (ERIC Report Retrieved from http://eric.ed.gov/PDFS/ ED443815.pdf

Finn, P. (1999). *Literacy with an attitude: Educating working class children in their own self interest.* Albany: State University of New York Press.

Greene, M. (1978). *Teaching: The question of personal reality. Teachers College Record 80*(1), 23–35. Retrieved from http://www.maxinegreene.org/articles.php

Haberman, M. (1987). Recruiting and selecting teachers for urban schools. Reston, VA and New York, NY: ERIC Clearinghouse on Urban Education Institute for Urban and Minority Education. Retrieved from http://www.getcited.org/pub/102744262

Kohn, A. (2004). *What does it mean to be well educated? And more essays on standards, grading and other follies.* Boston, MA: Beacon Press.

Ladson-Billings, G. (1996). Your blues ain't like mine: Keeping issues of race and racism on the multicultural agenda. *Theory into Practice, 35*(4), 248–255.

Ladson-Billings, G. (1997). *Dreamkeepers: Successful teachers of African American children.* New York, NY: Jossey-Bass.

Lorde, A. (1982). *Zami: A New Spelling of My Name.* Berkeley, CA: The Crossing Press.

Meier, D., & Wood, G. (Eds). (2004). *Many children left behind: How the No Child Left Behind Act is damaging our children and our schools.* Boston, MA: Beacon Press.

Murrow, S. E. (2006). Charting "unexpected territory" in the social foundations: Pedagogical practice in urban teacher education. *Educational Studies, 43*(3), 296–312.

Orfield, G. (n.d.). School desegregation 50 years after *Brown*: Misconceptions, lessons learned and hopes for the future. *The Center for the Study of Ethics in Society, 15*(3), 1–22. Retrieved from *http://www.wmich.edu/ethics/pubs/vol_xvi/orfield.pdf*

Otterman, S. (2011, July 21). Ed schools pedagogical puzzle. *The New York Times.* Retrieved from http://www.nytimes.com/2011/07/24/education/edlife/edl-24teacher-t.html? pagewanted=all

Perrone, V. (1988). *Teacher with a heart: Reflections on Leonard Covello and community.* New York, NY: Teachers College Press.

Public Agenda. 2000. A sense of calling: Who teachers and why. Thomas B. Fordham Foundation. Washington, DC: Steve Farkas, Jean Johnson, Tony Foleno.

Rist, R. (1970). Student social class and teacher expectations: The self-Fulfilling prophecy in ghetto education. *Harvard Educational Review, 40*(3), 411–451.

Schön, D. (1983). *The reflective practitioner*. New York, NY: Basic Books.

Schön, D. (1987). *Educating the reflective practitioner*. San Francisco, CA: Jossey-Bass.

Schön, D. (1991). *The reflective turn: Case studies in and on educational practice*. New York, NY: Teachers Press.

Seller, M. (1988). *To seek America: A history of ethnic life in the United States*. Englewood, NJ: Jerome S. Ozer.

Selwyn, D. (2006). Teacher education left behind: How NCLB harms the preparation of new teachers. *Rethinking Schools Online, 20*(2).

Strong-Wilson, T. (2008). *Bringing memory forward: Storied remembrance in social justice education with teachers*. New York, NY: Peter Lang.

Sunderman, G., Kim, J., & Orfield, G. (2005). *NCLB meets school realities: Lessons from the field*. Thousand Oaks, CA: Corwin Press.

Tripp, D. (1993). *Critical incidents in teaching: Developing professional judgement*. London, United Kingdom: Routledge.

U.S. Department of Education Office of Postsecondary Education. (2002). *Meeting the highly qualified teachers challenge: The Secretary's annual report on teacher quality*. Retrieved from http://www2.ed.gov/about/reports/annual/teachprep/2002title-ii-report.pdf

· 9 ·

Early Childhood Collaborations

Learning from Migrant Families and Children

ELIZABETH P. QUINTERO

Scholars, dedicated teachers, and community activists have documented the fact that many immigrant students come from a variety of backgrounds with different "funds of knowledge" (Moll, Gonzalez, & Amanti, 2005; Quintero, 2010; Steinberg & Kincheloe, 2009) for contributing to our communities and educational programs. We know that this knowledge is often considered to be in terms of specific skill sets, of practical knowledge such as plant husbandry, natural herbal medicines, or mechanical expertise. What is often overlooked is how much knowledge parents have about child rearing and the required conditions for their children to develop and learn optimally. I found that the parents in our project—who were migrant farmworkers, some who had received formal education in their home country, and some who had absolutely no formal education—had knowledge and passionate determination about what they want for their children. And, through interview and informal conversations, the parents shared their personal narratives with student teachers enhancing optimum understanding and learning.

What the Parents Know

Most of the parents interviewed in the study described in this chapter mirrored the following answer from a respondent to the question of what would be the preferred language in early and general education for her children: "Bilingual, English and Spanish and another language if possible."

Participants were also asked whether it is important that teachers understand or know of their home culture, and they answered, "Oh yes, because we all come from different cultures. For example, I am from Oaxaca and my culture is totally completely different from a person's from Michoacan and Guanajuato."

What the Children Know

It is a common stereotypical notion that children who live in relative poverty, whose parents don't speak the dominant language of the society and who haven't had access to many educational experiences may not be curious about their learning. Yet after working for two semesters with children from low-income families who are migrant farmworkers, one participating student teacher writes:

> If I made a book of the observations I took during this work I would title it *Inquisitive Minds*. I was amazed at the things I observed! From ladybug hunting, to finding leaks in hoses, to following photo directions, to inquiring about print, I was amazed at the variety of interests of the children that varied day by day, week by week, and month by month. What I noticed consistently was that children were deeply involved in their learning and were creating meaning through their work.

Purpose

This research story addresses issues of access and quality in early care and education for children of migrant farmworkers. Migration, language, culture, power, ethnicity, race, and class enter into the complex consideration of how the profession serves the needs of this population. Early-childhood student teachers approaching curricula from a participatory critical theory framework study and work to create responsive, high-quality early care and education for children of migrant farmworkers. The students rethink curriculum for young children of migrant farmworkers through their university coursework, by learning from the families and children of the workers, the employers of the families, and the early care and education staff who serve families through licensed programs and who have many years of experience working in Southern California.

The Early Childhood Studies Program at my university focuses on preparing student teachers to work with the families of migrant farmworkers by offering the teachers opportunities to become knowledgeable about serving the needs of this population in the United States and Southern California. This is done through providing student teachers with three components of curriculum work—qualitative methods including participant observation and narrative documentation, curriculum development, and authentic assessment based on the learning story model of early childhood assessment in New Zealand (New Zealand Ministry of Education, 2010).

In particular, the program focuses on working with and learning from migrant farmworkers. Research has shown that quality early care and education positively influences children's success in school and later in life (Loeb, Fuller, Kagan, Carrol, & Carroll, 2004; Shonkoff & Phillips, 2000; Schweinhart, Barnes, Weikart, Barnett, & Epstein, 1993). This is true for all children and particularly important for children of recent immigrants, who are often beginning to learn English and who have a rich cultural history as well as diverse needs.

It is a well-documented reality that by the year 2030, over half of students in schools within the United States will be students of multilingual and multicultural backgrounds. Acculturation and language acquisition are impacted by the process of aligning new societal expectations and requirements of immigrants with previous cultural norms, individual perceptions, and experiences preeminent in their lives; yet, these urgent issues are often ignored. By virtue of the fact that many immigrant students come from a variety of backgrounds with different "funds of knowledge" as Moll, Gonzalez, and Amanti (2005) report, it is urgent that university education students learn the complicated practice of recognizing, acknowledging, and incorporating learners' background knowledge while providing them access to new and necessary knowledge for successful participation in the 21st century. The research described provides a focus on this work in ways that currently aren't often discussed in literature in the field.

In Southern California, there is a sizable workforce of families with young children who are farmworkers (Figure 9.1). Findings from a needs assessment conducted in 2009 (Quintero, 2010) show that safe, reliable, and affordable childcare is not available for the children of farmworkers, which has a negative impact on the employment of migrant farmworkers from the standpoint of lost productivity and worker anxiety. In addition to this needs assessment, data show that at each ranch participating in the survey, some employees miss work up to seven to nine days a month because of stress related to lack of quality childcare.

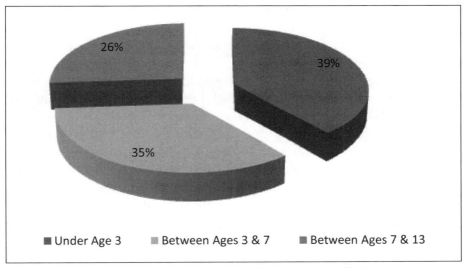

Figure 9.1 Percent of Farmworkers Who Have Young Children.

Context of Early Childhood Majors

At our university, in the final year of our Early Childhood Studies major, university students concurrently study in courses and spend 30 days in county programs working with experienced teachers, staff, and preschool and primary school-aged children during the fall semester and infants and toddlers in the spring semester. In the university courses, knowledge and research are presented to students so that they can continue to synthesize their understanding of child development, community contexts, and the various models of service delivery for programs with young children. Students are supported in this process through providing them the use of qualitative methods for observing and documenting children's learning. The students review theoretical models that have served young children's education around the world and investigate the latest findings in child development, which include studies in brain research as related to curriculum development and assessment. These Early Childhood majors are required to become experts at observing children's strengths and needs and then are required to develop their own curriculum plans for work-ing with a particular group of children. Finally, in this ongoing research study student teachers participate in cutting-edge authentic assessment design through the study and adaptation of the New Zealand learning story model (New Zealand Ministry of Education, 2010). In doing so, they work with early-care and education staff and parents from local families, write and implement curricula, practice collaborating with parents to assist with curriculum devel-opment, and provide insights from these experiences as they continue their uni-versity coursework.

This chapter documents the ways in which university student teachers are able to support the learning potential of all children within the context of their home, school, and community. Because of its participatory nature, using nar-ratives written by children, parents, and "teacher scribes," the New Zealand learning story model for assessment in Early Childhood is used to assess the out-come of this project. Although there are obvious contextual differences between early childhood programs in Southern California and those in New Zealand, there are some important similarities, both in terms of context, regarding col-laborators in the education of young children, and in terms of the demands that this emphasis on participatory collaboration creates regarding curriculum devel-opment and assessment. In New Zealand, early care and education experts have made dramatic historical progress with bilingual, bicultural program design and authentic assessment. Carr et al. (2009) address the importance of thinking about children's learning in all aspects of their lives as follows:

> The cultures that develop in early childhood centers and school classrooms can be described as 'dispositional milieux'; they may be overt and public, or subtle and covert; they may support the spirit and intent of a curriculum document or they may not. . . . We suggest that learning dispositions are features of places, in the case of early childhood centres, school classrooms and homes. These dispositional milieux are affor-dance networks: networks of useful resources, including people, that provide, *or appear to provide*, opportunities and constraints for the learning that the individual has in mind. (p. 8)

Our Early Childhood Studies Program in California has begun to make con-nections with these affordance networks as a framework for encouraging our university students and ourselves to see our work as teacher researchers, cur-riculum developers, activity facilitators, evaluators of programs, and assessors of children's growth, development, and learning as a holistic connection that spirals and connects and reconnects in a variety of ways.

Methods

Three aspects of the overall study are:

1. Qualitative research methods,
2. Curriculum development, and
3. Authentic assessment.

From these three features the Early Childhood teacher education students study, design, implement, and assess curricula based on critical theory. The participation and data collection methods involve participant observation, interviews with families, teacher journals, and collections of learners' work samples during their interaction with curricula. The data are analyzed by the categories that emerge, particularly as they relate to the theoretical perspective of critical theory.

The theoretical framework for this research is critical theory. The multidisciplinary knowledge base of critical theory affirms the role of criticism and rejects the radical differentiation between theory and practice as two separate poles of a dualism. Critical theory encourages the production and application of theory as a part of the overall search for transformative knowledge. Paulo Freire (1985) popularized critical theory and emphasizes participation through personal histories, the sharing of multiple ways of knowing, and transformative action. According to Freire (1997), freedom can only occur when the oppressed reject the image of oppression " . . . and replace it with autonomy and responsibility" (p. 29).

Those who adopt Freire's pedagogy need to be aware that it is not made up of techniques to save the world; rather, he feels that "the progressive educator must always be moving out on his or her own, continually reinventing me and reinventing what it means to be democratic in his or her own specific cultural and historical context" (Freire, 1997, p. 308). In other words, a progressive educator must continually strive to reinvent herself/himself and strive to adapt to the realities of what being democratic means in a particular context. A critical theory framework supports working with migrating families from a variety of historical contexts, language groups, and life experiences.

As this research and the resulting implications have revolved around participatory learner-driven curriculum and assessment, I have taken advice from Pinar concerning the interpretation of the developing work. Pinar (2004) advises: "The complicated conversation that is the curriculum requires interdisciplinary intellectuality, erudition, and self-reflexivity. This is not a recipe for high test scores, but a common faith in the possibility of self-realization and democratization, twin projects of social subjective reconstruction"(p. 8).

Collaborating Participants

This ongoing qualitative study includes students from the senior-level Early Childhood Studies Program in their undergraduate major, parents and children from families of migrant farmworkers in various classrooms, university supervisors, teachers, and assistant teachers from county early-care and education programs for pre-K to second grade classrooms and for infant and toddler programs.

The primary collaborators in this ongoing study are members of migrant farmworker families—adults and children. Parents have concerns regarding issues of quality and appropriate early care and education for their children. Agricultural workers in our county include families from Mexico and Central America and a large, close-knit indigenous group of families from Oaxaca and Mexico, known as the Mixtecs.

The Mixtecs are indigenous inhabitants of southern Mexico whose language and culture predate the Spanish conquest by hundreds of years. There are an estimated 500,000 Mixtec speakers today; almost one-fifth live in the United States for at least part of their lives. Mixtec language and culture are as different from Spanish as Navajo is from English. The Mixtecs' beliefs about health, religion, and family include many traditional concepts and are often at odds with Western concepts. Along with other indigenous cultures, the Mixtec's unique language, art, and culture are in danger of being lost forever. Many of the immigrant families who arrived in the United States in the 1970s and '80s raised their families here—and now have children in college or who are successfully employed. Many have become U.S. citizens (Fox & Rivera-Salgado, 2004).

However, there are barriers for many of the Mixtec people living in California. Many are illiterate, and some speak neither Spanish or English but only their native language, Mixteco or another indigenous language. As a result, they face exploitation and discrimination in labor, housing, and everyday life. Most live in extreme poverty and lack basic provisions such as adequate housing, food, clothing, and other necessities of life. Central to their struggle is the fact that they cannot communicate with people beyond their own indigenous community, thus impeding their ability to obtain appropriate health care, educate themselves and their children, negotiate with their employers to improve their work situation, and exercise their basic civil rights (Wright, 2005).

Qualitative Methods for Curriculum Development and Data Collection

The teacher education students participate in a variety of problem-posing activities (based on critical theory) in teacher education courses before they begin planning and implementing similar activities for the children they work with. They begin writing their autobiographical narratives and doing their qualitative research (Ely, Anzul, Friedman, Garner, & McCormack-Steinmetz, 1991) at the outset of their participation and continue throughout their program of study with the use of problem-posing critical literacy in their own learning as adults and then with young learners in their classrooms.

In curriculum classes beginning their senior year of undergraduate study, students practice qualitative narrative assignments, such as: (a) writing a narrative description (from journals) of children's development, strengths, and needs and the context of the classroom, (b) writing a brief account of children in school in their native language (other than English), addressing the following questions: "What do the children say?" "When do they use their home language?" "What supports their doing this? (The adults, the children, the materials, the personality of the child?)," and (c) noticing details about children's literacy and mathematics knowledge (at the placement), answering the following questions: "What do you see as the children's strengths?" "What do they know?" "How do you know they know this?"

The teacher education students participate in in-class activities involving reviewing research and discussing multicultural literature in order to become more adept at recognizing and documenting strengths, funds of knowledge, and the needs of families and communities. They learn to listen to families. In addition to doing class work related to collecting data about children and cultural contexts, students are assigned to conduct ethnographic interviews with parents of some of the children in their student-teaching classrooms. In addition, student teachers interview children about their life experiences.

Narrative Study Begins

Student teachers then begin developing content-learning experiences for children focusing on the history and culture of the farmworkers' families. It is important that the student teachers "tune in" to the children and their families and build upon their strengths, never minimizing their responsibility to provide opportunities for teaching strong academic foundations for future educational success. At the beginning of their study of curriculum development for preschoolers through second graders, the teacher education students practice noticing and documenting examples of children's use of critical literacy. One assignment early in the course is:

1. Observe a child or group of children in your field placement classroom and document an example of them using critical literacy. What happened? What did they do? What did they say? What was the transformative action?
2. Document an adult demonstrating or supporting a child using literacy in a community, school, or home context.

Based on the above assignment, one student writes in her reflective journal:

One concept that the children are exploring in the classroom is the concept of light via an overhead projector that projects onto the ceiling. There are several children pushing colored jewels and a stencil onto the projector. They push them around and are experimenting with how the objects appear on the ceiling when moved. Nearby, there are children indirectly associated with this activity. One child is drawing on a whiteboard the images she sees on the ceiling. The child next to her is engaged in the same task. She says, "La mariposa está muerta." She continues drawing the image.

I think this demonstrates critical literacy because the children are changing different medium of understanding to demonstrate the concept of storytelling through their work. While one child is using objects to tell their story on the overhead, another child is transforming this activity to tell their story via images.

I saw a teacher supporting children's literacy by sharing an exciting story with them at circle time. The teacher uses storytelling techniques, which draws the children in. She asks questions to spark curiosity. They seem very interested. The teacher lets the children know that the book is available in the library. She encourages children to visit the library to read books during free time. The next time I visit there are children in the library. The teacher tells me later that she was concerned because the children never visited that area of the classroom and wants to encourage the children to read independently.

Another student writes:

Recently I observed a child with special needs developing critical literacy in her personalized way. She is three years old and naptime is the most difficult time of day for her. She is rarely able to take a nap, and has never taken a nap during naptime at her program. On goods days she can lie quietly for most of the time, but it is a constant struggle for both the child and the teacher. Her most successful coping mechanism is reading a book. She only has very basic literacy skills, such as naming letters and the corresponding sounds. However, this child will flip through each and every page and tell herself a reasonably complex story that is consistent with the pictures in the book. When she is finished with one book, she will begin with the next book.

I would give her age-appropriate books to read and allowed her to spend any amount of time with one book until she was ready for another book. Though naptime is a quiet time for the children, I encouraged her to whisper to herself at a reasonable volume. It seemed essential.

The child is not only using her imagination to create a storyline, but she is also learning a useful coping mechanism in order to behave appropriately. By practicing coping skills, she is developing her intrapersonal intelligence and is learning how to assert her control in a positive manner. During a good day, when naptime ends her increased confidence in her abilities is obvious.

The university class studies research that documents teaching with critical literacy using problem posing that focuses on children's lived experiences and children's literature. This method nourishes an integrated curriculum that supports young children's meaningful learning (Quintero, 2010; Quintero & Rummel, 2010). Simply defined, the problem-posing method is comprised of several components. These are: *Listening, Dialogue, and Action*. In this method, participants:

- listen to their own histories through reflective writing and sharing of participants' stories, and gather new information in the form of minilectures, expert presentations, or scholarly research and academic information;
- dialogue about information that was shared and presented during the listening activities; discuss issues of power that have shaped their identities and current families, schools, and community contexts; and make connections to the situations of the children and families they work with using personal and historical information;
- collaborate on various curricular activities that encourage and support action or transformation on the part of children, families, and educators.

The adult student teachers practice in the university class and brainstorm with peers and instructors about ways problem-posing might be used with young children.

In the Early Childhood curriculum classes, the listening aspect of the class, for example, might begin with a minilecture reviewing curriculum theory and reiterating the connections of this work to early childhood foundational theories and models. Then, Early Childhood teachers and education students might be asked to journal about their personal research framework for early childhood education. They first reflect on their own experiences with emerging literacy development in their own lives.

The following example exemplifies the complexities of early literacy, showing the rich data that could be used for the next class period's discussion. This assignment, and "*Action* Homework," involved students reflecting and writing about their earliest personal memories of literacy in their family contexts. One student writes:

> I do not recall my mother of father ever reading, since my mother dislikes reading and my father was to busy working. Though, I do remember my family was full of stories. We would all gather around and listen to each other tell myths, scary stories, stories of their own lives and history. I remember sitting around the adults and listen to them, mesmerized by what they were telling. Even though my parents did not read to me, I had wonderful teachers that did. Mrs. Ryan was my first grade teacher and I loved how she read to us, with so much enthusiasm, she made the stories come to life. That is when I first started to care for books and I loved it when my classroom went to the library. From the library, I always got books that seemed interesting and at home since my parents did not read to me, I ended up "reading" them to my stuff animals. I may have just looked at the images and figured out a story from there so that I can "read" it to my stuff animals.

In a subsequent class, after a short video clip of an interview with Sandra Cisneros in which she discusses her revelation when she entered graduate school that her own history, language, and set of cultural experiences in Chicago were never included in the narratives she studied in school—ever. These personal narratives became the basis of her writing for *The House on Mango Street*.

In the Dialogue section, students are asked to discuss their chosen memories of their family literacy history with a partner. Following the discussion, information is distributed related to the history, language, and culture of the Mixtec people. Students then work in small groups to consider ways to incorporate some of the information into the curriculum activities that they are planning.

The class agenda for a related class session followed the following format:

1. *Listening:* The students listened to author Sandra Cisneros reflect on the issue of connecting personal family history to writing.
2. *Dialogue:* The students shared aspects of their memories of their

family literacy history with a partner, and discussed ways that their thinking about these experiences related to the issues Cisneros discussed.

3. *Action:* The teacher distributed information related to the history, language, and culture of the Mixtec people, and in small groups students worked on using some of the new information as a part of their lesson development for young children.

Soon after the reflections and discussion, the instructor addressed the topic of curriculum standards, stressing that some curriculum standards are the result of work by early childhood professional organizations and other standards are developed by state and federal groups and mandated for various age groups and grade levels. In this discussion, the levels were:

1. *Listening:* The instructor gave a minilecture about curriculum standards in general and early childhood education in particular.
2. *Dialogue:* The instructor asked the university students to discuss with a partner the connections they saw between professional curriculum standards and their own views of curriculum (philosophical and theoretical frame). The instructions were given as follows: "Please discuss in small groups ways that you see your own philosophies and views of curriculum relate to, are similar to, or are different from some of the 'model standards' that were shared in the minilecture."
3. *Action:* Students investigated the Web sites of professional organizations and government departments of education to view a variety of examples of standards and guidelines for curriculum development. Another dialogue activity followed the Web search, in which students were asked to discuss the ways in which their research frames influence their choices for curriculum development. For action homework, the university students were asked to write a detailed narrative describing the context of the program they are student teaching in, including information about the community of the families, the philosophy of the program, the environment of the classroom, and details about a few of the children's strengths and needs. When the university students brought their narratives back to class and discussed them, they were asked to reflect on and write about whether standards and curriculum guidelines enhance our work to support all families and children or inhibit this work.

In addition to studying curriculum standards and guidelines, critical literacy, issues of access, and family strengths and needs, the university classes allocate an hour or more each week for students to participate in activities that use children's literature as a focal point to integrate other content areas such as math and science into curriculum design. For example, the focus may be on problem-posing with math and storybooks. A variety of storybooks appropriate for four- to eight-year-olds was distributed to each table of four university students. The task was for the four students at each table to choose a storybook and agree on an age group of children for which they would create a problem-posing lesson that integrates literacy, math, and at least one other content area.

For the listening section, each group appointed a reader to read the book their group chose aloud. For the Dialogue section, they were asked to discuss the story in their groups and plan a problem-posing lesson (instructional sequence) related to it for their target age group. The group then made connections and/or suggestions based on Smith (2005) and were asked to include aspects in their activity that relate to literacy and at least one additional content area. For the Action section, the groups charted their problem-posing/instructional sequence on white paper to display. As they shared their planning with the class, the groups were asked to lead a discussion about other activities that would give children opportunities to develop this math concept in their classes, paying attention to maintaining opportunities for the children to make choices in their learning. They were encouraged to explore possible connections to children's culture, home language, and daily experiences.

Supporting Multilingual Learners

Another important focus of both the curriculum development and assessment is related to the Early Childhood Studies Program's commitment to support English Language Learners. The following example of a series of university class lessons illustrates the importance of focusing on the content as well as the process in curriculum development and in the ways the narrative supports the learning.

For the opening activity in the listening section, students are asked to review their personal field journals for information about children's use of their home language (other than English) in school and to answer the following questions: "What do they say?," "When do they use their home language?," and "What supports their doing this (the adults, the children, the materials, the personality of the child)?"

In the Dialogue section, students are asked to discuss what they had noted about children's use of their home language and explain that in detail to their small groups. Then, for the Action section, they are asked to analyze the following questions about their observations of their journals: "Is this critical literacy?" and "In what ways does this relate to your research frameworks?"

Then the class continues with another Listening section. The instructor reads the storybook *I Love Saturdays y Domingos* by Alma Flor Ada, which tells the story of a girl's life with both her English-speaking and her Spanish-speaking grandparents. For the Dialogue section, students are asked to relate the story to issues discussed that night in class. They then go back to Listening section, listening to *Friends from the Other Side: Amigos del Otro Lado* by Gloria Anzaldúa, which is a story about a young girl befriending a boy who had recently moved to an American neighborhood from Mexico with his mother but without documentation. The story includes issues of friendship, coping with bullying, experiences related to way political situations in communities affect children, and cultural traditions including sharing food and natural healing.

For the Dialogue section, the students participate in a large group discussion that addresses the topics surrounding appropriate ways to address controversial issues and teachers' responsibilities to do so. For the Action section, students read and share some teacher research articles addressing controversial issues from.the journal *Rethinking Schools Online*. Then, in groups, they are asked to plan centers that could be set up to go with the themes addressed in the story.

Early Childhood Assessment Adapted from New Zealand

In the practice that I recorded in this study, looking at the work of New Zealand researchers and teachers, I have realized that we can borrow and adapt some of the research and practice-based structures that they have been using for the past decade and a half. The beginnings of the work of this study will contribute to a model of early childhood assessment that has aspects that may be replicated, aspects that require adaptation for different contexts of learning, and aspects that contribute to a system for both summative and formative evaluation that may be studied across programs and sites.

Assessment is a complex topic in every situation. In the field of early care and education, the dilemmas of authenticity, ethics, efficacy, and consistency are mind boggling. On a national basis, there are several initiatives to implement assessments in early childhood settings that are meant to be developmentally and culturally appropriate. Many of us in the field maintain that the initiatives are lacking in many ways. One assessment is the Early Childhood Environment Rating Scale (ECERS). According to the National Network for Child Care Web site (2002), the ECERS

> provides an overall picture of the surroundings that have been created for the children and adults who share an early childhood setting. The ECERS consists of 43 items that assess the quality of the early childhood environment including use of space, materials and experiences to enhance children's development, daily schedule, and supervision. (first paragraph)

This ECERS evaluates personal care routines, space and furnishings, language-reasoning, activities, interactions, program structure, parents and staff on a scale from 1 to 7. A ranking of 1 indicates inadequate conditions, whereas a ranking of 7 indicates excellent conditions. A training video, an instructor's guide, and a video guide and training workbook are available to assist with training. Yet in spite of supporting programs carefully looking at their environment and its effect on learning, and the ongoing technical assistance provided in many cases, the assessment doesn't support professional development for teachers of young children in a deep or generative way.

Another assessment tool that has become popular nationwide and has been adopted by Head Start is the Classroom Assessment Scoring System (CLASS). Brookes (2008), the Web site marketing this product, emphasizes the system's the primary focus as follows:

> The importance of positive early childhood teacher–student interactions (is) the primary ingredient in creating quality educational experiences that launch future school success. With CLASS, educators finally have an observational tool to assess classroom quality in pre-kindergarten through grade 3 based on *teacher–student interactions in the classroom* rather than evaluation of the physical environment or a specific curriculum. (first paragraph, italics author's)

Although, of course, teacher–child interaction is of great significance in early learning settings, it is just one piece of a complicated web of interactions. Child–child interactions are also of ultimate importance, as well as the children's need to experience small-group and large-group social competence. Furthermore, as any early childhood teacher will affirm, focusing on one-on-one child interactions is a luxury that most teachers are not able to ethically or practically do for long periods of time due to the numbers of children in each setting. Based on the adult/child ratios and budget cuts as well as having fewer parent volunteers, a teacher's primary responsibility is to the whole group of children in his care.

I believe that the New Zealand model of learning story assessment is more comprehensive and more appropriate for participation among teachers, children, and parents, and therefore more authentic. At the same time that university students are beginning their study of curriculum development and working in their student teaching placements, they are also taking a concurrent assessment class along with the curriculum class. The textbook for the assessment class is *Assessment in Early Childhood Settings: Learning Stories* by Margaret Carr. The professors and students also relied heavily on the New Zealand Ministry of Education Web site about early childhood assessment (http://www.educate.ece.govt.nz/learning/curriculumAndLearning/Assessment forlearning/KeiTuaotePae/Book17.aspx).

The university assessment class uses problem-posing (based on critical theory), similar to that used in the curriculum class, to support students' understanding and use of the information in the curriculum as they grapple with issues of assessment. For example, in the listening section of one assessment class, the students were asked to review the field notes in their journals and identify a child or a small group of children that they had been focused on, noting patterns in the day-to-day experiences of the children. In the *Dialogue* section, the students shared their data about the children with a partner. Then in the Action section, they participated in jigsaw activity about a certain topic, such as Learning Dispositions in the Carr (2001) text. Then, they were asked to refer to the Early Childhood Education Web site and use the learning story of one toddler, Daniel, as a guide, review their own journal notes about children they were working with, and make an outline of a learning story about literacy learning on chart paper. They then shared their thoughts with the whole class. The structure of the learning stories in these examples was a simple narrative description that answered the following questions:

1. What's happening?
2. What aspect of competence does this assessment exemplify?
3. How might this documented assessment contribute to developing competence?
4. What might this assessment tell us about informal noticing, recognizing, and responding that occurs in this setting?
5. What's next?

In an Action homework assignment given toward the end of the semester of the combined curriculum and assessment class, students are assigned activities such as the ones listed below, in which they continue practicing going into more depth with the curriculum work and understanding the assessments. The activities include:

- Look at your own plans and write about new learning, creativity, excitement, or constructed knowledge that children will potentially experience. Your cooperating teachers have led children through lots of conceptual development and learning to date. Your work should not repeat that learning but build upon it.
- Choose a learning story handout as a model, and write a learning story about a child doing her work.
- Read Chapter 9 in Carr and write a personalized reaction

Preliminary Findings

Through ethnographic interviews, narrative documentation of observations, and other in- and out-of-class assignments, the Early Childhood student teachers maximized their thinking about and understanding of the cultural, economic, and sociopolitical contexts of families who work as farmworkers. Students interviewed Mixtec parents of young children. The patterns of information they gathered are startling in terms of debunking stereotypes. Parents with little or no formal education have profoundly specific hopes, expectations, and aspirations for the education of their young children.

One student teacher attended a Social Justice in Education conference hosted by the university. At the conference, a group called the Tequio Youth Group, which is affiliated with the Mixteca/Indigena Community Organizing Project, came to speak about discrimination against Mixtec children as well as other indigenous Mexican populations. She writes the following note related to the conference:

> After the presentation I spoke with one young man and asked him why he thought that my very young children that I work with weren't speaking Mixteco to each other and instead were choosing to not speak (particularly at the beginning of the school year). The young man replied that many children already know the shame associated with being Mixteco and hide it from a very young age. When I heard this, I knew that this work we are doing is extremely important and that we need to create stronger and more positive home and school connections.

Another student teacher asked for help from some Mixteco-speaking parents in her classroom to help her write an English/Mixteco bilingual "quick guide for communication" to share with other teachers. The beginning of the guide reads:

MIXTECO TRANSLATIONS THAT CAN BE USED IN THE CLASSROOM.
1. What's your name? (Sha nano?)
2. Do you want to eat? (Conu cushu acon?)
3. Thank you. (Tashiovio.)
4. Do you want to play? (Conu cusiqiu?)
5. Let's go. (Coee.)
6. Please. (Kano conu.)
7. Do you need to go to the restroom? (Conu cuu banu?)
8. We are going to eat. (Coo cuche.)
9. Come here. (Na acusho.)
10. Water. (Chi qui.)

The totality of our data show that 99% of the Mixtec parents want teachers and caregivers who are bilingual in English and Spanish with some knowledge of Mixteco (their home language) and knowledge of their culture. A student teacher commented:

> I spoke with a limited number of family members during my research, but I spoke with a couple of parents who I knew well from my previous work with the children. Both family members conveyed the importance of their children being able to learn English as well as maintain their home language and cultural knowledge and awareness. The families also wanted for their children to have "educational experiences" at school. Interestingly enough, these are the same things reported by a multitude of families by other students in the semester. I think we had all come to the conclusion that we needed to find a way to value the family's culture at school.

The learning that came from the Early Childhood student teachers collaborating with county teachers and assistants was important as well. Another student reported:

> I soon turned to the teachers who have been working with the children I was observing, as well as working with this community for several years. The teacher who I worked most closely with said that she thinks it is extremely important to bring families into the classroom to share something they know how to do with the children. This helps to value to family as well as what they know how to do. This teacher conveyed that often families are working extremely long hours and are never present to

speak with personally during the school day. In this case she has found how important it is to make phone calls to these families as well as send home letters to let them
know about activities and important things that are happening in the classroom. I also
spoke with the site supervisor at this school and she conveyed the importance in making strong connections between staff and families in order for the family to feel valued in the program.

A related finding in our data shows that 98% of families prefer licensed early
care and education programs, and 99% want their children to have access to
educational activities and nutritious food. All of them are adamant that they
need access to affordable quality child care seven days a week because of their
work in the agricultural fields.

Finally, an example of a writing that shows an Early Childhood student
teacher moving from narrative study to action (in the sense of transformative
action of critical pedagogy) follows:

One of my concerns when working with parents was that some of them were unable
to read and/or write. I found out that in the Mixteco families many of the women have
little or no literacy skills. One of my interviews was with Ms. AG, a 62 year old
woman. She had a rough childhood. She was the oldest of a family of 12. She took care
of her brothers and sisters and she didn't get the opportunity to go to school and learn
to read or write. Ms. G would like to take classes to build her skills in reading and writing. She feels very frustrated and stressed because she wants to become an American
Citizen and she finds it impossible.

Ms. I D is a 48 year old woman who came from a small village from Mexico. She
never learned to read nor write. She also took care of her younger siblings, just as Ms.
G did. In the small village the parents decided if they wanted to send their children
to school Ms. D's parents didn't want to send their oldest girl to school. She was more
useful to them in taking care of her siblings. Ms. D has learned to obtain information
and communicate with others. She has learned to copy her name and has mastered the
bus schedule. Some of these families lack the simple skills that are essential for daily
life. They have come to me to get assistance with filling out a simple application, reading medicine labels or understanding simple written text. There are some programs in
our community that can help adults with literacy, but not enough.

Among other activities, I conducted a parent workshop (within my regular class
routine in the classroom with children) was to introduce an activity making it clear
that Early Literacy was an important part in children's education and together we can
help children obtain language and start an early enjoyment to literacy. The purpose
for this activity is to have parents and children begin an Early Literacy Interaction by
exposing children to the joy of reading, to establish a routine, and introduce early literacy at home. A wide selection of books is place in a basket for allowing children to
have a selection of books. I started giving one book every Monday, each child has plastic zip bag in that bag they will place their book of choice, in addition to a half sheet

of paper is provided in the bag. A half sheet paper includes 3 questions (in Spanish) parents are to involve children by asking questions and writing down what children say. The questions are: Who was in the story? What happen in the story? What happened at the end? Parents or other family members can read the story two or three the together parent/child answer questions. The parents only write what children say, at the end of the school year teacher/parents can see the growth of children's vocabulary and language. After 2 weeks parents asked if they could borrow books to take home and read to their children, so I develop a book borrowing system so parent could have the opportunity to check out books on a daily basis. Children enjoyed taking their books and pretending they had homework with their parents. It was a wonderful activity to do with the families.

The student teacher, now a graduate and lead teacher, then wrote:

After reviewing this information it inspires me to continue with these activities, to promote early literacy not just to young children but also develop literacy with adults. One of my goals is to continue building relationships with families and get to know them, then create programs and parent education meetings to help them meet their needs. These needs consist of getting involved in parent education, participating in job training opportunities, and enabling them with the skills necessary to read to their children and help them with homework. Also, the most important outcome is to help these individuals become well-educated consumers, active citizens, informed voters, and take an active role in their child's education.

Voices of Possibility

The poet Gloria Anzaldúa speaks of surviving in borderlands, of being a crossroad. I believe that the current world, in which borders are in a state of flux with tenuous peace and in which governments come and go, families and schools become the crossroads. The international voices of teachers, of students, and of families and friends in our communities can be voices of possibility if only we can listen and learn from each other. According to Anzaldúa (1999, p. 195),

To survive the Borderlands
you must live sin fronteras
be a crossroads.

Reflective Questions

The following questions are designed to help student teachers practice with the problem-posing method of Listening, Dialogue, and Action:

Listening

1. Journal briefly about your earliest memories of literacy (oral, print, visual, music, etc.) in your own experience as a young child.
2. Write about experiences you have had with and knowledge about young children in migrant education programs. Do you believe that their life experiences and situation of possible poverty and oppression prevent their learning curiosity? In what ways? What is your evidence?
3. Write about an instance when you observed children using their home language in school, during play, and in situations of new learning.

Dialogue

In small groups, the following questions can be discussed:

1. What opinions do you believe migrant families have about the most optimum situations for childcare for their young children?
2. What are your thoughts about migrant families wanting their children to only learn English and not develop home languages that may be different from English?
3. How would you explain any connections you see between memories of your early experiences and the experiences of some of the children you work with?

Action

1. Observe a group of children in an early childhood program. What do they do, what do they say, and how can you tell what they know? How would you describe this knowledge in a narrative format?
2. Describe a child, from your observations, using critical theory or critical literacy in the context of his life.

Visit the following Web site to investigate the information about Learning Stories and discuss it with your classmates: http://www.educate.ece.govt.nz/learning/curriculumAndLearning/Assessmentforlearning/KeiTuaotePae/Book17.aspx

References

Anzaldúa, G. (1999). *Borderlands: The new mestiza/La frontera*. San Francisco, CA: Spinsters/Aunt Lute Press.

Brookes. (2008). *Classroom Assessment Scoring System*. Retrieved from http://www.brookespublishing.com/store/books/pianta-class/index.htm

Carr, M. (2001). *Assessment in Early Childhood Settings: Learning Stories*. Thousand Oaks, CA: Sage.

Carr, M., Duncan, J., Lee, W., Jones, C., Marshall, K., & Smith, A. (2009). *Learning in the making: Disposition and design in early education*. Rotterdam, Netherlands: Sense.

Ely, M., Anzul, M., Friedman, T., Garner, D., & McCormack-Steinmetz, A. (1991). *Doing qualitative research: Circles within circles*. New York, NY: Routledge.

Fox, J., & Rivera-Salgado, G. (Eds.). (2004). *Indigenous Mexican migrants in the United States*. Stanford, CA: Center for Comparative Immigration Studies.

Freire, P. (1985). *Politics of Education*. Granby, MA: Bergin & Garvey.

Freire, P. (1997). *Pedagogy of hope*. Granby, MA: Bergin & Garvey.

Leonardo, Z. (2004). Critical social theory and transformative knowledge: The functions of criticism in quality education. *Educational Researcher 33*(6), 11–18.

Loeb, S., Fuller, B., Kagan, S. L., Carrol, B., & Carroll, J. (2004). Child care in poor communities: Early learning effects of type, quality, and stability. *Child Development, 75*(1), 47–65.

Moll, L. C., Gonzalez, N., & Amanti, C. (2005). *Funds of knowledge: Theorizing practices in households, communities, and classrooms*. Mahwah, NJ: Lawrence Erlbaum Associates.

National Network for Child Care. (2002). *Early Childhood Environment Rating Scale*. Retrieved from http://www.nncc.org/Evaluation/ecers.html

New Zealand Ministry of Education. (2010). Retrieved from http://www.educate.ece.govt.nz/

Pinar, W. (2004). *What is curriculum theory?* Mahwah, NJ: Erlbaum.

Quintero, E. P. (2010). Something to say: Children learning through story, *Early Education & Development 21*(3), 372–391.

Quintero, E. P., & Rummel, Mary K. (2010). Problem Posing, Reflection, Action: Literature and Our Lives, in Rhodes, C. (Ed.) *Literature and social justice*, International Reading Association.

Schweinhart, L. J., Barnes, H. V., Weikart, D. P., Barnett, W. S., & Epstein, A. S. (1993). *Significant benefits: The High/Scope Perry Preschool Study through Age 27*. Ypsilanti, MI: High/Scope Press.

Shonkoff, J., & Phillips, D. A. (Eds.). (2000). *From neurons to neighborhoods: The science of early childhood development*. Washington, DC: National Academy Press.

Smith, S. S. (2005). *Early Childhood Mathematics*. New York: Allyn & Bacon.

Steinberg, S., & Kincheloe, J. (2009). Smoke and mirrors: More than one way to be diverse and multicultural. In S. Steinberg (Ed.) *Diversity and multiculturalism: A reader*. New York, NY: Peter Lang.

Wright. A. (2005). *The death of Ramón González*. Austin: University of Texas Press.

· 1 0 ·

Who Am I?

Urban (ELL) Teachers and Students Create Narratives and Professional Stance Through Cultural Texts

BRETT ELIZABETH BLAKE

Explorations in linguistics show that narrative traditions differ significantly across cultures—in structure, schemas, rhetorical styles, storytelling conventions and devices and embody cultural values that are particularly evident in judgments as to which events are considered salient and tellable. (Pavlenko, 2002, p. 214)

Elsewhere in this book, narrative has been alternately described as a "way of knowing," a "positive source of insight," a method to conduct "inquiry," an "opportunity to advance thinking about education and practice," a "window to Reader Response," and, of course, as an avenue for teachers to construct, reflect upon, and potentially reconstruct their personal theories of teaching (in a particular field) into what was outlined in the introductory chapter as a teacher's "professional stance."

In this chapter, I want to shift gears just a bit. Because I have spent my entire adult life working with, teaching, and writing about urban students who have primarily been English language learners (ELL), my perspective on narrative and its benefits for teacher education is, perhaps, more of a "global" one—that is, I believe that the power of narrative not only lies in its ability to provide insight across disciplines for both teachers and students, as described throughout the previous chapters but also in its ability to provide insight across all other branches of human and natural science (see Chapter 2). And yet, both our own and our students' narratives as a professional stance are powerfully shaped by the cultural, social, and historical conventions of our own culture(s) and our position in that culture on a macro- and microlevel—in terms of our language, social status, gender, and so on.

For example, in the United States, as well as in other Western cultures, historical autobiography has, as Pavlenko (2002) puts it, "evolved as a Western construction" (p. 214); one that is held in high status as evidenced by the numerous reviews each week in the Book Review section of *The New York Times*. In other cultures, life identity stories may not exist as a genre, or if they do, they are not constructed and/or told the same way that we might expect in our own classrooms (see Quintero's chapter on migrant families and their children, for example). And, more important, these written works may not be interpreted using the same background knowledge of a culture's particular language and language structure. That is, when we, as United States teachers of ELLs, seek to use story as a powerful tool with which to "get at" our teaching in more productive ways as well as to get at our ELL students' lives in richer ways, we run the risk, quite simply, of imposing our narrative stance and therefore our voice and our *meaning* onto those of our students. Such an imposition actually works against the great benefits of using narrative (as defined in previous chapters) in our classrooms. But that does mean we should not use narratives.

In this chapter, I want to first discuss the place and importance of using "voice" and the idea behind using cultural texts to discuss narrative and story within the contexts of urban ELLs in today's global society. Then, I will present students' "identity stories" and other narratives as a response to various classroom activities (i.e., responses to literature, process-writing activities, and poetry), in order to highlight how these stories of being an ELL, an immigrant, and/or the "Other" have helped shaped teachers' narratives. Their narratives, in turn, afforded these teachers the ability to reflect on their own identities and develop their own set of narratives and professional stances of who they are as teachers of urban ELL students. Finally, I will emphasize the importance of interpreting students' narratives in multiple, and critical, ways, and from multiple points of view, taking great care to legitimize all stories so that we do not run the risk of silencing voices in the classroom that are different from ours.

Developing Voice

Voice is an elusive and problematic construct, and yet its expression remains a central struggle among our urban ELLs today (especially amid increasing standardized testing and teacher/student accountability both across grades and across disciplines) for two major reasons: First, too often voice is equated with empowerment or cultural identity (Cummins, 1986; Ferdman, 1990). The implicit assumption in this belief holds that by giving students the opportunity to create narrative—or story—through bringing their own personal experiences into the classroom, they can move closer to their true cultural identity, thus being empowered, or "given voice" by the teacher and/or the experience itself. Ferdman's (1990) central thesis rests on just that notion: He suggests that students (especially those from "minority" backgrounds) can be empowered by being "permitted to discover and explore ethnic connections" (p. 20).

Second, voice (and, thereby, the created narrative) runs the risk of being the construction of someone else's (e.g., the teacher's) interpretative stance— a stance that may be altogether different from that of the diverse urban ELL, for example, but one that is fully determined—by students wishing to please the teacher and/or to receive a good grade from her. Delpit (1986, 1988) reminds us that too often, "a certain paternalism creeps into the speech of some of our liberal colleagues as they explain that our children must be 'given voice'" (1986, p. 384).

Both the terms *empowerment* and *interpretation*, then, must be viewed with a critical eye; that is, because voice and therefore the construction and the writing/rewriting of a piece is always done from an interactive, sociocultural-constructivist point of view and is heavily (and inescapably) situated in the various historical contexts that have helped shape what both the writer *and* the reader bring to a text. Just as a text is never neutral, neither is voice; it cannot be devoid of the contexts that traditional literacy and literature theorists might suggest (especially regarding our schools' and on our states' standardized exams). Rather, voice is developed and expressed through a wide range of contexts and experiences, contexts that are always present and never static. Voice is marked with the voices of both prior and present contexts. In other words, there is always a multitude of often-competing contradictory voices emanating through a single narrative or a single story, by both the writer and the reader. And both sets of voices are the voices of intent, experience, knowledge, and opinion, as well as of culture.

However, acknowledging this interplay among voices, by allowing both readers and writers to not only recognize but also to appreciate diverse students' stories, does not automatically ensure that this diversity is expressed by the students in an honest and meaningful way. After all, the dominant discourse remains dominant because students are so well trained to appropriate that which they know is most revered, most acceptable. In short, the expression (of voice) itself does not ensure that the voice (throughout the narrative) is authentic, and it certainly does not mean that those of us who interpret the piece "get it right." As Ruiz (1991) so eloquently argued several years ago, "to have a voice implies not just that people can say things, but that they are heard" (p. 220).

Developing Cultural Texts

When one composes a text, one indeed composes a social self (Bakhtin, 1981, 1986; Dyson, 1992, 1993). As students write, they weave in stories of their lives and experiences, shaping their texts as they shape their identities, linking themselves to their worlds and to the worlds of peers and school through their words. According to Bakhtin, the act of composing a story is always an act of "dialogism." That is, as Ewald (1993) describes, when a student uses his words to create and recreate, he "necessarily engages or responds to past and present discourses," as each word "smells of the context(s) in which it has lived its intense social life" (p. 332). A cultural text, then, is a text that "smells" of context, of experience, of the students' realities. In the urban ELL classroom, for example, it is a text that releases scents of gender, of race, of class, of linguistic heritage, and of community—a narrative that reflects particular aspirations, struggles, challenges, hopes, and aspirations (Figure 10.1). And like all the narratives we have read in previous chapters, it too is a narrative that deserves to be heard.

Student and Teacher Narratives: Who Am I?

Jose, a seventh grader, writes the following impression of racism in the United States:

> Racism is a major problem in this country. I think that a law should be passed to restrict racism and get cops to arrest anyone who is being racious [sic]. Still, this might not fix the problem, so there are alternatives. One thing that should be done is to teach young kids from an early age why racism is bad and what should be done to help get rid of it. This will end up stopping racism dramaticly [sic]. Another useful tactic to stop racism

would be to show how each of us are different and unique but it should be known as a [sic] amazing thing, not a bad thing. This might help people change or have a change of heart. (seventh-grade math classroom)

Ms. L. (reluctantly and under my guidance in a graduate human relations course) posed the question that Jose responded to above ("What does racism mean to you?") to her students. As a first-year seventh-grade urban math teacher, Ms. L. did not feel that the math classroom was an appropriate place to ask students to write, especially about something so dangerous and so obviously not in the state math curricula. But she did, and this is what she had to say:

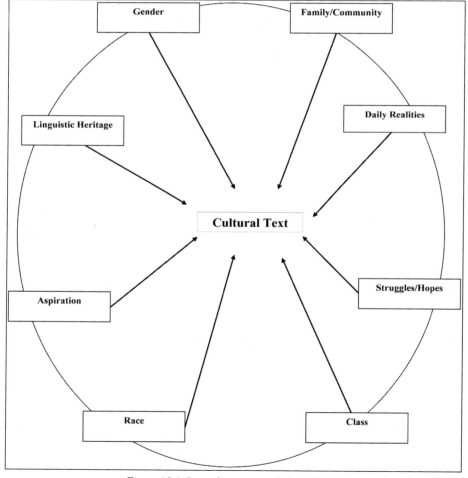

Figure 10.1 Interplays among Cultural Text

After reading the stories of some of my students I was able to understand the differences between them. The stories revealed that many of my students have been through a lot at their young ages. I teach Mathematics so doing a task like this is a little more difficult because I deal with numbers. These writings have helped me to appreciate my students more, and it has also helped them to feel much more comfortable with me. When you learn about your students and you show that you care it is easier to teach because you form a connection and create strong bonds. My reflections have helped me to become a better teacher. The reason for this is because I had never been asked to write about something as sensitive as race, immigration, etc. The messages we send to our urban children are negative. We need to create a classroom culture that is supportive. [All student and teachers' names are pseudonyms; all writing has been left as the original text except where meaning might be lost.]

Other preservice and in-service teachers whom I have worked with over the last several years developed other avenues in which they could tap into their students' notions of "who am I?" learning that these responses might help them become better teachers of an often-challenging population. (Most of these data comes from students in an in-service graduate class, many of whom were "career changers," students who were leaving other professions such as law, social work, and engineering, usually in midlife, to come to teaching. The class was a required human relations in inclusive setting course that (loosely) focused on topics of identity, race, class, gender, immigration, educational practices, and policies. It is not my intent here to describe my methodology; suffice it to say I used qualitative inquiry in discovering and uncovering themes and categories around student and teacher stories and narrative. For example, one of my kindergarten preservice teachers used an activity called Circles of My Multicultural Self (Gorski, n.d.) to discuss the meaning of diversity at a large public school in New York City. The preservice teacher explains (see Figure 10.2):

The students and I read the short poem together while using our fingers to point to the different objects and body parts mentioned. The goal was to help these 20 students from various cultures, ethnicities, and religions to understand that although we may all look different, we are all the same and we all need love. Then, I introduced a Venn diagram activity—My Partner and I: Same and Different. I explained to the students what a Venn diagram is and how it works. It was pure joy to observe the children ask each other questions and get to know each other better. It was even more joyful to hear some students exclaim that they never knew certain facts about their classmates. And both I and the teacher learned that even kindergarten students can learn about the crucial issue that faces them on a daily basis: diversity.

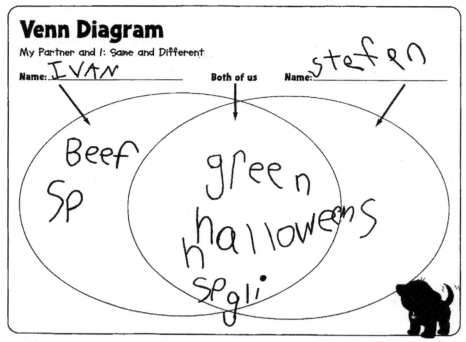

Figure 10.2 My Partner and I: Same and Different sample from Kindergarten class.

Here is what one of my third/fourth grade (combined classroom) teachers said about learning to work with her urban ELLs after designing a (very!) creative activity around flavors of ice cream (See Figure 10.3):

> Recently, I conducted an identity profile activity with my students. I teach a combined 3rd and 4th grade class where children are at the age of developing their self-image and confidence. To introduce the activity, I asked my students to imagine themselves at an ice cream truck on a warm summer day. I asked them to think of what flavor of ice cream they would most like to order—I told them that just as they enjoyed different flavors of ice cream, they had different aspects of their personalities and of their cultures to share. I felt this identity profile went over well with my students. Students were eager to share their work and by completing this activity, I feel my students were able to get a better sense of who they were—their qualities, their interests, and characteristics—as well as their classmates, and I learned that the more they know about each other, the better self-images they have and the better they seem to get along!

Figure 10.3 Grade 4 student ice cream cone as a representation of diversity of self.

Student and Teacher Narratives: Evolving Identities

Once students enter the middle grades, the subject of identity and "who am I?" seems to play an even more pivotal role. Struggling with the new and often more demanding content in various classrooms, the onset of adolescence can be daunting to any child. And for urban ELLs, add a new language and a new school culture, as well as a new societal one, and you have a mix for a challenging teaching situation! This seems especially true in today's school culture, as middle school is the place where name calling and bullying of all forms (e.g., cyber-bullying) is said to reach its peak. One of my sixth-grade teachers, Ms. F., felt so strongly about the bullying in her urban middle school classroom that she took time out of each day to ask students to write and talk about this very real problem. Here is the end of what Ms. F. says after she had successfully created activities that would evoke students' stories of their bullying:

I think all teachers should be required to ask students to write some sort of identity story with their students at least once a year. Not only could it help defend children against bullying and name-calling, but it will help students to develop a healthy self-identity, and that makes my job easier!

She continues:

We hear about it all the time. The news broadcasts it as another child who has taken their own life because of bullying. It starts with simple name-calling, a sort of "past-time" of American schools. My students are sixth-graders who are naturally starting to discover who their real friends are. Due to this, we have been dealing with name-calling and bullying on numerous occasions. I decided to help my students understand the impact of this and to provide them with a way to combat it. So, I had them write down a list of hurtful names they have been called in their lives. Then they wrote down feelings and aspects of their personalities they wish the name-callers knew about them.

Here are three sample narratives of what the students had to say:

Student 1

Names I have been called: Rudolf the Red nose reindeer, Buck tooth, ugly

How I felt when I was called those names: When I was called these names I felt angry. I felt angry because the people who called me these names had taken the time and effort to think of a pointless name (one not so original) just to make me feel bad. But later I didn't feel angry I felt a little happy because I stuck out to them. Out of everyone else they saw me/doesn't sound right. Sounded better before I wrote it.

Something you wish a person knew about you: Something I wish a person would know is that I'm a nice person. I've never hurt anyone and I would never hurt someone because I would get nothing from it.

Student 2

Names I have been called: Stupid Egyptian, Asshole, Idiot, Faggot, Dumbass

How I felt when I was called those names: I felt left out, I just wanted to kill myself and just quit my sports' teams and quite everything. I would just want to stay home for the rest of my life. I would want to ask that person why does he curse and make fun of me. (Not suicide. I'm not crazy).

Something you wish a person knew about you: I would wish to tell that person that I can beat them in academics and sports. After that he will be sorry.

Student 3

Names I have been called: Stupid, dumb, seriously skinny, and that I have problems, terribLe at math.

How I felt when I was called these names: I didn't want to talk, burst into tears, go home, lock myself in a room and never show my face.

Something you wish a person knew about you: That I am a survivor, when I was little I had kidney surgery. I actually had it twice when I was born. I didn't have enough blood, and I had little of a kidney, so they cut it off. Doctors didn't know if I was going to live.

Ms. F. says in response to the narratives:

After reading these, I realized that the students also needed an avenue in which they could express positive aspects of themselves, and so I designed an activity where they could highlight the positive dimensions of themselves. First, I asked students to use a web to enter descriptors (words) of themselves that were positive and important to them. Then, I ask them to write short paragraphs or stories to three prompts.

Here is what the same three sixth graders had to say in response to the follow-up prompt for an activity, "Share a story about a time you were especially proud to identify yourself with one of the descriptors you put in the web."

Student 1. I am very proud to be althetic because one day I saved my little brother in the pool because I knew how to swim.

Student 2. Well, I am proud to be an Egyptian and British mix because both countries are good with awesome history and of course great food.

Student 3. When I scored the first goal.

Here is what they say in response to the prompt "Share a story about a time it was especially painful to be identified with one of your words above":

Student 1. It was painful to be latino one day because I went to a store and bought something, then the manager told me that I took something, just because I am Spanish.

Student 2. When I went to Egypt 2 years ago, I went to eat at a restaurant, so the waiter asked what religion am I, and I told them I'm a Coptic orthodox. So they kicked me out.

Student 3. It sometimes is hard to be a girl because boys think they're better than girls. Also because boys play rough so they don't want you to get hurt.

Here is what they said in response to the prompt "Name a stereotype associated with one of the groups with which you identify that is not like who you are": "I am [blank] but I am NOT [blank]."

Student 1. I am latino but I am NOT stupid.

Student 2. I am funny but I am NOT dumb.

Student 3. I am a girl, but I am NOT dainty.

Student and Teacher Narratives: Power and Honor

In high school, student narratives tend to shift from the name calling, bullying, and "who am I?" in terms of ice cream flavors, to real-world exclamations of who they are as human beings in an urban context—as "minority," poor young men and women who truly struggle with the injustices they see around them. Ms. L., an urban public school student herself many years ago, says,

Through their narratives, it became very clear to me that they all want to be successful, they care about their communities, they love their families and they are cognizant of racism and prejudice. Here are excerpts of my students' narratives:

Sample 1. Who am I? Who shall I be? Where shall I go? Why am I here? I love to be powerful and honored in great ways. I don't look for comfort, but inspiration to do great things that would better me and my community.

Sample 2. I wish the government would help this community more but there are a few people like me in my community who care and want change. Clearly, I am an understandable young woman who likes to fight to make wrongs right. I would like to see and watch people that I talk to go through changes. I like to help and would love to stay and be a successful female in America.

Sample 3. Being a Hispanic young mother, people have many prejudices against you. You'll end up on welfare, uneducated and depending on everyone else. Not me. I plan on becoming a teacher. I'm ready to provide for my child....I'm not going to be a statistic or failure.

Sample 4. One stereotype that I know people have against African Americans is that we steal all the time and have no home training. Racism in my world exists . . . racism comes in different forms. It can be in small gestures or in big words.

A former corporate executive turned New York City Teaching Fellow, Ms. L. concludes:

> It became apparent to me [through these stories] that we became educators because we wanted to make connections with young people, some of us realized that working in corporate environments would never provide great rewards but excellent financial bonuses while others realized that there is great satisfaction in watching other people accomplish a goal because of our help and wisdom.

Mr. F., another former business executive, reflects on his own life as an immigrant to connect to his students:

> I have learned to be patient with parents who don't speak the language. We need to focus on our own cultural histories to fully help our students. Using my experience as a child of immigrants who believed in education, but were unable to help me with homework, I always felt that students had no excuse for not doing well in school. But I have to remember how challenging and confusing school was for me as I'm sure it is for today's students. Their cultural identity is no doubt a factor to their confusion. Wishing to be part of the dominant culture and being true to their ethnicities may conflict with each other. This year, I focused simply on education and learning and never tried to make a cultural connection. I felt that I had failed them. . . .

In other classes, high school teachers tried to move beyond the "simple" narrative of identity or "who am I?" by using literature and poetry writing to get at their students' stories. As a junior/senior-level English teacher, Mr. C. remarks,

> Narratives, where they existed, often followed their immigration experiences (as I had seen before when reading their college essays). Frequently, they expressed a lot of the same difficulties we had seen in class: learning English, making friends, approaching school as an outsider. It was interesting to me to see how many of them took it in this direction. One of the great things about being an English teacher [though] is one of the great duties of literature . . . Who Am I? . . . It's a question that goes all the way back to Plato! So perhaps it is my duty to highlight literature that encourages students

to ask questions of themselves. . . . Toni Cade Bambara's "The Lesson" and Alice
Walker's "Everyday Use" both talk about the way African-Americans construct personal and social identities.

And in another high school English class, Ms. S. tells us:

Many of my students identified with a Caribbean county as home. Over 50% were born
elsewhere and of the remaining, most were first-generation. The pride in their country
was strong. As an educator I value presentations and poetry in the classroom. For my
student pieces, we were working on the novel *The Outsiders* by S. E. Hinton. In groups
they created a BioPoem for the character, "Ponyboy." Then, using the same format below,
created one that reflected their own self.

Line 1:   Your first name only
Line 2:   4 traits that describe you
Line 3:   Daughter/son of *or* sibling of
Line 4:   Who loves (3 items, places, or people)
Line 5:   Who feels (3 items)
Line 6:   Who needs (3 items)
Line 7:   Who gives (3 items)
Line 8:   Who fears (3 items)
Line 9:   Who would like to see (3 items)
Line 10:   Who lives in
Line 11:   Your last name only

The sample (with names changed) of one student, Maria, reads:

Mean, cold-hearted, heartless, nice
Daughter of Naomi and Jose Reyes
Who loves hearing emo and rock music, on computer and drawing
Who feels nothing for other, mean, and sometimes happy
Who needs help with problems at home, money myself
Who give no feeling for other and their suffer, meaning and nothing
Who fears my own weakness, emotions, and past-life
Who would like to see Mexico, Honduras and other places
WHO LIVES IN NEW YORK CITY IN BROOKLYN
REYES

Ms. S. writes:

As I began to reflect [on what they had written] I realized that in my minority classroom, I am the "outsider" until I shed those layers like I had asked them to through

their poetry. [In my first year of teaching], I never connected with my students, nor did I understand their traditions. I was a minority. Even among the staff, I was the only Caucasian teacher. The few Jamaican women who made up the majority of the teachers, had their own language, sayings, and culture I longed to understand.

Teacher Narratives: What Have Students' Stories Told Us? Who Am I as a Professional? How Have Student Narratives Made Me a Better Teacher?

Next, I present the short narratives of various (and potential) classroom teachers as they reflect on just exactly how students' stories can open their eyes to becoming better teachers to developing that professional stance we have talked about throughout this book. Here, I have identified each teacher by race/ethnicity in shorthand terms, that is, by designating one as African American and another as Asian, for example, knowing that these simplistic labels only capture a very small part of who they are—but a part that others certainly see immediately: skin color, gender, shape of face, dress, and when one opens one's mouth—dialect.

Mr. A (African-American)

At 10 years old I learned that being black had limitations. You did not have the privileges the members of the dominant culture enjoyed. For example, you were restricted to where you wanted to go eat in public places. Every student has a story too . . . I feel that I become a better teacher by listening to my students' stories.

Ms. D (Angla)

I would have them base their narratives on their own personal experiences, so that the class can learn from this; especially extracting the various diversity elements as a teaching tool.

Ms. C. (Latina)

A student's story will help me to see them not as deficient but as different. I never want to blame to student's family life or community for any kind of deficiency. I want to be able to understand a student's differences and bring those differences into a positive light.

Mr. G. (Anglo)

Stories highlight elements in a student's life that may have been difficult or painful. Being able to relate to your students is one of the most imperative and challenging tasks for today's inner-city teachers. It is a personal look into the strengths and weaknesses, but also shows us what students know best and thrive on.

Mr. W. (Asian)

I have been able to sympathize with the student stories I've been reading, especially the foreign students who had the hardest time adjusting to America. While reading passages about their confusion and tears in the classroom, I felt their pain as if I was suffering along with them. I hope I can become a more sympathizing teacher in the future instead of a controlling one.

Ms. P. (African American)

While I don't think I ever believed that my students lacked the characteristics to succeed in school, I do think I was easily swayed into the idea that the institutionalized racism that they have dealt with their entire school careers could somehow excuse lower expectations for them. When students didn't perform as expected, I quickly blamed society on their behalf and was often, albeit unintentionally, less diligent in my search for ways to make them succeed. I know that I can't dismiss the impact of institutionalized racism in my students' education, but I do have to be careful not to use it as an excuse either. It is my job as a teacher to give them tools to overcome the roadblocks and the injustices that they have faced and will inevitably face after they leave my classroom.

Ms. O. (Angla)

In order to more clearly understand who we are as individuals, we need to better understand who we are as a society and culture . . . understanding our culture will help us understand ourselves and others. This works both ways: an understanding of individual identities promotes a greater understanding of societies and cultures. One of the biggest challenges facing teachers today, whether in-service or pre-service is how to be effective with all learners. As shifting demographics in schools provided greater ethnic and linguistic diversity, teacher candidates continue to be predominantly white, middle-class, and female. How can a white middle-class teacher best instruct an impoverished person of color from an unstable family background whose first language is not English?

A simple answer to the above question would suggest that a teacher candidate should do some student teaching in schools with diverse student populations and to get to know her students as well as possible in order to best accommodate their needs. The real work of overcoming prejudices in the classroom begins with an honest examination one's own personal bias and racism and deep reflection on how to overcome this. As I continue on my journey as a teacher and strive to become better with each class I teach, I am humbly reminded that I have much to learn from my students and an ever-growing admiration for those students who achieve success despite overwhelming odds. We enter into this noble profession with high ideals of academic success for those we will teach; we must always be mindful that this opportunity must be available to all.

Final Thoughts and Reflective Questions

Throughout this chapter, I have highlighted three interrelated findings about using narrative and/or story in our urban ELL classrooms: First, when we as teachers write stories about our lives, it helps us to learn about ourselves—our own prejudices, biases, expectations, or understandings of the world around us—which in turn allows us to see our students better. Second, by proceeding to ask our urban students to tell us the stories of their lives, however challenging or frightening they may be, we are then in the position to do the "critical work" involved with becoming "better" teachers. And finally, using narratives and story in our classrooms helps us—whether by teachers or students—to shape our cultural identity and situate ourselves and our stories, we hope, in a larger globalized context that acknowledges and appreciates the diverse voices from around the world.

This critical work or critical response to the texts of our students and to our own lives, we believe, is the most powerful way to get at this thing we call teaching. Teaching framed from this perspective, according to Kincheloe (2010) and others, is based on the tenets of "critical pedagogy," which Kincheloe (2010) says is:

- grounded on visions of justice and equality;
- concerned that students don't hurt students—good schools don't blame students for their failures or strip students of the knowledges they bring to the classroom
- enacted through the use of generative themes to read the word and the world
- centered on the notion that teachers should be researchers—here teachers learn to produce and teach students to produce their own knowledges

- concerned with "the margins" of society, the experiences and needs of individuals faced with oppression and subjugation;
- attuned to the importance of complexity in constructing a rigorous and transformative education; and
- grounded on the notion that teachers become researchers of their students, in that as researchers, teachers study their students, their backgrounds, and the forces that shape them. (p. 10).

I believe that in all areas of teaching, such a critical response to our students' texts takes center stage in our quest to become critical pedagogues. According to Pavlenko (2002), in doing so successfully, we:

> uncover how particular configurations of power relations allow some learners, but not others, access to linguistic resources, whether to learn a language, or to tell their own story. Most important, such an approach will allow us to examine our own roles in privileging certain narrative styles over others and in silencing certain voices while emphasizing others—thus moving us forward in the implementation of more critical approaches. (p. 217)

Reflective Questions

1. Who are you? Design a web with your name in the center—branch out from the center circle emphasizing the cultural (family, religious) aspects of your life that are important to you. Be as creative as you like. Which aspects are most important for you as teachers to acknowledge in your students?
2. What is the difference between what the author terms a cultural text and what all previous authors have called narrative or stories? Are these distinctions important? Why or why not?
3. Ask your students to design a cultural web like the one previously described, adding a short narrative explaining their choices. Read their responses and ask yourself what you have learned about your students that will now make you a better teacher. Why? How? What are some other specific techniques you will use in your classrooms to better get at your students' cultural identities?

References

Bakhtin, M. (1981). *The dialogic imagination*. Austin: University of Texas Press.

Bakhtin, M. (1986). *Speech genres and other late essays*. Austin: University of Texas Press.

Cummins, J. (1986). Empowering minority students: A framework for intervention. *Harvard Educational Review, 56*(1), 18–36.

Delpit, L. D. (1986). Skills and other dilemmas of a progressive Black educator. *Harvard Educational Review, 56*(4), 379–385.

Delpit, L. D. (1988). The silenced dialogue: Power and pedagogy in educating other people's children. *Harvard Educational Review, 58*(3), 84–102

Dyson, A. H. (1992). Whistle for Willie, lost puppies and cartoon dogs: The sociocultural dimensions of young childrens' composing. *Journal of Reading Behavior, XXIV*, 443–462.

Dyson, A. H. (1993). *Social worlds of children learning to write in an urban primary school*. New York, NY: Teachers College Press.

Ewald, H. R. (1993). Waiting for answerability: Bakhtin and composition studies. *College Composition and Communication, 44*(3), 331–348.

Ferdman, B. M. 1990. Literacy and cultural identity. *Harvard Educational Review.60*, (2), 181–204.

Gorski, P. C. (n.d.) Circles of My Multicultural Self. Retrieved from the EdChange Web site: http://www.edchange.org/ multicultural/activities/circlesofself.html

Kincheloe, J. L. (2010). *Knowledge and critical pedagogy*. London, United Kingdom: Springer.

Pavlenko, A. (2002). Narrative study: Whose story is it anyway? *TESOL Quarterly 36*(2), 213–218.

Ruiz, R. (1991). The empowerment of language minority students. In C. E. Sleeter (Ed.), *Empowerment through multicultural education* (pp. 217–227). Albany, NY: SUNY Press.

Afterword:
Telling Stories out of School

WILLIAM AYERS

In the 1930s over 100,000 people of African descent were still alive who had once been held as chattel slaves inside the United States. In just two years, from 1936 to 1938, writers and historians who were part of a federal program called the Works Progress Administration (WPA) interviewed over 2,000 formerly enslaved people and collected their stories and narratives by hand, without benefit of audio or video recorders. A rich archive of first-person accounts was created, and not a moment too soon—the last generation of people held in bondage was aging and passing away, and with them all the textured and nuanced memories of the experience of slavery, all the specific meaning and interpretations of historic events as seen through the eyes and the unique lenses of people who had endured slavery from the inside. The slave narrative archive provides an essential resource for understanding the period generally, as well as the lived lives of the millions of human beings who suffered the "peculiar institution" that so profoundly shaped, and continues to shape, the American story. This archive combined with the discovery and dissemination by scholars of earlier autobiographical accounts of slavery (mostly unpublished) transformed the field of antebellum history. No honest history of the US written in the last half century has been able to ignore the power of the slave narratives.

The Writer's Project of the WPA engaged 6000 writers, and slavery was only one focus; others included agriculture, mines, factories, music, and folklore. A stated goal of the project was to "turn the streets and the hiring halls into literature"; indeed over 800 books were eventually published based on this work, and writers like Studs Terkel, Richard Wright and many others earned their chops in these fields. More recently *Voices of Freedom*, a published oral history of the great Black Freedom Movement in the US, contains over 1000 interviews that were conducted and edited, sent to participants for clarification and further editing, and then presented in relation to key events from the Movement. This is "event-driven" oral history, as opposed to person-centered work. And in 2010, Isabel Wilkerson published *The Warmth of Other Suns*, an oral history of the Great Migration of six million Blacks from the South to the North in the US, "the biggest under-reported story of the Twentieth Century." Wilkerson conducted 1200 interviews, returned to do 36 in greater depth, and ended with three fully developed narratives.

These examples begin to show a range of what is possible in both the execution and presentation of narrative research—in one approach there is a kind of democratic stance, or "documentary populism," that seeks the collective voice, the grassy grass roots, the more the merrier, and the uncommon common person: if you talk to enough folks, you'll get to the full human story. In another there's a push to find that key informant, the individual who through memory and story-telling skill can take us deeper and deeper: if you talk to the right person (Malcolm X, Nate Shaw) you'll illuminate the real human condition. And in another the author accounts for and sets up as a central character the self in dialogue with another: if I follow an interview far enough, talk to myself along the way, and get into a huge and heated argument between "I" and me as I pursue that elusive interview subject, I'll come to the root of the human experience. Surely none of these is easy; none can be done without lots of thought and experience and courage and energy, and each—and everything between—can be right and useful in separate contexts and under different conditions.

Robert Blake and Brett Elizabeth Blake enter this field with a focus on teachers and teaching—also not a moment too soon. Education is under unprecedented fire, after all, and the fate of public schools hangs in the balance; education at the end of empire is education in crisis and contestation. The outlines of the agenda of the powerful are increasingly apparent: privatization, drastically lowered expectations for students and families, the demonization of teachers, zero-tolerance as a cat's paw for surveillance and control, sort-and-punish curricula, a culture of obedience and conformity, a narrowing definition of learning as job-training and education as a product to be bought and sold in the market. On the other side there is a growing fight-back based on the principle that all human beings are of incalculable value, and that life in a just and free society must be geared toward and powered by a profoundly radical idea: the fullest development of all human beings—regardless of race or ethnicity, origin or background, ability or disability—is the necessary condition for the full development of each person; and, conversely, the fullest development of each is the condition for the full development of all. These narratives add to the natural history and specific experiences of this contested space and this political moment.

Stephen Jay Gould asserts that "we live in a world of detail, and diversity just is." Gould defends natural history as the painstaking work of observing and developing case studies, one by one. "You may view this as discouraging," he goes on, "if your temperament be dark. You may also find in [it] the essence of freedom."

Narrative, too, is interested in a world of detail and diversity. It tends to thick and nuanced stories that describe a whole—an entire cultural universe—as it is experienced by participants. It further attempts to capture the *relationship* of this particular cultural universe, this whole unit, to the larger and smaller units in which it is embedded. It emphasizes *qualities* instead of *quantities*. It asks, "What the hell is going on?" "How do people make sense of life here and now."

In these narrative efforts a helpful guiding light is the core belief that *every person a philosopher/every day another story*. We create as rich and varied archives as we can and hope that participants will see themselves in this collection as three-dimensional, grass-roots makers of history, and that their descendants will better understand how their ancestors—like all human beings: free and fated; fated and free—shuffled through this mortal coil. Future educators and historians will find material to aid in their own searches for deeper meanings and fuller understandings. This will add ground-level, individual perspectives toward uncovering and teaching reality, and in this way, through narrative, to assist the process of truth-telling.

Although narrative is as old as Aesop, in contemporary culture it is expressed through a growing diversity of media. And while oral history and narrative standing alone are surely inadequate, often distorted, and always incomplete, any attempt to write contemporary history or understand current events that ignores or displaces first-person accounts and oral sources is wrong *by definition*—wrong in the sense of inaccurate but also wrong in the sense of immoral.

How do people make sense of their experiences and their lives? We note that there is never a single story to tell, but rather each story is embedded in many other stories. We seek out the people Studs Terkel called, "the etceteras of the world," the extraordinary ordinary people who might tell their truths against all conditioned clichés, speaking in the "poetry of the everyday."

The focus is life as it is *lived*, meaning as it is *constructed* by people in their circumstances—something not easily fitted into disciplines or departments. This leads us to approaches that are person-centered and unapologetically subjective. Far from a weakness, the voice of the *person*, the subject's own account, is the singular *achievement* of this work. These are actually ancient approaches to understanding human affairs, relatively new only to social science researchers.

We struggle to understand both the importance and the elusiveness of meaning for human beings—we understand, for example, that you can't get a joke by following objective laws or logical progressions, nor can you grasp the reason for a rebellion or the workings of a school from a mathematical model. We know that knowledge is not, and cannot be a disembodied view from nowhere, something mechanically attained, free of perspective, point of view, or situation. We see knowledge as entangled, rooted, complex, and various. And we seek, therefore, consciousness, the root of meaning, rather than an unreasoning or automatic apparatus.

We note that the times are messy and that life itself is a Catch-22. We didn't choose our time or place, and we can't determine when or how we are thrust into the world. Our choice is to step aside and cover our heads or to embrace the lives we are given and live them fully. We can dive into the contradictions, seize the little moments and teach/organize/live toward freedom, joy, and justice. In the words of W. H. Auden we must love one another or die.

In a free society people are encouraged to think for themselves and to develop minds of their own, to make judgments based on evidence and argument, and to build capacities for exploration and invention. They are encouraged then to ask the most fundamental and essential questions that are always in motion, dynamic, and never twice the same: Who in the world am I? How did I get here and where am I going? What in the world are my choices and my chances? What's my story, and how is it like or unlike the stories of others? What is my responsibility to those others?

The dominant metaphor of the rich and powerful posits schools as businesses, teachers as workers, students as products and commodities, and it leads rather simply to thinking that school closings and privatizing the public space are natural events, relentless standardized test-and-punish regimes sensible, zero tolerance a reasonable proxy for justice—this is what the true-believers call "reform." The hijacking of school reform by the neo-liberal corporate planners, the US Chamber of Commerce and the Business Roundtable, US government strategists and the education elites intensifies an attack on teachers, unions, teacher education, schools, and the kids themselves. The aim is to recreate the privileges of the powerful while forging a generation of technicians and passive followers and disciplining the lower classes to accept their place in the matrix. The gravitational pull of this narrative is so great that everyone finds themselves re-voicing the deceptive goals and the phony frames. This is the power of narrative and points to the necessity of counter-narrative.

We live in a time when the assault on disadvantaged communities is particularly harsh and at the same time gallingly obfuscated. Access to adequate resources and decent facilities, to a relevant curriculum, to opportunities to reflect on and to think critically about the world is unevenly distributed along predictable lines of class and color.

Two framing questions might serve as organizing principles in the years ahead, questions to pose and discuss at every turn:

1) How do we tell our stories and work within the contradictions as we re-frame the issues shaping the educational debates today, neither collapsing in the face of oppressive situations—standardized testing, say—nor simply setting ourselves apart as critics or cynics flying above the fray? How do we teach/organize/intervene in a hopeful and affirmative way, one foot in the mud and muck of the world as it is, one foot moving toward a world that could be but is not yet?

2) How can we do our daily work and re-imagine it as an act of movement-building? How does this speech, this lesson, this letter, this gathering connect with and build toward a powerful social movement larger than the specific speech or lesson or letter?

Contributors

Editors

Robert W. Blake, Jr. is an Associate Professor in Elementary Education at Towson University, Towson, Maryland. Dr. Blake has a Ph.D. in Curriculum Design from the University of Illinois at Chicago, a MAT in Biology from Brown University, and a BS in Biology from the State University of New York at Albany. He is a former high school and middle school science teacher and has extensive experience in elementary pre-service and in-service teacher preparation; both in general teaching and the teaching of science. He has been collecting elementary pre-service teacher narratives of science teaching for over ten years and has numerous national/international presentations. His latest book, *Inside-Out, Environmental Science in the Classroom and the Field, Grades 3–8* (NSTA press) has been critically acclaimed.

Brett Elizabeth Blake is a Professor in the Department of Curriculum and Instruction, School of Education, at St. John's University, Queens, New York where she is also a Senior Research Fellow in the Vincentian Center for Social Justice and Poverty. Dr. Blake has worked extensively with linguistically diverse adolescents in a wide variety of settings including migrant camps and jail classrooms in an effort to ensure that they too have equitable access to language and literacy acquisition strategies for academic achievement. Her latest research and teaching takes her into private Islamic schools in New York City where she is working with middle schools girls on their writing development. Dr. Blake holds an MA in linguistics from Northwestern University and a Ph.D. in Curriculum Design from the University of Illinois at Chicago.

Contributing Authors

Sandra Schamroth Abrams is an Assistant Professor in the Department of Curriculum and Instruction at St. John's University, New York. Her research, publications, and presentations concentrate on learning environments, power structures, social dynamics, and contextual knowledge related to digital literacies and new media. Her recent *Teacher's College Record/National Society for the Study of Education Yearbook* (NSSE) edited volume with Jennifer Rowsell, entitled *Rethinking Identity and Literacy Education in the 21st Century*, and her current and forthcoming publications explore how digital literacies both disrupt and create conventions and provide new avenues for pedagogical discovery.

Robert W. Blake is Professor Emeritus, Education and English, State University of New York, College at Brockport. He has authored, co-authored, or edited 21 books. His latest book, *Literacy: A Primer* from Peter Lang Publishing was co-authored with his daughter, Brett Elizabeth Blake. Currently he is working on a new book, *How English Has Changed—and Is Still Changing*. He may be reached at *bobbillydumpling@aol.com*

Julie H. Carter is an Associate Professor at St. John's University in New York City teaching courses in sociological foundations of education. Her research attempts to explore the means by which new teachers frame their work in broad theoretical terms and situate themselves within useful communities of practice as well as how urban agriculture youth programs can create critical learning spaces for youth and seeds of eco-justice for urban neighborhoods and communities.

Darlene Fewster is an Associate Professor of Special Education at Towson University. Dr. Fewster received her master's degree in Clinical Psychology from Loyola University, Maryland and her doctorate in Special Education from the Johns Hopkins University. Dr. Fewster has taught more than fourteen undergraduate and graduate courses and has extensive supervisory experience in Professional Development Schools (PDS). She has presented at numerous international/national conferences on such topics as Teacher Education, Learning Disabilities, Traumatic Brain Injury, Assessment, Mathematics Instruction, and Neuroeducation.

Helen M. Garinger is currently a Lecturer and the Associate Director of Counselor Training, at the University of Pennsylvania. Dr. Garinger began her career in public education as a K-8 Art instructor. She taught thousands of students over twenty years, gaining extraordinary insight into child development. She then became a middle school counselor and clinical practitioner. For the past ten years Dr. Garinger has taught graduate students to become effective school and mental health counselors.

Elizabeth Quintero's early childhood work as preschool teacher, curriculum specialist, and university teacher educator spans years in different states and countries. Programs that serve families in multilingual communities representing rich culture and history are her passion. She is currently a Professor of Early Childhood Studies at California State University Channel Islands. Quintero was recently appointed as an Associate Editor at the research journal, *Early Education and Development*.

Mary Beth Schaefer is an Assistant Professor with the School of Education at St. John's University. She holds a doctorate in literacy from the University of Pennsylvania. Her research interests include social-cultural influences on readers' responses to literature, college and career readiness, and middle school curriculum. Her latest piece, "From Loathing to Love: Sandy's Reading Journey" appears in Kathleen Malu's edited collection, *Voices from the middle: Narrative Inquiry by, for, and about the Middle Level Community*, Information Age Publishing (IAP), 2010.

Index

Studies in the Postmodern Theory of Education

General Editor
Shirley R. Steinberg

Counterpoints publishes the most compelling and imaginative books being written in education today. Grounded on the theoretical advances in criticalism, feminism, and postmodernism in the last two decades of the twentieth century, Counterpoints engages the meaning of these innovations in various forms of educational expression. Committed to the proposition that theoretical literature should be accessible to a variety of audiences, the series insists that its authors avoid esoteric and jargonistic languages that transform educational scholarship into an elite discourse for the initiated. Scholarly work matters only to the degree it affects consciousness and practice at multiple sites. Counterpoints' editorial policy is based on these principles and the ability of scholars to break new ground, to open new conversations, to go where educators have never gone before.

For additional information about this series or for the submission of manuscripts, please contact:

Shirley R. Steinberg
c/o Peter Lang Publishing, Inc.
29 Broadway, 18th floor
New York, New York 10006

To order other books in this series, please contact our Customer Service Department:

(800) 770-LANG (within the U.S.)
(212) 647-7706 (outside the U.S.)
(212) 647-7707 FAX

Or browse online by series:
www.peterlang.com

BECOMING A TEACHER

Studies in the
Postmodern Theory of Education

Shirley R. Steinberg
General Editor

Vol. 411

The Counterpoints series is part of the Peter Lang Education list.
Every volume is peer reviewed and meets
the highest quality standards for content and production.

PETER LANG
New York • Washington, D.C./Baltimore • Bern
Frankfurt • Berlin • Brussels • Vienna • Oxford